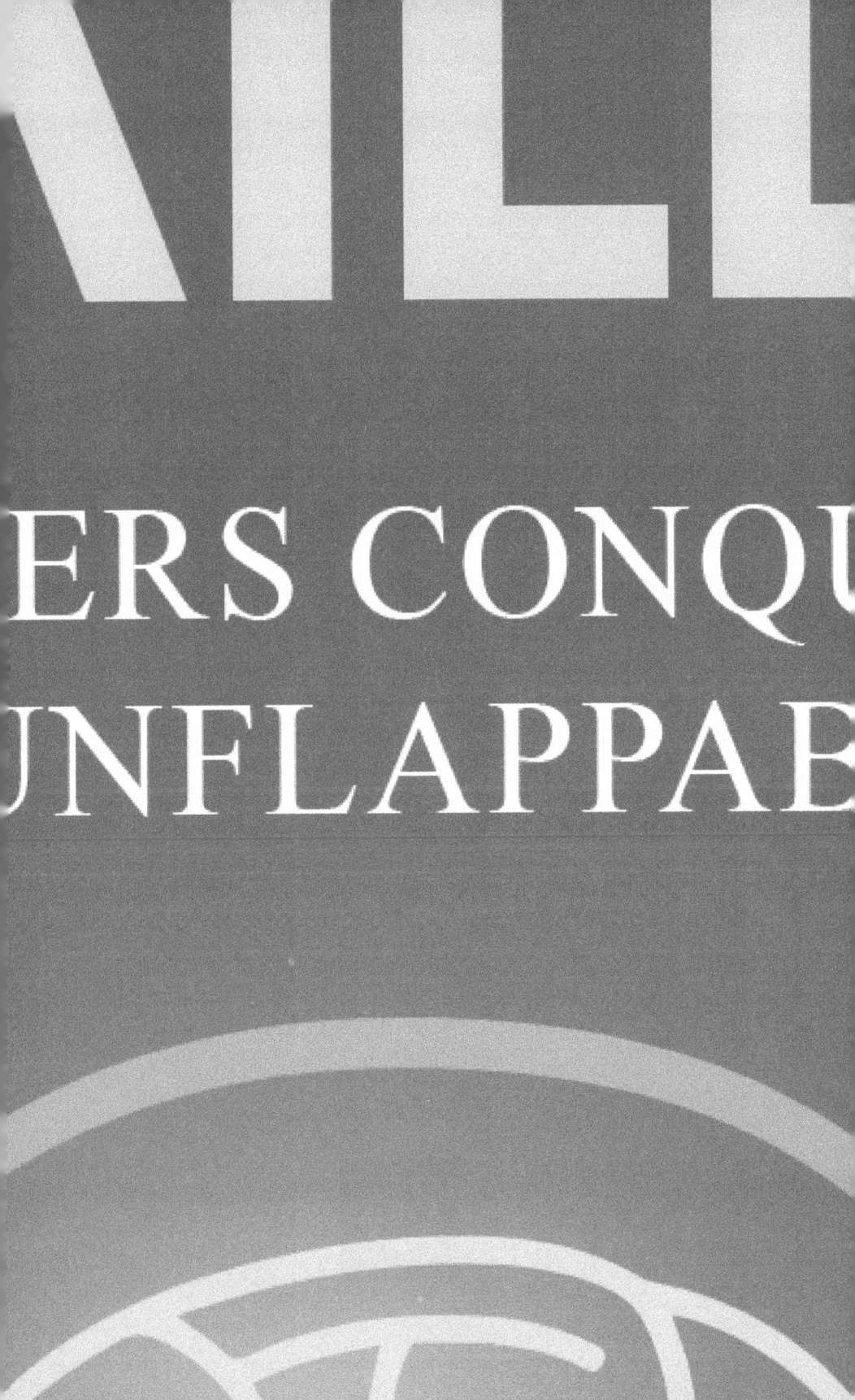

NEURO-RESILIENCE SKILLS
HOW LEADERS CONQUER STRESS & BUILD UNFLAPPABLE TEAMS

HUMAN FLOURISHING SERIES
BOOK 1

PAUL O'NEILL

For Gillian—

whose grace under pressure has taught me more about resilience than any theory ever could.

Your presence has stilled all my storms—and still, my love for you rages on.

And for Carmen—

may you grow up knowing that your infectious joy is your mightiest strength.

You are the rhythm behind every word in these pages.

This book may be about staying grounded—

but you both elevate me every day.

RECOMMENDATIONS

"It's rare that I would use such a word but it's extremely well-earned in Paul's case: he is a visionary. His ability to make the complex simple, to get to the heart of an issue and to recommend an effective solution is outstanding. His vitality and energy is infectious"

Emma Jensen, Head of Go-To-Market, OPTUS

"Through the lens of research in neuroscience, Paul can forge interventions that promote resilience. His type of coaching allowed me to be better equipped to cope with stress and adversity, at my level, but also recognising the signs in other people and helped me being a better manager"

Jessica Scalzo, Variety Improvement Manager at COSTA

"Paul is one of the energizing and gifted leaders I know. He is also one of the most skilled NLP practitioners I have had the good fortune to meet"

Tim Dalmau, CEO at Dalmau Consulting

"As a leader, Paul has a unique quality rarely seen in today's leaders and that is: the ability to find and bring out 'the best' in people"

Tony Enache, CFO at Farm Pride Foods.

"Paul offers a refreshing take on leadership and workplace change strategies. He provides time efficient tailored insights and solutions to support and equip leaders to develop, reframe perspectives and shift the status quo to deliver positive outcomes suited to today's dynamic work environment"

Elizabeth Brockbank, Environmental Manager at ALCOA

"Paul demonstrated a balanced consultative senior management approach that could quickly interpret and translate detailed plans and how they could consolidate into overall strategies for KPI success"

Peter Sheehan, Director GM, Western Sydney Airport.

"Paul is an excellent trainer who has transformed my life. His amazing skills, dedicated care and consistent emotional intelligence has opened a new world for me to view"

Philip Hoang, Data Engineer at CBHS

"Paul has been an invaluable asset to both myself personally and in my business strategies. Paul and his unique skill set have aided constant changes in the business and personal arena that mean I achieved positive rather than negative outcomes personally and financially"

Ben Kavich, Director at Workhorse Group of Companies

"My life was just like 'work-retire-die'. But this has changed dramatically after I had couple of sessions with Paul. With his help, I can recognise myself, again. I learned to love myself and make myself a priority, again. Paul's training has not only changed my life, it changed my whole family's life"

Iris Huangfu, Accountant, Sydney, Australia

"Paul's intervention and guidance was a game changer. It's not easy to put into words the impact that his NLP practice had as it wasn't singular nor limited to just myself or to that point in time. Personally, I was brought back to a feeling of inner strength and reminded, not through words or description, but through creating an experience, that I can be in control of how I feel and create calm from within my own skin"

V. Madsen, Perth, Australia.

"I would like to thank Paul for transforming my life. He helped me find a completely different mindset, which you will find will help you discover the keys to the life that you deserve, too. As a female going through the beginnings of divorce, it has not been easy. But I have now gained a deep sense of security and confidence. And I have the excitement of a wonderful new future"

L. Diaz, Sydney, NSW.

"Paul is a fantastic hypnotist who has helped me with a lot of my deep personal issues, both for work and my private life. Every time, he works his magic. Truly, he is simply the best!"

A. Gonzales, Registered Nurse, Sydney, Australia.

"The tools / techniques I learnt through my time with Paul will stay with me a lifetime, and why wouldn't I want that when I'm feeling like I'm floating in champagne bubbles"

Jacqueline D., Palates Instructor, Queensland, Australia

CONTENTS

Preface — xi

PART ONE
THE INNER GAME

Section One — 3
1. INSTINCTUAL CONTACT — 7
2. INSTINCTUAL AWARENESS — 13
3. INSTINCTUAL ACUITY — 25
Section One Summary — 39
Section Two — 53
4. CORE SKILLS — 57
5. INTERMEDIATE SKILLS — 67
6. ADVANCED SKILLS — 79
Section Two Summary — 89
Section Three — 103
7. WHEN SAFETY IS RUPTURED — 107
8. RUPTURE REPAIR COACHING — 117
9. RUPTURE PREVENTION — 143
Section Three Summary — 161
Conclusion to Part One — 167

PART TWO
THE OUTER GAME

Section Four — 187
10. THE HIVE MIND — 197
11. SAFETY-EMBEDDED STRUCTURES — 211
12. SAFETY PRIMING SKILLS — 241
Section Four Summary — 261
Section Five — 275
13. THE ELUSIVE OBVIOUS — 279
14. NON-VERBAL ACUITY — 285
15. THE SUBTLE SKILLSET — 293

Section Five Summary	313
Section Six	317
16. OF SENSE & MEANING	323
17. "BAND OF BROTHERS"	343
18. "LES MISÉRABLES"	363
Key Insights	386
Section Six Summary	389
Conclusion	401
Afterword	427
Appendix	431
Notes	437
Bibliography	445
Index	449
Acknowledgments	455
About the Author	457

PREFACE

The weight of leadership has never been heavier. Every day, leaders are expected to drive results, manage crises, and navigate complexity—often with fewer resources, tighter deadlines, and unrelenting pressure. Yet, the numbers paint a sobering picture:

> *94% of middle managers feel under-skilled.*
> *85% of new executives either fail or remain mediocre.*
> *79% of change initiatives collapse within two years.*

Why? Because leadership today isn't just about operational discipline, technical expertise, or sound strategy—it's about navigating the relentless unpredictability of human systems with clarity, resilience, and purpose.

The problem isn't that leaders lack intelligence or work ethic. It's that they've been trained to suppress their most valuable asset—the instincts that have guided humans through uncertainty for thousands of years. In a world that prizes intellect above all, instincts are dismissed as primitive, unreliable, or impulsive. But what if that thinking is flawed? What if the very reflexes we've been taught to ignore are, in fact, the key to leading with clarity, confidence, and control?

Think about it: when crises strike, when pressure mounts, when the path forward is unclear—what separates those who crack under the weight from those who rise to the moment? It isn't just intelligence. It's the ability to harness raw instinct, to remain calm under fire, and to translate chaos into decisive action.

In *Neuro-Resilience Skills: How Leaders Conquer Stress & Build Unflappable Teams*, you will discover a new paradigm for leadership—one that doesn't pit reason against instinct but fuses them together into a powerful, adaptive force.

This is not a book of abstract theory. It's a practical guide to mastering your inner game—the foundation of all great leadership. Before you can lead others, you must first learn to lead yourself. You'll develop real-time resilience skills, turning stress into strength, fear into focus, and uncertainty into deliberate, decisive action.

Couched in cutting-edge science, you'll learn state-of-the-art human change techniques—like the *Tension Releaser* and *Dual-Mind Reflection*—you'll gain the tools to ground yourself in high-pressure moments, enhancing composure, clarity, and control. You will cultivate the kind of steady presence that doesn't just sharpen decision-making—it instinctively reassures and inspires those you lead. But leadership is never a solitary act. The second part of this journey focuses on the outer game—the ability to create environments where others can thrive. Here, you'll master:

- Emotional & Psychological Safety—so teams feel empowered to innovate and take ownership.
- Non-Verbal Communication Competence—so your presence conveys authority and trust before you even speak.
- Aligning Group Instincts with Shared Goals—so collective energy is harnessed, not fractured.

Leadership, at its core, is about connection—uniting people around a shared vision, forging trust, and turning collective uncertainty into collective momentum.

Take a moment. Picture the leader you aspire to be. Imagine stepping into even the most chaotic situations with an unshakable calm. See yourself guiding teams that trust each other, adapt under pressure, and thrive in the face of challenge. This isn't an abstract ideal. It's an attainable transformation.

At the heart of *neuro-resilience* is the truth that leadership isn't about perfection—it's about integration. It's about bringing together intellect, instinct, and emotion so that your decision-making is sharper, your presence is stronger, and your leadership is felt.

So, take a deep breath. Step forward. The leader you're striving to become is already within you. Let's unlock that potential—together.

Paul O'Neill

November 2024

PART ONE
THE INNER GAME

SECTION ONE
INSTINCTUAL FOUNDATIONS

*And when everyone's screaming,
nobody hears the truth*
George Orwell

Leadership is often depicted as a cerebral endeavour, demanding strategic thinking, clear decision-making, and logical precision. Yet beneath the veneer of calculated reasoning lies a primal force that shapes our choices more than we realise: instinct. The *Instinctual Foundations* section of *Neuro-Resilience Skills* invites readers to explore this hidden dimension of leadership, where ancient neural pathways and gut-level reactions coalesce with current challenges. Through three chapters—*Instinctual Contact, Instinctual Awareness,* and *Instinctual Acuity*—this section offers an illuminating journey into the unconscious drivers of decision-making, helping leaders refine their instincts for better outcomes.

Human instincts, developed through millennia of survival, are as relevant in the boardroom as they were on the savannah. Consider the snap of a twig in a dark forest: your heart races, muscles tense, and senses sharpen, ready for fight, flight, or freeze. This primal response, orchestrated by the ancient structures of the brain, serves as a compass during moments of uncertainty and potential threat. In our time, however, this same mechanism often misfires, interpreting subtle workplace tensions as life-or-death scenarios. Leaders must therefore learn not only to understand these instincts but to master them.

Chapter 1, *Instinctual Contact*, begins with an exploration of our "gut feelings"—those visceral reactions that guide decisions before conscious thought intervenes. From the immediate physiological effects of stress to the intricate dialogue between the gut and the brain, this chapter unravels the neuroscience behind instinct. It introduces techniques like the Tension Releasor, a practice designed to ground leaders in moments of pressure by fostering a state of metabolic congruence. By understanding how instinct manifests in physical sensations, leaders can develop a keener sense of when to trust their gut and when to question it.

In Chapter 2, *Instinctual Awareness*, the focus shifts to the *Triune Brain Theory*, a model that illuminates the interplay between our instinctual, emotional, and rational minds. While neuroscience highlights the interconnectedness of brain functions, the *Triune Brain* provides a practical framework for understanding leadership behaviours. The *Reptilian Brain* governs survival instincts, the Mammalian Brain navigates social connections, and the Primate Brain enables strategic thinking. This chapter explores how these layers interact in high-stakes scenarios, offering exercises like the *Dual-Mind Reflection* to help leaders balance gut reactions with rational analysis.

The final chapter, *Instinctual Acuity*, delves deeper into the unconscious processes that guide our decisions. Drawing on the concept of neuroception—our nervous system's ability to detect safety or danger without conscious awareness—it reveals how leaders can hone their instincts for greater precision. Techniques such as *The Worry*

Solver and *Connect with Yourself* help leaders transform stress into clarity, tapping into their "Unconscious Navigator" for more effective decision-making. Through case stories, such as contrasting leadership styles of risk-averse and bold decision-makers, this chapter illustrates how instinct can be both a strength and a liability.

Collectively, these chapters offer more than just theoretical insights. They provide practical tools and exercises to help leaders engage with their instincts, build resilience, and navigate the complexities of modern leadership. By increasing their instinct awareness, refining their unconscious patterns, and balancing primal impulses with deliberate reasoning, leaders can unlock a deeper level of personal and professional mastery.

The *Instinctual Foundations* section is a call to action for leaders to embrace the wisdom of their bodies and minds. It challenges the dichotomy between reason and intuition, offering a pathway to integrate the two. In doing so, it equips leaders not only to survive in the high-pressure environments of today's world but to thrive—leading with clarity, confidence, and congruence.

ONE
INSTINCTUAL CONTACT

*Fear, relentless and inescapable,
fastens upon the hearts of men.*
Homer

YOU ARE VENTURING through a dense woodland with your family as twilight descends. The air is crisp, and the forest hums with the subtle rustling of leaves and the distant calls of unseen creatures. Suddenly, the snap of a twig echoes nearby. Instinctively, your heart quickens, muscles tense, and senses sharpen. Without conscious deliberation, you're poised to react—fight, flee, or freeze. This immediate, instinctual response emanates from a deep-seated part of us often referred to as the "Gut"[1]. It's a primal compass, honed over millennia, guiding us through moments of uncertainty and potential danger.

In the realm of leadership, this primal instinct plays a pivotal role, influencing decisions and actions in ways we might not fully comprehend. Our 'gut reactions', rooted in the ancient structures of the brain and influenced by unconscious non-verbal cues, are ever-present forces shaping our leadership styles and organisational cultures. Understanding the influence of 'the gut' is essential for navigating the complexities of today's leadership, where swift judgement, adaptability, and emotional intelligence can make the difference between success and failure.

Consider the case of Sharon, a seasoned CEO facing a critical decision about a potential merger. The numbers look promising, the market analysts are optimistic, and her team is enthusiastic. Yet, as she sits in the boardroom, poised to sign the agreement, a nagging feeling in her stomach gives her pause. Something doesn't feel right. In that moment, Sharon faces a quintessential leadership dilemma: should she trust her gut instinct or proceed based on the rational analysis before her?

This scenario illustrates the double-edged nature of instinct in leadership. On one hand, Sharon's gut feeling could be drawing on years of experience and subconscious pattern recognition, alerting her to subtle red flags that her conscious mind hasn't yet processed. On the other hand, it could be an irrational fear response, perhaps triggered by a past negative experience that bears no relevance to the current situation. The challenge for Sharon, as for all leaders, lies in discerning when to heed these instinctual warnings and when to override them.

The concept of "gut feeling" is more than just a convenient metaphor. Recent advances in neuroscience have revealed a complex network of neurons lining our digestive tract, often referred to as the "second brain"[2]. This *enteric nervous system* communicates bidirectionally with our central nervous system, influencing and being influenced by our emotional states and cognitive processes. When we speak of having a "gut reaction", we're acknowledging a very real physiological phenomenon—one that has profound implications for how we make decisions, especially under pressure.

. . .

Somatic Honing

> *The conscious mind may be compared to a fountain playing in the sun and falling back into the great subterranean pool of subconscious from which it rises*[3]
> **Sigmund Freud**

Let us embark on an exploration of instinct and awareness, a practice designed to help leaders tune into and achieve increased awareness of their physical sensations. In particular, those subtle signals that so often go unnoticed (or we choose to ignore) but can shape our decision-making in profound ways[4]. This exercise is about cultivating a sharper awareness of your body's responses—responses that, if listened to, can ground your thinking and sharpen your instincts.

Start by finding a quiet space where you won't be disturbed. Sit or lie down, whichever is most comfortable for you. This practice works best when you are completely at ease, allowing your attention to gently turn inward.

Begin by focusing on your breath. Take a slow, deep inhale through your nose, and then exhale through your mouth. Repeat this a few times. There is nothing complicated about this; it's simply a way to settle your mind, to remind your body that it can relax into the moment. Feel the rhythm of your breathing, and let it become an *anchor* for your attention.

Now, let's shift your focus to your toes. Bring your awareness there, as though you are scanning them with the light of your attention. What do you notice? Is there tension, warmth, or perhaps a neutral stillness? The key here is not to change anything, but to observe. Let your body reveal its sensations to you without any interference.

Gradually, move your attention upwards. Slowly, methodically, focus on your feet, ankles, calves, knees, and thighs. As you bring awareness

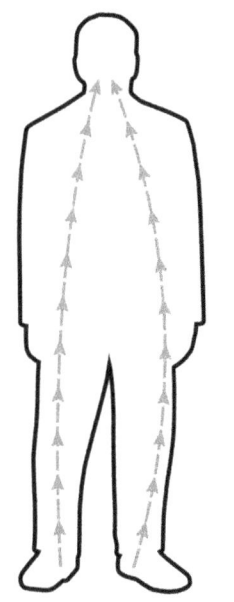

Somatic Honing Body Map

to each area, you may notice certain sensations—tension, comfort, even a subtle vibration. Observe these sensations as though you are an explorer, encountering them for the first time. There's no need to analyse or react, simply allow your awareness to pass through, like a gentle breeze.

As you continue upward, pay close attention to your abdomen and chest. This is often where your gut instincts live, where emotional responses can manifest as tightness, discomfort, or a sense of ease. Take your time here. What does your gut feel like in this moment? Is it calm? Is it tense? Simply notice without judgment. This is where much of our intuitive intelligence resides, often giving us subtle hints before our conscious mind catches up.

Next, bring your focus to your shoulders, neck, and head. These areas tend to be reservoirs for stress. Scan through them carefully, noticing if there is tightness in your neck, tension in your jaw, or pressure in your temples. Again, observe without trying to force anything to change.

Once you've completed this body scan, return to your breath. Take several deep, calming breaths, and with each exhale, let go of any residual tension you may still feel. Focus on the areas that stood out the most during your scan—the ones that felt tight or uncomfortable. As you exhale, imagine that tension gently dissolving.

Now, reflect for a moment. What did you learn from this process? Did you notice any signals—perhaps from your gut or areas of tension—that might be speaking to you about something in your life? This awareness is not just a passive observation; it is a tool you can carry forward. When making decisions, return to this feeling. Ask yourself, *"What is my body telling me?"*

This practice is not just about calming the mind, though that is a natural by-product. It's about fostering a more intimate relationship with your own internal signals, the subtle cues that often guide us when we listen. By increasing your instinct awareness, you'll find yourself making decisions that are more grounded, more intuitive, and more in tune with your deeper sense of knowing.

In time, this connection with your physical self becomes second nature, offering a source of clarity and insight that enhances your leadership and personal growth.

As we delve deeper into the neurological underpinnings of leadership instinct, we'll explore how this ancient compass within us operates in the boardrooms, team dynamics, and organisational challenges of our current era. We'll unravel the complex interplay between our reptilian instincts, our mammalian emotions, and our higher cognitive functions. Through this journey, we aim to equip leaders with a deeper understanding of their internal processes[5], enabling them to harness the power of instinct while mitigating its potential pitfalls.

In the chapters that follow, we'll embark on a fascinating exploration of the neuroscience behind instinct, examining how our brains process information and make split-second decisions. We'll investigate the role of non-verbal communication in triggering instinctual responses, and how these subtle cues can ripple through an organisation, shaping its culture and performance. We'll delve into the concept of the collective reptilian brain, understanding how instincts can spread through a group, sometimes leading to innovative breakthroughs, and other times to destructive groupthink.

Crucially, we'll also explore the vital role of psychological safety in leadership, understanding how leaders can create environments that allow for healthy expression and modulation of instinctual responses. We'll introduce the concept of neuro-resilience, a set of skills that leaders can develop to better navigate the often-turbulent waters of instinct-driven decision making.

As we progress, we'll grapple with the leader's dilemma—how to balance the often-contradictory pulls of instinct, emotion, and reason. Through case stories and practical exercises, we'll provide leaders with tools to refine their instincts, making them more reliable guides in complex and chaotic situations.

Our journey through the realm of gut instinct in leadership promises to be as challenging as it is enlightening. By the end, we hope to have provided a comprehensive map of this internal terrain, enabling leaders to navigate with greater confidence and skill. After all, in the fast-paced, ever-shifting sands of leadership at this time, our ancient instincts may well be our most valuable compass—if we learn to read them correctly.

TWO
INSTINCTUAL AWARENESS

To know thyself is the beginning of wisdom
Socrates

GUT INSTINCTS often guide our leadership decisions. To understand them, we must first embark on a journey into the intricate workings of the human brain. Our destination? The ancient neural structures that have been shaping our responses to the world long before we developed the capacity for complex thought.

The *Triune Brain Theory*[1], first proposed by neuroscientist Paul D. MacLean in the 1960s, offers a compelling framework for understanding the evolutionary layers of our brain and how they influence our behaviour. While neuroscience has revealed that brain function is more interconnected than this model suggests, however, the Triune Brain remains a useful tool for thinking about the brain's core functions. Just as Newtonian physics is sufficient for most non-physicists, unless you need to delve into Einstein's theories, the Triune Brain provides a practical way for leaders to understand how instinct, emotion, and reason shape our responses in leadership contexts.

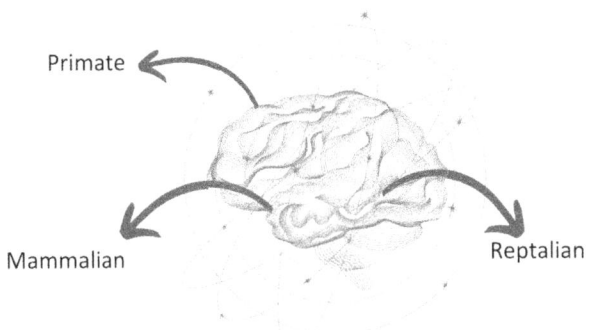

Think of our brain as a city built and rebuilt over millennia. At its core lies the old town, with narrow, winding streets and ancient structures—this is our *Reptilian Brain*[2]. Surrounding it is a bustling medieval quarter, filled with the hustle and bustle of emotion and social connection—our *Mammalian Brain*. Finally, enveloping it all is a futuristic metropolis of towering skyscrapers, representing our *Primate Brain*, capable of abstract thought and complex problem-solving. Now, let's take a closer look at each of these "districts" in our neural city:

Primal Puppet Master

At the base of our brain, sitting atop the spinal column, lies the most ancient part of our neural architecture—the *Reptilian Brain*. This includes structures like the brainstem and cerebellum, which govern our most basic survival functions. Think of it as the ever-vigilant night watchman of our neural city, constantly scanning for threats.

The Reptilian Brain is responsible for our most instinctual responses: fight, flight, or freeze[3]. It's the part of us that reacts before we have time to think, the source of that gut feeling that something isn't quite right[4]. In leadership contexts, this part of our brain might cause us to bristle at a perceived challenge to our authority or instinctively back away from a risky proposition.

Looping back to Sharon, our CEO facing a crucial merger decision:

As she sits in the boardroom, her Reptilian Brain *is scanning the environment, picking up on subtle cues—like the tension in a colleague's voice or the slight shift in another's body language. These signals are processed below her conscious awareness. However, even though she is not consciously aware that they are happening, their affect is still contributing to that uneasy feeling in her stomach. While the Reptilian Brain's immediate responses can be lifesaving in truly dangerous situations, because they are a binary light-switch, not an analogue dimmer-switch, they can lead us astray in much more nuanced contexts of progressive leadership, where 'threats' are more 'concerns', requiring more subtle and require nuanced responses.*

As Sharon is in a fight-flight mode, not a calm social engagement mode, her metabolism is out of sync with her environment. The first part of being congruent when engaging with stakeholders, is to be metabolically congruent with the environment in which you engage them. That requires that you engage with yourself to begin with. Once you feel grounded and centred, your metabolic, emotional and behavioural responses will pivot into your social engagement mode, naturally and without volition.

TENSION RELEASOR

With that in mind, let's turn our attention to a practice that offers a gentle yet effective way to soothe the mind and body quickly—a practice rooted in self-awareness and soft, deliberate action. The goal here is not only to relax but also to engage in a quiet dialogue with yourself, inviting deeper awareness into how you carry tension and how you can let it go.

I call this technique the *Tension Releasor* because stress builds tension in one's body and it stays there until it is released. Going on holiday, having a massage, making love, and a relaxing in a nice warm bath will all release tension. However, such activities tend not to be available whilst at work, which is where this technique comes, requiring just fifteen-twenty minutes, initially. With practice, you'll be able to get the same affect under five minutes, even as you in the middle of a meeting with your eyes wide open.

Begin by settling into a comfortable position, preferably somewhere you won't be disturbed directly – there may well be ambient noise but that's alright. If you're ready, gently close your eyes and take a moment to acknowledge how you feel right now. Notice any tension, whether it's in your body or mind. This simple act of recognition is the first step—it's as if you're introducing yourself to the feeling, making it less elusive.

Now, hear a calm, kind voice in your mind. It's your voice, but gentler, quieter. This voice is going to guide you through the next few moments. The tone is important—it's somewhere between a loving command and a gentle suggestion, it's a warm invitation for your body to let go of any tension it doesn't need anymore.

You're encouraging yourself to soften, to relax, but you're doing it in a way that feels effortless, as if you're gently coaxing your body and mind into a calmer state. We'll begin at the top of your head and slowly move down through your body. As we move through each part, focus your awareness there, and if you find tension, picture that area being softly massaged, the way a skilled hand might ease out a knot. Before you begin, read and fully understand the instructions. In support, a short form version of the exercise is in the end of this section.

Start with your head and, ever so gently, ever so softly, say:

- *"My scalp can soften and relax now..."*
- *"My eyes can soften and relax now..."*
- *"My mouth can soften and relax now..."*
- *"My tongue can soften and relax now..."*
- *"My jaw can soften and relax now..."*

Feel each area gently yielding, as if tension is dissolving with each word.

Now, let's move to your neck, shoulders, and arms. This area often holds more strain than we realise:

- *"My neck can soften and relax now..."*
- *"My shoulders can soften and relax now..."*
- *"My arms can soften and relax now..."*
- *"My hands can soften and relax now..."*

Imagine that tension slipping away, your muscles becoming lighter, looser.

Next, we focus on the back and the muscles that support your posture:

- *"My upper back can soften and relax now..."*
- *"My lower back can soften and relax now..."*
- *"My glutes can soften and relax now..."*

Here, picture the tension evaporating from you, like steam from a coffee cup.

And finally, bring your awareness to your legs and feet, grounding your relaxation:

- *"My thighs can soften and relax now..."*
- *"My calves can soften and relax now..."*
- *"My feet can soften and relax now..."*

As you move through each part of your body, feel the subtle shift, the softening that comes with attention and suggestion.

Now, allow your awareness to rest on your mind itself:

- *"And now, my mind can soften and relax more and more..."*

Let this be a moment of surrender, as if your mind is letting go of what it used to 'need' to hold onto and now is a choice to let go.

Pause here for a while. Simply notice how you feel. You might find that you're more relaxed than when you began. You can stay in this feeling for as long as you like, and if you wish, you can repeat the process, perhaps finding new areas that need softening.

When you're ready to return to full awareness, know that you'll feel refreshed, clear, and alert, as though this moment of calm has gently reset your mind and body. In practising this, you're not just releasing tension—you're cultivating a deeper connection with your own capacity for peace, a resource you can return to again and again.

This is the art of softening, and in mastering it, you'll discover how to ease the everyday tensions that life brings while opening yourself to a deeper relationship with your own inner self; as well as, for leadership purposes, your sense of centredness will translate into non-verbal congruence.

Emotional Compass

Encircling our reptilian core is the *Mammalian Brain*, also known as the limbic system. This is the realm of emotion, motivation, and social bonding. If the Reptilian Brain is our night watchman, the Mammalian Brain is our social secretary, constantly navigating the complex web of relationships and emotional cues that define our social world.

Key structures in the Mammalian Brain include the amygdala, which processes emotions like fear, and the hippocampus, crucial for memory formation. This part of our brain allows us to form attachments, feel empathy, and navigate social hierarchies—all vital skills for effective leadership.

In our neural city metaphor, the Mammalian Brain is where social life thrives—in bustling markets and cozy taverns, where alliances are formed, trust is built, and emotional intelligence is developed.

For Sharon, her Mammalian Brain allows her to read the room, sensing excitement or apprehension from her team members. It helps her form bonds with colleagues, inspiring loyalty and commitment. However, it can also introduce biases, such as instinctively trusting someone who reminds her of a mentor or distrusting someone based on past experiences.

The *Mammalian Brain* adds complexity to our instinctual responses. It's not just about survival but about thriving in a social context. This can lead to more sophisticated gut reactions, like "This person feels trustworthy" or "This deal feels right."

Reason & Foresight

> *We can be blind to the obvious,*
> *and we are also blind to our blindness.*
> **Daniel Kahneman**

Finally, we come to the most recent addition to our neural architecture—the *Primate Brain*, primarily comprising the neocortex. This part of the brain distinguishes humans (and other primates) from most mammals, enabling our highest cognitive functions: abstract thinking, language, planning, and consciousness itself[5]. In our neural city, the Primate Brain is the gleaming financial district, where complex deals are struck, and innovation happens. It gives us the ability to step back, see the bigger picture, and weigh the pros and cons of a decision with logical precision.

But here's the paradox: even as our Primate Brain enables careful, rational thought, it doesn't operate in isolation. Beneath the surface, the older systems of our brain—our emotional Mammalian Brain and instinct-driven Reptilian Brain—are constantly influencing our decisions. This interplay between instinct and reason is what Daniel Kahneman famously described in, *'Thinking, Fast and Slow'* as the tension between *System 1*, our fast, automatic, and intuitive mode of thinking, and *System 2*, our slow, deliberate, and analytical mode.

As leaders, understanding how these three layers of the brain interact is crucial. In high-pressure, high-stakes situations—like responding to a crisis—we may need to rely on the quick, instinctual reactions of our Reptilian Brain. But for long-term strategic planning, our Primate Brain's capacity for abstract thought is essential. And yet, in the most pivotal moments, neither can act alone. Great leadership isn't about choosing one over the other—it's about integrating these different brain functions into a cohesive decision-making process.

This means learning to respect the speed and efficiency of our instinctual reactions while tempering them with the clarity and depth of rational analysis. Kahneman's work reminds us that both systems have their strengths: instinct can guide us toward insights we might otherwise overlook, while reason ensures we don't fall prey to biases or emotional impulses.

Now suppose you're facing an important decision—one of those moments when the pressure is on, and your instinct is to act quickly. This is where the balance of these two systems becomes critical. Instead of rushing, I want you to consider the value of a pause. This pause isn't just about slowing down; it's about creating a moment of reflection to access the strengths of both systems.

What we're going to explore is a technique I like to call the *Dual-Mind Reflection*. It's a structured way to engage both your rational mind and your instinctive gut feelings before making any major decision. Let's walk through it step by step, and you'll see how this process can help you navigate those critical moments with more clarity and balance.

Dual-Mind Reflection

The first step is surprisingly simple yet often overlooked: *acknowledge the decision point*. You need to consciously recognise that you're about to make a choice. It sounds obvious, but by merely acknowledging it, you're already shifting from a reactive mode—where you might be driven by urgency or impulse—into a more reflective, deliberate state. This awareness is crucial because it sets the stage for everything that follows.

Now, once you've recognised the decision, I want you to take a deep breath—but don't underestimate the power of this breath. This isn't just a casual inhale; it's a signal to your body and mind that you're taking a moment to pause. A deep breath helps to disengage any immediate emotional reactions that might cloud your judgment. It gives you space, a bit of room to think.

Next, let's *engage the 4-7-8 Breathing Technique*. It's simple but remarkably effective at calming the nervous system and clearing the mind. Here's how it works: inhale through your nose for a count of four seconds. Hold that breath for seven seconds. Then, exhale slowly through your mouth for eight seconds. Do these three or four times. What this does, physiologically, is slow down your heart rate and give your brain a chance to shift out of its reactive state and into a more reflective one.

Once you've calmed your body, it's time to focus on the *rational aspects of the decision*. What are the facts? What do you know for sure? What are the pros and cons? This is the moment to engage your analytical mind. Look at the data. Examine the situation logically. Ask yourself: what does the evidence say? This step is all about detaching from any emotional noise and seeing the decision through a purely rational lens.

But we're not stopping there, because decisions aren't made in a vacuum of pure logic. Now I want you to *shift your attention to your gut feelings*. How does this decision make you feel? Beyond the facts and figures, there's often a more visceral reaction we have to major decisions. Do you feel a sense of excitement? Maybe hesitation or discomfort? These feelings are important. They're not just background noise—they're your body and mind giving you subtle feedback that might not show up in your rational analysis. So, take a moment to honour those feelings, whatever they may be.

At this point, you're going to *scan your body for any physical sensations*. Pay attention to areas like your gut, your chest, your shoulders. Is there tension? Are there any tight spots? Often, your body will reveal stress or unease before you're fully conscious of it. These sensations can be clues about how you really feel about the decision, even if your mind hasn't quite caught up yet.

Now comes the interesting part: *balancing the two perspectives*. You've looked at the rational side, and you've explored your gut instincts. Are they aligned? Do they point in the same direction, or are they pulling you apart? This is the moment of synthesis, where you take stock of the full picture. If the rational and instinctual sides agree, great—you've got a clear path forward. If they don't, that's okay too. It means there's more to consider, and that's precisely what this check-in is designed to reveal.

Finally, once you've given space to both your reason and your instinct, it's time to *proceed with your decision*. The point of this exercise isn't to second-guess yourself endlessly, but to pause just long enough to gain a fuller understanding of what's really going on—both in your head and in your gut. By taking this pause, you can move forward with a greater sense of confidence, knowing that you've considered both the logical facts and the emotional insights.

This process, the *Dual-Mind Reflection*, isn't about choosing between logic and intuition. It's about recognising that both play a role in our decision-making, and the best choices are often those that incorporate both. By practising this, especially under pressure, you'll develop a more nuanced, thoughtful approach to leadership—one that's both rational and deeply attuned to your own inner signals.

As you continue to explore your instinctual patterns, ask yourself:

- *"When have I overridden a gut instinct in favour of rational thought?*
- *Did it lead to a better outcome, or were there unforeseen consequences?"*

CONVERSELY:

- *"Have there been times when trusting my instincts led me to success?"*

These reflections will help you hone the balance between intuition and logic, ultimately strengthening your leadership effectiveness.

THREE
INSTINCTUAL ACUITY

> *There is more wisdom in your body than in your deepest philosophies*
> **Friedrich Nietzsche**

NEUROLOGICAL UNDERPINNINGS of our instinctual responses now explored, we now turn our attention to how these ancient systems operate in the current spheres of leadership. Our focus shifts to what we might call the "Unconscious Navigator" - the part of our mind that guides our actions and decisions below the threshold of conscious awareness.

Always On, Always Alert

Recall our earlier metaphor of the brain as a city, with the *Reptilian Brain* serving as the vigilant night watchman. This primordial part of our neural architecture never sleeps, constantly scanning our environment for potential threats or opportunities. In leadership contexts, this translates to an ever-present undercurrent of instinctual responses that can significantly influence our behaviour and decision-making.

Consider our CEO, Sharon, in a highly tense negotiation. While her *Primate Brain* is occupied with the complex details of the deal, her *Reptilian Brain* is ceaselessly monitoring the room. It's attuned to subtle shifts in tone, tiny changes in body language, and barely perceptible alterations in the emotional atmosphere. This unconscious vigilance can manifest as seemingly inexplicable hunches or gut feelings.

For instance, Sharon might suddenly feel a need to change her approach, even though she can't articulate why. Perhaps her *Reptilian Brain* has detected a slight tensing in the jaw of her counterpart, signalling growing resistance that hasn't yet been verbally expressed. This instinctual nudge, if heeded, could lead Sharon to adjust her strategy before the negotiation reaches an impasse.

However, the always-on nature of this system can also lead to false alarms. In our ancestral environment, it was better to overreact to a potential threat than to underreact. But in the corporate environment of this era, this hair-trigger response system can sometimes lead us astray, causing us to react defensively to situations that don't actually pose a threat.

The Body's Threat Detection System

Central to understanding our *Unconscious Navigator* is the concept of *neuroception*[1], a term coined by Stephen Porges as part of his *Polyvagal Theory*. Neuroception refers to our nervous system's ability to detect safety or danger in our environment without conscious awareness.

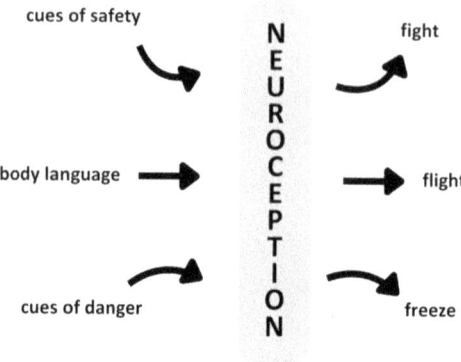

Polyvagal Theory: Reaction Function

This subconscious threat detection system is remarkably sophisticated. It doesn't just respond to obvious dangers, but also to subtle cues that might indicate a shift in the social environment. For a leader, this could mean unconsciously picking up on signs of disengagement in a team meeting, sensing growing tension between colleagues, or feeling a nascent opportunity emerging in a casual conversation.

Let's return to Sharon for an illustration. She's giving a presentation to potential investors. Midway through, she finds herself inexplicably stumbling over her words and feeling a creeping sense of unease. Unbeknownst to her conscious mind, her neuroception has detected signs of scepticism in her audience - perhaps a pattern of crossed arms, averted gazes, or subtle head shakes. Whatever it is, her body is reacting to this perceived threat before her conscious mind has had a chance to process it.

This unconscious threat detection can be incredibly valuable, allowing leaders to respond to situations even before they've fully understood them consciously. However, it can also be misleading if not balanced with conscious reflection. A leader's neuroception might be oversensitive due to past experiences, leading them to perceive threats where none exist. Part and parcel of this aspect is our ability to develop a worry habit.

Let's explore a way to transform worry into something useful and productive—a practice I call *The Worry Solver*. This process invites you to engage with your concerns in a way that turns them from burdens into opportunities for clarity and control.

THE WORRY SOLVER[2]

Start by bringing to mind something that's been causing you concern. This might be a small worry or something that has been looming large in your thoughts. Don't rush through this step; take a moment to really notice what's been on your mind. Acknowledge the worry for what it is—a persistent thought, trying to capture your attention.

Now, ask yourself a simple yet profound question:

"What is the underlying purpose of this worry?

Consider this carefully. As I say to my clients:

"The body complains. It doesn't explain. It leaves that to the brain; and the brain most often get it wrong"[3].

Worry, as frustrating as it can be, often has a 'hidden' purpose. This purpose is hidden because it is often buried somewhere in the *subconscious*; which, as the name implies, is below our conscious awareness.

For example, your body might be trying to protect you. Stephen Porges tells the story about a Fire Chief who called his team to evacuate a building moments before the floor collapsed. He had no cognitive understanding, but he trusted his neuroception's unconscious ability to sense danger. In doing so, he saved himself and his team[4].

Alternatively, your body maybe attempting to prepare you for something. Perhaps there's a big event coming up – a major presentation, a meeting with a disgruntled key client or even a big trip that needs to go well.

There's a phenomenon that I call the *Weekly Worry Pattern*. This is a 'pattern of protection' where the human body is readying itself for danger or threat. It often besets leaders and managers on a Sunday evening, typically any time from 3pm. The bad feelings cause them to scan their work week to find all the likely suspects to explain why they are feeling bad. They then brood, mull and get worked up over all imaginary events that were not bothering them at all at 2pm.

This is a great example of the body complaining and the brain getting it all wrong. There's a better way: If you find yourself worrying, just take a moment and get centred. Perhaps do the *4-7-8 Breathing Technique* and/ or the *Tension Releasor*. Whatever works best for you, once your rational *Primate Brain* is back online, ask yourself:

"How is this worry trying to help me? What does it provide or protect me from?"

You may find that the answer is something related to feeling safe, avoiding risk, or safeguarding a certain outcome. Whatever the reason, it's important to recognise that your worry has a <u>*purpose*</u>, even if it's not serving you in the best way right now.

Once you've identified the reason that resonates with you, it's time to challenge the worry. Here's where we shift from concern to creativity. Ask your mind to come up with at least three different ways to achieve that same positive outcome, but without the stress and discomfort that worrying brings. These new methods should feel like genuine alternatives, ways to keep you safe, prepared, or in control, but in a calmer, more effective manner.

Take a moment to really explore these new options. Do they feel right to you? Does each one offer a solution that brings the same benefits as worrying, but without the emotional toll? If you feel any reluctance or hesitation, pause and ask your mind to resolve any inner disagreements. It's important that you feel at ease with these new approaches, and you'll know you're ready to move forward when you feel a sense of peace and confidence about them.

Now, let's take it a step further. Visualise yourself applying these new strategies in the future. Picture how you might handle similar situations using these calmer, more effective methods. See it, feel it, experience it as though it's already happening. The more you envision this, the more natural it will feel, as though it's the way you've always handled things.

In practising *The Worry Solver*, you're not just managing worry—you're rewiring your response to it. You're training your mind to find solutions that offer the same protection, but with less strain. Over time, this practice will allow you to face life's challenges with a sense of calm confidence, knowing that you have the tools to handle whatever comes your way.

Case Stories

The way our unconscious navigator guides us can vary significantly from one leader to another, shaped by individual experiences, cultural background, and personal temperament. Let's explore the contrasting styles of two brothers, who own and run several small-to-medium sized businesses together.

When the *Reptile* Dominates

Meet Mick, known for his cautious, discipled and methodical approach to business. His leadership style is characterised by a strong aversion to risk, a preference for established procedures, and a tendency to react defensively to new ideas or challenges to the status quo.

We can perceive his leadership style is influenced from an overactive *Reptilian Brain*, due to past experiences of failure, paternal and fraternal conflict in business contexts. Mick's neuroception is hyper-tuned to potential threats, causing him to perceive danger in situations that others might see as opportunities. He uses the word 'No' every time he hears a new idea in order to feel safe.

While this cautious approach can protect the company from certain types of risks, it has also stifled innovation and growth. Mick's team often feel discouraged from presenting new ideas, knowing they're likely to get a 'No' response. Over time, this has led to a stagnant company culture and missed opportunities in the market. In addition, Mick's fight-flight response kicks in immediately after any aspect of his life veers off its prescribed path. His demeanour becomes gruff and surly, treating those around him as if they are the problem.

In leadership, there's often an elusive but undeniable sense we call gut instinct—those moments when your internal compass seems to pull you towards a decision without an obvious logical rationale. Honing this instinct can elevate your leadership to a new level, and the best way to sharpen it is through thoughtful reflection and tracking. That's where a *decision journal* comes into play. By keeping a record of these gut feelings, along with their outcomes, you'll be able to spot patterns, learn when your instincts are sharpest, and improve your overall decision-making process.

Decision Journaling

> *In my experience, the biggest challenge people face is learning to get out of their own way*
> **Richard Bandler**

⁵First things first, you'll need a system that works for you: a digital journal—something like *Evernote*, *OneNote*, or a simple document—or, if you are old school like me, a physical notebook. Your preference doesn't matter. What does matter is self-discipline and consistency. Every time you log a gut feeling, be sure to include these basics:

- *Date* of the decision
- *Description of the decision* you're grappling with and the feeling it stirred
- *Context* and environment (Were you rushed? Was the decision complex?)
- *Rationale-to-Instinct* (R/I) *Ratio* (How much of this decision was driven by logic versus instinct?)
- *Expected Outcome* versus *Actual Outcome*

This framework will guide you in building a clearer picture of how your instincts play out over time.

Start by becoming more mindful of those moments when your gut feeling kicks in. They can sneak up on you during a meeting, as you respond to emails, or when you're making a high-level strategic call. When you sense a strong gut reaction, jot it down. Here's how you can make that entry more meaningful:

1. Be Specific About the Feeling

Don't just record "I had a bad feeling." Be precise: Was it excitement or fear? Did it feel like a 'yes' or a 'no'? Was the decision attractive or repulsive? The more you label the feeling, the more you'll start to understand its origins.

- **Pro tip**: *Notice where in your body the feeling appeared first. Was it in your chest? Did it move to your stomach? Perhaps it stayed in one spot or looped back around. Getting granular like this can help uncover patterns you might not notice otherwise.*

2. Context is Crucial

What was happening around you at the time? Were emotions running high? Did you have all the facts, or were you shooting from the hip due to time pressure? By capturing the context, you'll start to see whether certain environments amplify or mute your instincts.

3. Track the Rationale-to-Instinct (R/I) Ratio

Reflect on how much of the decision was based on cold, hard facts and how much relied on your gut. Use simple ratios like 50:50 or 80:20. Over time, you'll get a clearer picture of when your gut is most reliable and when it might need a logic check.

Monitor the Outcome

Decisions unfold at their own pace. Some outcomes are immediate, while others take weeks or months to come into focus. To make sure you don't forget, set reminders in your calendar or task management apps to review each decision at an appropriate interval.

When you come back to it, update your journal:

- Was the decision successful?
- Did your gut feeling guide you well, or did the outcome stray from your expectations?

- Were there any external factors or new information that changed the result?

This follow-up step is essential to learning from your instincts and improving your decision-making.

Review and Reflect on Patterns

Now that you've been logging your decisions, it's time to step back and review. Aim to do this once a month or once a quarter, depending on how frequently you've made entries. As you go through your journal, start identifying patterns:

1. **Look for Common Themes**

Are your gut instincts sharper in certain situations, like high-pressure environments or people-focused decisions? Or, conversely, are there times when they've led you astray, like when you didn't have enough data or felt rushed?

2. **Refine Your Self-Awareness**

Based on your reflections, fine-tune your approach. Are there moments when you need to trust your instincts more? Or situations where external pressures, biases, or emotions might cloud your judgment? This ongoing self-assessment will make you more conscious of when and how to rely on your gut feelings.

CONSISTENCY IMPERATIVE

The secret to success with this system is *consistency*. Keep up with your journaling, and over time, you'll collect enough data to see real patterns in your decision-making. But don't be too rigid either. The goal here is not to put your gut instinct on autopilot, but to blend it thoughtfully with rational analysis for more well-rounded decisions.

By consciously reflecting on your gut instincts, you can deepen your understanding of when to trust them and when to back them up with logic. The result? More informed, confident decisions—and leadership that feels both intuitive and grounded in reason.

This approach creates a reliable framework for personal growth and development, making you not just a leader who follows their gut, but one who hones it into a trusted tool for long-term success.

Balancing Instinct with Reason

In contrast with Mick, his brother, Ben, is known for his bold, innovative approach. Ben's leadership is characterised by quick intuitive decision-making, a willingness to take calculated risks, and an ability to inspire his team to push boundaries.

Ben's unconscious navigator seems to be calibrated differently. His neuroception is less sensitive to potential threats and more attuned to opportunities. This stems from a history of successful risk-taking.

While Ben's approach has led to breakthroughs and rapid growth, it also comes with its own set of challenges. He often overlooks genuine risks, pushes his team too hard in pursuit of his vision. His deep trust of his intuitions means that he will commit to large capital expenditures, without seeking Mick's agreement. To put it mildly, this 'seek forgiveness not permission' approach has become a source of explosive tension with Mick, who then obsesses about the downside.

Both Mick and Ben could benefit from a greater awareness of how their *unconscious navigator* is influencing their leadership style. For Mick, this has meant learning to question his instinctive caution, consciously looking for opportunities where his gut tells him to retreat. For Ben, it could involve developing practices to pause and reflect before acting on his intuitions, ensuring his risk-taking is truly calculated rather than impulsive.

Let's consider the practice of *Connect with Yourself*—that part of you that I've labelled *Unconscious Navigator*[6]. A rather simple yet profoundly effective method for those moments when life overwhelms you, when stress invades your body or your thoughts swirl restlessly. This technique offers not only rapid relief, often within a mere minute, but also the potential for deeper insight into how you might improve your current circumstances[7].

Connect with Yourself[8]

> "When you practice using your brain in this way, you will find yourself feeling really good a lot more often"
>
> **Richard Bandler**

First, acknowledge the stress you're experiencing. It's crucial to recognise when your body is holding onto tension or when your mind is entangled in an endless loop of racing thoughts. This act of recognition is the initial step towards regaining control—almost as if, by merely noticing it, you begin to dismantle its grip.

Next, shift your attention to one inch below your bellybutton. There's something curiously grounding about this. Think of a colour which, for you represents joy. Any colour will do, so long as it means joy to you and a light with that right there. Place your hand gently over the light, just under your bellybutton. Let your focus settle on the sensation of your hand resting there.

Take three slow, deliberate breaths and breathe into your 'joy' light. Feel your tummy move gently in and out. It's not the breath itself that's the magic here—it's the concentration, the return of your awareness to the body's centre, to your core, that initiates a calming effect. With each breath, you'll likely feel a gentle release, a loosening of that earlier tension.

Then, recall a moment of joy. It could be anything—a memory of happiness, love, or deep contentment. Allow yourself to step back into that experience fully. What can you see, what can you hear, how does it feel? Engage with the memory as though it's unfolding again right now, in the present. Let the colours become brighter and more vivid, and the sounds be crisper and richer. And let the feeling be stronger and more intense. In doing this, you're not simply distracting yourself; you're actively shifting your emotional state, reorienting your mind and body towards positivity.

And here's where it becomes interesting: as you settle into that feeling of grounded safety, imagine that your *Unconscious Navigator* can speak. What might it tell you? What advice would it give you in this moment? This isn't about grand biblical revelations but rather subtle wisdom—often your body knows what you need before your mind has had a chance to catch up.

Finally, act on what you've learned. Whatever small or large step emerges from this quiet dialogue with yourself, follow through as soon as you can. It's the act of listening and then doing that transforms this simple practice into something truly powerful.

By engaging in this, you're not just calming yourself; you're developing a deeper relationship with your own inner signals—signals that, more often than not, offer a clearer sense of direction than the noise of everyday life.

SECTION ONE SUMMARY

*The answer, my friend,
is <u>not</u> blowing in the wind*
Keith McCullough

The *Instinctual Foundations* section of *Neuro-Resilience Skills* delves into the primal instincts that underpin leadership decisions and behaviours. By examining the neurological and physiological roots of gut instincts, this section empowers leaders to understand, refine, and leverage their natural responses to navigate the complexities of leadership effectively.

The journey begins in Chapter 1, *Instinctual Contact*, which explores the visceral, immediate reactions that arise from our ancient survival mechanisms. These instincts, honed through evolution, serve as our primal compass in uncertain or threatening situations. The chapter explains how our "second brain," the enteric nervous system, communicates with the central nervous system, influencing both our emotions and decisions. Leaders are introduced to the *Tension Releasor*, a technique for achieving metabolic congruence—aligning their internal state with the external environment to foster clarity and poise under pressure.

Chapter 2, *Instinctual Awareness*, introduces the Triune Brain Theory as a framework for understanding how instinct, emotion, and reason interplay in decision-making. The Reptilian Brain governs our survival instincts, the Mammalian Brain manages emotions and social bonds, and the Primate Brain enables logical reasoning and foresight. Leaders learn how to recognise when these brain layers align or conflict, particularly in high-stakes scenarios. Through the *Dual-Mind Reflection*, they are guided to pause, assess, and harmonise gut feelings with rational analysis, achieving more balanced and effective decisions.

In Chapter 3, *Instinctual Acuity*, the focus shifts to the unconscious processes that guide our behaviours and perceptions. The concept of neuroception—our nervous system's ability to detect safety or danger without conscious thought—takes centre stage, revealing how these subtle cues shape our responses. Leaders explore how unconscious vigilance can provide invaluable insights but also lead to overreactions if unchecked. The chapter introduces techniques like *The Worry Solver*, which transforms stress into actionable clarity, and *Connect with Yourself*, which helps leaders ground themselves in moments of overwhelm. By honing their "Unconscious Navigator," leaders can develop sharper instincts and greater self-awareness, enabling them to make more confident, congruent decisions.

Throughout the section, real-world examples and case stories illustrate how instincts play out in leadership contexts. From a CEO grappling with a major merger decision to contrasting leadership styles driven by risk-aversion or boldness, these narratives highlight the dual-edged nature of instincts. Leaders are encouraged to reflect on their own patterns and biases, using the tools provided to refine their instinctual responses.

SECTION ONE SUMMARY

The *Instinctual Foundations* section equips leaders with a deeper understanding of their primal instincts, helping them harness these ancient systems to thrive in modern leadership. By integrating instinct, emotion, and reason, leaders can foster resilience, clarity, and congruence in their decisions and actions.

Techniques Introduced:

- **Somatic Honing** – Develop grounded, intuitive decision-making.
- **Tension Releasor** – Achieve metabolic congruence and calm under pressure.
- **Dual-Mind Reflection** – Balance gut feelings with rational analysis.
- **The Worry Solver** – Transform worry into actionable clarity and control.
- **Decision Journaling** – Track and refine instinct-driven decisions.
- **Connect with Yourself** – Reduce stress and foster self-awareness.

These techniques form the foundation for leaders to develop greater neuro-resilience, integrating their instinctual and rational capacities for more effective and balanced leadership. By mastering these skills, leaders can navigate uncertainty with confidence and authenticity, leveraging the wisdom of their instincts as a powerful leadership tool.

Instinctual Awareness Exercises

Somatic Honing

1. Relax into a comfortable position in a quiet space where you won't be disturbed
2. Begin by taking a few slow, deep breaths
3. Inhale through your nose and exhale through your mouth
4. Focus on the rhythm of your breathing to settle your mind
5. Beginning at your toes, shift your attention slowly upwards through your body
6. As you do so, notice any sensations, such as tension, warmth, or discomfort
7. As you move up your legs, just sense without judgment or the need to react
8. Move your attention to your tummy and all the area below your diaphragm
9. Become aware of any sensations that you feel whether comfortable or stressful
10. Feel the effect your breath in your tummy and then feel it in your chest
11. Bring awareness to your shoulders, neck, and head
12. Observe any tension or relaxation in your muscles and your jawline
13. Once you've scanned your entire body, take five deep, cleansing breaths
14. Recall the sensations you noticed, especially in your tummy, chest, neck and head.

Tension Releasor

As this works best as an 'eyes closed' process, as it removes visual stimuli and allows you to focus on physical sensations. It's a straightforward technique but read the steps through a couple of times.

1. Inside of your mind, use a *calm gentle caring <u>inner</u> voice* to narrate the words below
2. Your words should feel like somewhere between a *command* and a *suggestion*; because it's a gentle *invitation* for your body, ever so softly, ever so gently, really relax
3. As you start engaging each body part, from the top of your head down to your feet, move your conscious awareness through to each body part.
4. If you find tension, move your awareness through it like a masseur would move their thumb gently through a knot
5. Take your time with each body part: be thorough before moving onto another.

Head

- My *scalp* can soften and relax now...
- My *eyes* can soften and relax now...
- My *mouth* can soften and relax now...
- My *tongue* can soften and relax now...
- My *jaw* can soften and relax now...

Neck, Shoulders & Arms

- My *neck* can soften and relax now...
- My *shoulders* can soften and relax now...
- My *arms* can soften and relax now...
- My *hands* can soften and relax now...

Back & Glutes

- My *upper back* can soften and relax now...
- My *lower back* can soften and relax now...
- My *glutes* can soften and relax now...

Legs & Feet

- My *thighs* can soften and relax now...
- My *calves* can soften and relax now...
- My *feet* can soften and relax now...

And now my **mind** can soften and relax still more and more...

Pause for a little while to notice the feelings and then, if you wish, repeat the exercise. Stay with this increasingly relaxed and calm feeling as long as you wish. You will be able to return to full waking alertness, refreshed and alert, as soon as you are ready.

Dual-Mind Reflection

Purpose:

The *Dual-Mind Reflection* trains leaders to take a brief pause before making major decisions. During this pause, they can reflect on both rational analysis and gut feelings. It helps leaders slow down and make more mindful choices, especially under pressure.

Steps:

1. When a major decision is required, mentally note that you are about to make a choice. This small step stops things just running automatically, creating the space for a more deliberate approach.
2. Before proceeding, take a slow, deep breath to signal a pause. This helps disengage any immediate emotional reactions and shifts your mind into a more reflective state.
3. Begin the 4-7-8 Breathing Technique
   - *Inhale* through your nose for a count of 4 seconds.
   - *Hold* your breath for 7 seconds.
   - *Exhale* slowly and completely through your mouth for 8 seconds. Repeat this cycle 3-4 times to calm your nervous system and clear your mind.
4. After calming your body with the 4-7-8 breathing, reflect on the rational aspects of the decision. What facts or data do you have? What are the logical pros and cons?
5. Now, shift attention to your gut feelings. How does this decision make you feel emotionally? Do you sense excitement, hesitation, or discomfort? Honour these gut reactions as valuable sources of insight.
6. Pay attention to any physical sensations or tension in your body during this pause. Areas like your gut or chest may provide clues about hidden stress or discomfort related to the decision.

7. Now that you've reviewed both your rational analysis and gut feelings, balance the two perspectives. Are they aligned? Do they offer contrasting views?
8. After reflecting on both the logical and intuitive aspects, proceed with your decision. Trust that by pausing, you've gained a fuller, more holistic understanding of the situation.

The Worry Solver

1. Begin by focusing on something that has been causing you concern.
2. Ask yourself:
    - "What is the underlying purpose of this worry?
    - How is it trying to help me?
    - What does it provide or protect me from?

Be specific because the answer is often something related to safety or protection

3. Once you've identified the reason that resonates with you, challenge your Primate Brain, the rational mind, to find at least three different way to achieve the same positive outcome without the burden of stress or discomfort that comes with worrying.
4. Make sure you feel completely at ease with these new options. If you sense any reluctance, take a moment to ask your mind to resolve any inner disagreements. You will know you're ready when you feel peaceful and confident about moving forward with these alternatives.

Finally, visualise yourself applying these new approaches in the future at least five times or until it feels natural, as though it's the way you've always handled things.

Decision Journaling

1. **Choose Your Journal** – Use a digital tool or notebook; consistency matters more than format.
2. **Log Your Decisions** – Track key moments in meetings, emails, and strategic choices:

- **Date** – When did the gut feeling occur?
- **Decision & Feelings** – Briefly describe both.
- **Context** – Was it rushed, complex, or personal?
- **R/I Ratio** – Estimate the mix of reason vs. instinct.
- **Expected vs. Actual** – Measure decision accuracy.

3. **Be Specific About the Feeling**
    - Was it excitement, fear, certainty, or doubt?
    - Where did you feel it first (chest, stomach, etc.)?
4. **Capture the Context**
    - What was happening? Were emotions high? Did you have all the facts?
    - Identify environments that amplify or mute your instincts.
5. **Track the R/I Ratio**
    - Estimate the balance (e.g., 50:50, 80:20).
    - Over time, notice when your gut is reliable vs. when logic is needed.
6. **Monitor the Outcome**
    - Schedule periodic reviews (monthly/quarterly).
    - Reflect: Was your gut right? Did new information change the result?
7. **Review and Identify Patterns**
    - When are your instincts sharpest? When have they misled you?
    - Recognise when to lean on instinct vs. reason.
8. **Stay Consistent**

- Keep tracking to refine your instinct-reason balance.
- Recognise that different decisions (e.g., lunch vs. house purchase) require different ratios.
9. **Learn and Grow**
    - Develop confidence in balancing intuition with logic.
    - Become a leader who makes informed, intuitive decisions.

Connect with Yourself

1. Recognise the tension in your body or the racing thoughts in your mind.

   - Notice how you feel. This recognition alone starts to lessen the stress, as you begin to take back control.

2. As you shift your attention to a point about one inch below your bellybutton:

   - Think of the kind of intense joy that child have
   - Visualise a colour that represents that level of joy
   - Let that colour form into a light on that spot below your bellybutton
   - Place your hand gently over this spot and focus on the sensation of your hand resting there.

3. Take three slow, deep breaths, focusing on your 'joy' light.

   - As you breathe, feel your tummy gently rise and fall.
   - With each breath, notice how the tension begins to loosen, as you centre your awareness on your core.

4. Think of a joyful memory—a time when you felt happy, loved, or content:

   - Relive that moment in your mind. What do you see, hear, and feel?
   - Engage with this memory fully, as though it is happening now
   - Allow yourself to immerse in the positive emotions it brings

5. Settle into the feeling of calm and safety

- Imagine that your *Unconscious Navigator* can speak to you.
- Use your intuition sense any insights or subtle wisdom.
- Ask yourself:
    - *"What might it say? What advice does it offer?"*

6. Act on Your Insight

- This wisdom comes from a part of your being. Whether it's a small adjustment or a larger change, follow through as soon as possible.
- Acting on this inner wisdom turns this practice into a powerful tool for personal growth and direction.

SECTION TWO
PERSONAL RESILIENCE SKILLS

*If you know the enemy and know yourself,
you need not fear the result of a hundred battles*
Sun Tzu

In a world increasingly defined by complexity, uncertainty, and relentless demands, resilience is no longer a luxury but a necessity. For leaders, the stakes are even higher. Whether navigating a high-stakes negotiation, leading a team through layoffs, or managing personal crises while maintaining professional poise, leaders face challenges that test not just their intellect but their emotional and physiological thresholds. The three chapters in this section—*Core Skills*, *Intermediate Skills*, and *Advanced Skills*—offer a roadmap for developing neuro-resilience, an essential skillset for thriving under pressure and emerging stronger from adversity.

At the heart of this journey lies an understanding of our most primal instincts. Conceive of the moment a gazelle, grazing peacefully, senses a predator nearby. Without conscious thought, its body shifts into mobilisation or immobilisation, survival strategies deeply ingrained in its neurobiology. While humans are far removed from the savanna, these instinctive responses persist, influencing how we react to stressors in the workplace today. Recognising and mastering these primal forces is the foundation of personal resilience.

Understanding the Core

In *Chapter 4: Core Skills*, we begin with the basics—an exploration of how our body's primal instincts manifest in everyday life. Drawing on principles from neuro-linguistic programming (NLP) and the wisdom of ancient maxims like "know thyself," this chapter invites readers to map their internal responses. By uncovering patterns in their sensory modalities—visual, auditory, and kinaesthetic—leaders gain a clearer picture of how their body reacts to both positive and negative stimuli. This deep self-awareness lays the groundwork for a nuanced understanding of stress responses and their influence on decision-making, social engagement, and professional performance.

Through practical exercises such as *Instinct Mapping* and *Finding Home*, readers learn to bridge the gap between their conscious and unconscious responses. These tools empower leaders to move from reaction to intention, transforming instinctive impulses into purposeful actions.

Steadying the Ship

Building on this foundation, *Chapter 5: Intermediate Skills* delves into strategies for maintaining balance in turbulent times. Neuro-resilience, as illustrated through the metaphor of a seasoned ship captain steering through a storm, is about navigating crises with clarity and composure. Leaders are introduced to techniques like *Stepping Out of Fear* and *Taming Vicious Memories*, which help recalibrate physiological responses to perceived threats. These methods are not just about managing stress but about reprogramming the mind to perceive challenges with curiosity rather than fear[1].

Through relatable case stories, such as Rebecca's journey from reactive to responsive leadership, readers see how these tools can be applied to real-world situations. By learning to distinguish between instinctual reactions and thoughtful responses, leaders gain the ability to make better decisions, inspire confidence, and create an environment of psychological safety.

Mastering the Inner Game

Finally, *Chapter 6: Advanced Skills* challenges readers to elevate their resilience to a level of instinctual intelligence. This is where the journey moves beyond self-awareness and self-regulation into the realm of mastery. Advanced techniques like *Turning Anxiety Around* and *Wrapped in Serenity* help leaders transform negative emotional states into positive, productive ones. By actively engaging with and manipulating their internal experiences, leaders learn to harness the power of their instincts rather than being dominated by them.

This chapter introduces a four-tier model of instinctual development: *Instinct Ignorance, Instinct Awareness, Instinct Acuity,* and *Instinct Intelligence*. The progression through these stages reflects a leader's journey from being at the mercy of their physiological responses to leveraging them as tools for growth, creativity, and leadership excellence.

Why Resilience Matters

The skills presented in this section are not theoretical abstractions; they are practical, actionable techniques honed through years of research and application. They are designed to help leaders confront the realities of today's business—a landscape fraught with unpredictability and high stakes. More importantly, they offer a path to personal growth that extends beyond the workplace. By mastering these inner games, leaders can bring their best selves to every arena of life, fostering trust, collaboration, and resilience within their teams and organisations.

This section is not just about survival; it's about thriving. It's about understanding that our instincts, while rooted in evolutionary biology, can be guided, shaped, and even rewired to serve us in today's complex world[2]. With these skills, leaders will be better equipped to face challenges head-on, emerging not just unscathed but stronger, wiser, and more capable than before. Welcome to the journey of mastering your personal resilience skills. Let's begin.

FOUR
CORE SKILLS

The body knows things about which the mind is ignorant[1]
Jacques Lecoq

PICTURE A GAZELLE GRAZING peacefully on the African savanna. Suddenly, it catches the scent of a predator on the wind. In an instant, its entire physiology shifts. Muscles tense, heart rate accelerates, pupils dilate. The gazelle is poised on a knife-edge, ready to explode into action at the slightest provocation. This is mobilisation in its purest form.

Now, imagine that same gazelle, but this time it's too late. The predator is upon it. In a flash, the gazelle's body goes limp, its heart rate plummets, and it enters a state of profound stillness. This is immobilisation—nature's last-ditch survival strategy.

In neither case does the gazelle cognitively chose the mobilised and immobilised responses. They are entirely chosen by the gazelle's *body* bypassing its conscious awareness. These *unconscious choices* are not merely the province of wild animals. They are deeply embedded in our own neurobiology too, as humans have a shared mammalian ancestry with the gazelle. As it was put more beautifully in *The Descent of Man*[2]:

> *Man still bears in his bodily frame the indelible stamp of his lowly origin*
> **Charles Darwin**

They continue to determine our responses to perceived threats in the digital age society, *including the workplace and including top executives*. You, that is, the conscious 'you', does not choose your response. Your body does that itself. The conscious 'you' come up with justifying reason 'why' your body responded that way, afterwards.

This is important because it doesn't feel like that, but that's how mammalian bodies function. The separation is not between the 'mind' and the 'body', it's a sequencing of the 'unconscious' and 'unconscious' responses in both the brain and the rest of the body. Let's consider how these primordial responses might manifest in our contemporary professional lives:

Picture Samantha, an experienced and capable Senior Business Development Manager. She is getting ready for a high-stakes meeting. As she prepares to present a crucial proposal, she feels her heart racing, her palms growing sweaty. Her senses sharpen, her mind becomes hyper-focused. This is mobilisation at work—her body preparing her to face a challenge, not so different from our gazelle preparing to flee from a predator.

In many ways, this mobilised response can be adaptive in the workplace. It can sharpen our focus, enhance our performance, and push us to rise to challenges. It's what allows us to meet tight deadlines, think on our feet during difficult negotiations, or rally a team in times of crisis.

In NLP, the qualities of our senses become hidden doorways to our primal instincts. We all experience those powerful instinctual responses that pull us towards something we desire or push us away from something repelling.

Through the following fascinating technique, you will learn how your individual sense modalities of seeing (**V**isual), hearing (**A**uditory) and feeling (**K**inaesthetic) are represented differently by our nervous system. The different qualities and characteristics of these VAK modalities are called _**sub**_modalities, which is where your unique patterns are hidden.

As inscribed in the *Temple of Apollo* at Delphi is a famous maxim, 'know thyself'. It is important to note that it is *your particular* nervous system that you are about to explore. It will be thinking about a particular thing that *you* have chosen to think about. As such, this is a study of *your* subjective experience, not someone else's and certainly not everyone else's. This is a good thing because you'll uncover the sensory patterns that underpin *your* primal responses, specifically.

Since you'll need a reasonable degree of concentration, settle in somewhere peaceful, free from distractions, so you can focus entirely on your internal world. This exercise is most effective when you can immerse yourself without interruption. Be clear of the mission: you're here to uncover how *your* primal instincts manifest in your VAK submodalities.

Instinct Mapping[3]

> *In order to change beliefs, we first need to learn a way of finding out the qualities of beliefs*
> **Richard Bandler**

First think of one "move towards" instinctual response that you enjoy, such as lust or greed or desire; as well as one "move away from" response that you strongly dislike, like disgust, fear, or sadness. Write them down ahead of time.

Close your eyes and summon a vivid memory of a time when you felt a deep sense of lust or greed. These are base primal mammalian instincts that might be inappropriate conversations in the staff canteen. However, they are a part of you and, for good or ill, these primal drives drive your decisions. So, to uncover their patterns, the intensity of these primal feelings needs to be life and death intensity; not like you're going window shopping.

So, if it's lust, think of a time you were emersed in a lustful moment, completely locked into to that primal desire. If it's greed, remember an experience that you were intensely feeling**, "I want that! I'm taking it! That's mine!"**.

Whatever the instinct that you have picked, you want to be as aroused and focused as a starving man smelling meat on the barbeque. That's the level of primal instinctive intensity you require.

So, re-live the moment clearly by: 1) seeing what you saw through your eyes at the time; 2) hear what you heard through your ears and 3) feeling the strong primal urge building in your body. Now, make the pictures brighter and bolder, make the sounds richer and crisper and allow the sensations to intensify.

Now, holding everything at max intensity, make a note of the VAK qualities:

- **Visual**: Is the image bright or dim? Is it a movie or a still? Is it in colour or black and white? Is it sharp and in focused or is it a grainy or blurry? Are the colours vivid or dull? Is the image close to you, or does it seem distant? Is it 3D or flat?

- **Auditory**: Are there sounds in this memory? Are they loud or soft? Is the sound clear or muffled? Do the sounds seem to come from inside your head going out, or do they seem external coming towards you? Are there voices present? If so, what's the tone—seductive, calm, or something else?

- **Kinaesthetic**: Where do you feel the sensation in your body? How does it move through your body? Is it moving down/ up or left/ right? Do they feel warm or cool, sharp or soft? Is it a heavy or light feeling? Are you breathing high and fast at the top of your chest or low and slow in your abdomen?

Use the '*Submodality Comparison*' sheets in 'Appendix' and check off/ tick everything you've noticed about the characteristics and the qualities of the pictures, sounds, and feelings of this positive, instinctual response. If you detect tastes or smells check off/ tick them too. Remember: this is all about how *your* body and brain codes your thoughts, feelings and memories.

Then re-run the exercise for the negative instinct. I know that it is not fun doing strong negative feelings, so I would encourage you to do them really well, otherwise you'll need to repeat it (which really sucks!). So, again, if it's fear, think of a time where you were really scared. If it's disgust, make it an experience you had that was absolutely gross. Whatever the negative instinct that you have picked, you want to be as aroused and focused as a terrified running for their lives. That's the level of primal instinctive intensity you require.

These are your experiences, so you might as well make the most of them and, hopefully, for the last time.

With both sets of notes before you, look for the *difference* not the similarities. For example, if both pictures are grainy doesn't matter. If the sounds are muffled in both, or you are panting in both, these qualities do not matter. However, if one memory had a yellow hue and the other was more of a blue hue; if one picture had a border around it and the other didn't, that's important.

If one had sound coming in from the left and the other from the right; or one was loud and the other was silent, that's important. If the feelings with one seemed to circle in the tummy and the other was like it was shooting up your legs, that's important. If you could taste or smell something in one and something different (or nothing at all) in the other, that's what is important.

When Your Body's Lost Its Way

By mapping and comparing the submodalities of different states, you've laid the groundwork to understand how you respond to life's most instinctual moments. This is your opportunity to calibrate to your unique internal patterns. By doing so, your *instinct acuity* is a magnitude higher than most leaders. You have begun to know yourself in a more useful and unique way. But as Sophocles put in *Oedipus Rex*:

"Alas, how terrible is wisdom when it brings no profit to the man that's wise!

Because we can all get knocked off kilter, from time to time, and lose our way. Perhaps something has happened in our personal relationship, or some other disappointment has befallen us. Either way, as professionals we need to be able to get back to how we normally are. Or perhaps it's a problem in business and we don't want to contaminate our home life, with cranky intolerance, domestic tension and interrupted sleep. How can we get our old selves back?

This is a great point in the book to learn a method that, with practice, will allow you to take control of your stress for the rest of your life. I call it the *Finding Home*.

This process is not about eliminating stress entirely—after all, some stress is part of being alive—but rather about training your mind to handle it with grace, to meet life's challenges from a place of calm, rather than tension.

FINDING HOME

We begin by bringing clarity to the present sources of your stress. Take a few moments now to reflect and identify the five most significant sources of stress that are weighing on you. Write them down, if you can. There's something powerful in the act of naming them—by writing them out, you begin to gain control over them, shifting them from vague feelings to clear, tangible things you can work with.

Once you've compiled your list, we will go through each stressor, one by one. This will be an exercise in reducing their power over you. By doing so, you're also training your unconscious mind to maintain a lower overall stress level, a more natural state of ease. Please read and understand (even write down) the instructions before you begin. As an aid, all exercises are in short form at the end of the section.

Let's start with one stressor from your list. I want to create a calm anchor. Remembering the feeling of calm in the 'Connect with Yourself'. Go can just re-live the exercise in your mind: see what you saw, hear what you heard and feeling that lovely feeling of calm. Make the colours, sounds and sensations beautiful to you. Then press your thumb and middle finger together. And, as you press them together, take a deep, steady breath and find that the corners of your mouth are turning up into a little smile.

Think of the face of your favourite comedian. Notice that their face alone can bring you a smile. Because, neurologically, when things that are fired together are wired together. Their face, perhaps their voice. But when you think of it, it triggers a smile. As that feeling of calm joy peak, again press your thumb and finger to together. This is called *anchoring* because it ties the stimulus to the response. When you *fire the anchor*, the body will recall the feeling.

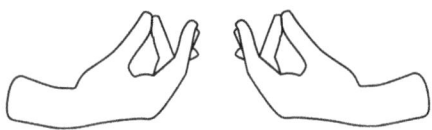

Now, bring to mind the stressful situation you've chosen, but hold it lightly. Picture yourself facing it, but with an unusual twist: imagine that you're looking at it with complete ease.

As this scene unfolds in your mind, let that sense of calm, initiated by your anchor, spread through your body. Now, visualise yourself moving through the situation smoothly. Picture what you'll see. Hear the sounds around you, the voices, the background hum of life. Feel how peaceful you are. Every movement, every decision, every interaction feels effortless. You are in control, not through force, but through calm presence.

Fire the anchor (press the thumb and finger together) and bring back calm and confident feeling. Now, bring the stressful situation to mind again, but this time, add a layer of complexity. Imagine that a few challenges arise—maybe the situation doesn't go perfectly, maybe things don't unfold exactly as planned. But here's the key: watch as you handle those challenges with the same calm ease. Again, see what you'll see, hear what you'll hear, and most importantly, feel the sense of calm as you navigate these obstacles effortlessly.

Pause for a moment. Reflect on how you feel now, in relation to that stressor. Does it feel different than it did a few minutes ago? Can you sense a shift in how your body is responding to it? If not, don't worry —sometimes these things take time, and *the beauty of this practice is in its repetition.* Simply repeat the process as needed, allowing your mind and body to adjust to this new way of being.

Now, repeat this exercise for the remaining stressors on your list. Take your time with each one, using your calm anchor to guide you back to that place of ease and control. With each round, you're not only reducing the power of these individual stressors, but you're also teaching your mind a new pattern. You're training it to generalise this calmness across your entire life, a calm that extends beyond these specific situations.

And here's the real power: as you continue to practice, you'll find that your unconscious mind starts adopting this lower stress level as its default state. Stressors will still come and go, but your baseline will be different—a foundation of calm resilience, ready to handle whatever life throws your way.

As we conclude this exploration of our body's responses in the workplace, let's return to our friend Sharon. Armed with this understanding of her own nervous system, she might approach that high-stakes presentation differently. She might recognise her racing heart not as anxiety to be suppressed, but as her body's way of rising to a challenge. She might use grounding techniques to modulate her activation, finding the sweet spot where she's energised but not overwhelmed.

And if she finds herself freezing in the face of harsh criticism? She might recognise this as an adaptive response to perceived threat and take steps to re-engage her social nervous system—perhaps by connecting with a supportive colleague or using breath work to shift her physiological state.

In our next chapter, we'll explore practical strategies for fostering this kind of nervous system literacy in the workplace, examining how organisations can create environments that support resilience, recovery, and the cultivation of our innate capacity for social engagement.

FIVE
INTERMEDIATE SKILLS

Rock bottom became the solid foundation on which I rebuilt my life
J.K. Rowling

SALTY SEAMEN STEERING through a perfect storm. The lashing rain and howling wind, the impenetrable blanket of darkness, and the relentless crashing of waves could easily overwhelm even the bravest souls. Yet, the captain stands steady at the helm, his demeanour a reflection of his calm poise and focus—a beacon of hope for the anxious crew. This is the essence of neuro-resilience in leadership—the ability to maintain equilibrium and effectiveness, even in the face of overwhelming challenges.

As we venture deeper into the complex terrain of instinct and leadership, we arrive at a critical juncture: how can leaders develop the personal capacity to navigate the turbulent waters of instinctual and emotional responses? And let's be honest, we've all been there, haven't we? Faced with unexpected challenges that trigger something primal within us? The answer lies in cultivating neuro-resilience—a set of skills that enables leaders not only to weather the storm themselves but also to guide their teams through it.

THE CASE FOR *Neuro-Resilience*

Present day leaders face unprecedented levels of complexity, uncertainty and stress, from rapidly changing demographics, to fluctuating regulations and exponential advances in technology. Have you ever noticed that no matter how much strategic planning you do, some situations hit you in ways you didn't expect? That's because many challenges trigger our most primitive instinctual responses, bypassing rational thought processes and leading to reactive, suboptimal decisions.

Take Gary, the factory general manager. His finance manager, Rebecca, is well-versed in strategic planning, financial analysis, and team management. But when faced with a crisis that triggered her fight-or-flight response, all that knowledge went out the window, as her reptilian brain took over. Sound familiar? After Rebecca's 'blank mind' moment, Gary had her trained in neuro-resilience skills.

Months later, Gary tells her to prepare the planning for a series of layoffs. This announcement jolts her and her body responds in exactly the same way. This time, however, Rebecca understands that her body is having a reflex-like instinctual response called 'fight-or-flight'.

She understands that her body has chosen to go through a series of physiological *patterns of protection*: her brain's alarm system, the amygdala, has kicked into gear; stress hormones, like cortisol and adrenaline, are flooding her body; her heart rate and blood pressure are spiking; and blood flow is being redirected from her primate brain to the limbs, priming her for battle or to run.

Recognising this change of state, Rebecca takes a moment to begin to autoregulate, in order to access the higher cognitive functions in her primate brain. She uses the *Stepping Out of Fear* technique which is designed to help step back from stressful thoughts, creating both distance and clarity.

STEPPING *Out of Fear*

This method is particularly effective when you find yourself overwhelmed by emotions tied to a specific situation. Remember, Rebecca's mobilised response is not because there is actual danger in front of her. Rather, her brain has conjured pictures and sounds that are believable enough to her body, which then shifts into 'fight-or-flight.' As imaginary problems require imaginary solutions, Rebecca understands that she must change the way she is imagining the situation to become calmer and more objective. Take a moment to read the instructions fully.

Start by bringing the source of your stress to mind. It could be a recent event or something from the past that still lingers. Perhaps it's a future worry that's playing on your mind. Whatever it is, take a moment to picture it.

This image might come to you as a collection of still frames—faces, locations, or specific moments. Or it could play like a short video, a scene unfolding in your mind. However, it appears to you is perfectly fine; the important thing is to bring it into focus in a way that feels natural.

Now, imagine stepping out of the scene entirely. Visualise yourself as if you were watching a film, but instead of being inside the action, you're floating gently away from it. Feel yourself moving back from your body, so you can now see the back of your head, as though you're observing yourself from a distance. Sometimes people find it easier visualising this by drifting out from the side and seeing themselves in profile. Whichever way works easiest, you will be able to see yourself in the movie. At the same time, your awareness is outside of the movie, watching it play out.

Keep moving away, until the scene is about three metres away from you. You're now viewing it from a safe distance, as though it's happening to someone else. In a similar way watching people on a rollercoaster from the ground is different from the firsthand experience of being in the rollercoaster. From this vantage point of three metres away, the situation feels less immediate, less overwhelming, allowing you to see it with a bit more objectivity.

Next, remove all the colour from the scene. Picture it as if it were an old black-and-white film. The vibrancy is gone, and with it, the emotional charge begins to dull even more. The movie is still playing, but it's stripped of the vividness that makes it feel so present.

Now, shrink the image down to a tenth of the original size. Picture the scene becoming smaller, more manageable. As it reduces in size, notice how your feelings towards it begin to shift. It's no longer looming over you—it is now something contained, something you can observe without feeling so affected.

Finally, make the image transparent. Let it fade, becoming lighter and more translucent, until it's barely there. You can still see it, but it no longer holds the same power. The scene, once so vivid and pressing, has now faded to a shadow of its former self[1].

With the emotional intensity reduced, you're in a better position to think clearly. Ask yourself: Are there any decisions you need to make about this situation? If so, make them now, from this calmer, more detached viewpoint. This distance allows you to see the problem without being entangled in its emotional web.

When you're ready, you can return to the present moment. The stressful image, now reduced, no longer holds the same weight. This practice, done regularly, can help you gain perspective on challenges that feel overwhelming, giving you space to respond thoughtfully rather than react emotionally.

In time, you'll find that this process becomes a natural response to stress, a way of reframing difficult situations and regaining your emotional balance.

Previous Bad Experiences

Rather than being triggered by imagining a danger that is not actually there, a fight-or-flight response is often triggered by memories of something that really happened. Because of their nature, these memories usually involve moments of adrenaline and noradrenaline associated with a mobilised response. Just as adrenaline in the body give us the energy to fight or escape, noradrenaline is the equivalent for the brain, where it seems to make things slow down, visuals become more vivid, and our hearing is more acute. Our survival wisdom has put our body on instant high alert.

In a world of sabertoothed tigers, it is easy to understand how the ability to be stronger, faster, with sharper senses is an advantage to survival. However, after the event, these vivid pictures, crisp sounds and negative physical arousal can come back as very disturbing memories. This is especially so as they stand out starkly from other everyday memories like having a wonderful day at the beach or lovely meal with the family.

Taming *Vicious Memories*[2]

Let's explore a powerful technique for transforming the emotional weight of a difficult memory. This exercise invites you to reframe the experience in a way that detaches it from the negative emotions that have been bound to it. Think of it as a kind of mental editing, where you become both the director and the viewer of your own film. All the exercises are listed in the end of the section in simple step 1, 2, 3 form. Before you do the exercises, read them through thorough here, so that you clear what to do.

To begin, see yourself sitting comfortably in a cozy cinema. The kind of seat that's so perfectly designed for relaxation, you feel at ease the moment you settle in. The lights are dim, the room is quiet, and everything is set for you to watch a film—not just any film, but one that you're going to re-edit for your own benefit.

Now, imagine that you can float out of your body, gently rising up towards the projection booth above. From this new vantage point behind the protective glass, you can see yourself seated below, completely relaxed, ready to watch the screen. You're still present, but in a way that feels distant from the scene unfolding before you.

On the screen, you're about to watch a troubling memory. But before it starts, identify two key moments: the first is just before the event took place—what you might call the **before** moment—and the second is just after you successfully navigated through the experience, the **after** moment. These two moments serve as the boundaries of the memory you're about to reframe.

Project a still image of the **before** moment onto the screen. From your safe spot in the projection booth, observe yourself seated in the cinema below, watching this image on the screen. This creates a layered distance between you and the memory—a gentle buffer of safety.

Now, let the film play. Watch the memory unfold from the **before** moment, moving all the way through to the **after** moment, where you've come out the other side. Once you reach the end of the event, freeze the frame on the screen at the **after** point, that moment where the difficult experience has passed, and you are safe.

Here's where the rewiring begins. In your mind, play the film in reverse, as quickly as possible. Watch everything rewind—the visuals, the sounds, even the sensations—all racing backwards to the **before** moment. Imagine the entire experience unravelling, like watching a tape reel spinning rapidly in reverse.

Repeat this process five times fast. Watch the memory play out, then swiftly rewind it back to the beginning. With each repetition, you will find that the emotional intensity lessens, you can recall the memory, but the intensity of feelings that you have are diminished. It's as if the memory has lost its sting, leaving you with a clearer, calmer perspective.

FAST & Easy Refresh

To further reinforce this process, consider engaging in regular relaxation practices, such as listening to a hypnotic trance, which can help dissolve any lingering discomfort.

SCAN THIS QR Code here for a lovely trance that lasts under ten minutes. It's a fast and easy way to move from the idea of altering your state to just doing it. I was asked to do a 'trance under 10' for someone in Orlando, Florida. This is a recording of that moment: cleaned up, enhanced and published.

Neuro-Spa

It can be done 'eyes open' or 'eyes closed' - it's under ten minutes long. Take the time and try both. Do then do it both ways a second time. Coming in and out of an altered state, trains your neurology to do it deliberately.

Through repetition, you're not just increasing your skill—you're training your mind to think in a different way, your body to feel a different way, which will lead you to choose do things differently. This is *personal freedom*.

Slowly *Then Suddenly*

We've discussed how getting sudden bad news or a sudden recollection of a bad experience can trigger a mobilised response, which downgrades our cognitive function. Another way leaders have learned to downgrade their cognition is by generating a gloomy view about themselves and their future.

It's not uncommon for even the best of leaders to hit a run of adverse results, none of which are directly related to their individual or even their team's performance. After all, in business, the 'Business Cycle' cycles through boom and bust. It is intellectually honest and will keep you grounded were you to admit it when your results are looking great without really deserving it. After all, sometime dumb luck can be lucky. On the other hand, congratulating yourself for good dumb luck is not only dishonest, but also deluded.

Dumb luck also has a double-edged sword because, at other times, dumb luck can be *unlucky*. Similarly, castigating yourself for bad dumb luck is not only dishonest, but also unnecessarily demoralising. Worse still, with a string of bad luck, you can begin to list into an emotional downward spiral, dragging your team along with you.

Once more, that spiral is a result of one's imagination, because you've built a belief from the conviction you have that the past predicts the future, the current trajectory will persist, and that cycles don't cycle. The brain then projects a visual hallucination of horrible things with a hideous internal dialogue pouring gasoline on the flames.

Again, this jolts your body into metabolic and behavioural *patterns of protection*. And, as long as the gloomy hallucinations continue, the protective patterns will continue; eventually becoming toxic. What is needed is a way of letting your emotional balance to naturally reset, creating the space for calm and clarity to emerge, once again.

. . .

SILENCING the Storm[3]

Bring to your mind a situation that has been causing you stress or worry. It could be something recent or a long-standing issue that seems to resurface time and again. Take a moment to let this situation come into focus.

Now, pause and reflect on the narrative you've been telling yourself about this situation. Often, these stories sound something like:

- "There's nothing I can do, it's all going sideways again."
- "This is just the way things are in my department. There's just no way out."
- "I don't think I can handle this anymore. I'm beaten."
- "Why can't we ever get a break?"

It doesn't matter if the story is perfectly clear in your mind or if it's vague and unformed—simply allow yourself to connect with whatever *inner dialogue* feels familiar. If necessary, feel free to create an example that fits the gist of how you are feeling.

Now, turn your attention to that voice, the one repeating the gloomy narrative. Where does it seem to come from? Does it come in from the front, the back, the left- or right-hand side of your head? Or does it come from the inside out? If so, in which direction is it coming out? Just notice from where this internal dialogue seems to arise and go to.

Next, visualise those words, in their written form, leaving your mind. See them drifting outward, like subtitles in a film. Now, hear the same voice three metres away from you. As you hear the voice over there, still gibbering and whining away about the same old nonsense as it did inside your head. However, notice how your feelings have changed.

What happens when that story is no longer sitting inside your head but out there? This shift in perspective—moving the voice outside yourself—creates a kind of emotional shift. It helps your mind reframe the story, creating distance between you and the old narrative. With that narrative no longer looming inside you, you'll find there's room for something new now—something closer, better and more empowering.

At your own pace, begin to lower the volume of that distant voice. Let it grow quieter, softer, until it's barely audible, a whisper on the edge of your awareness. And as the volume fades, notice how it feels to no longer be tethered to that old story. And, in this newly cleared space, recognise that you have the freedom to create a new narrative.

By engaging in this practice, you are not just quieting the noise of self-doubt and worry—you are actively regulating your emotions, repairing your own safety. Preparing the groundwork for a better that moves you forward. And the more you do this, the more practice you put in, the more natural it will become, allowing you to regain your sense of safety.

By learning to *rewire* how the brain has encoded a horrible event, both real from the past and think about the present or the future, you open the door to a mind that is not only capable of healing but also of growing stronger through each of challenges. That is part of what I call the *Inner Game* of neuro-resilience skills.

SIX
ADVANCED SKILLS

So throw away your baggage and go forward
Aldous Huxley

THERE ARE LEVELS TO NLP. As such, we shall continue practical applications to build the skills and learning that leaders need to grow:

1. *Instinctual Ignorance* – where their metabolism and behaviours shift in a Pavlovian manner, which they do not understand but then justify to themselves after the event.
2. *Instinctual Awareness* – where they become conscious of how their instincts manifest in the feelings and sensation in the different part and all over their whole body.
3. *Instinctual Acuity* – where they become nuanced about their own neurological impulse that move us towards and away from things; how they manifest in their subjective experience, their VAK submodalities; how patterns of

protection present themselves; and how they affect their decisions.
4. *Instinctual Intelligence* – where they learn to trust their instincts when appropriate; as well as to engage with them to think differently, feel differently and act differently. They know umpteen ways to dial their negative feelings down, when they are being counterproductive. They know how to return to a state of safety, from the skin in, to make social engagement, problem-solving and decision-making fully available to us.

In the strategies in the last chapter, we learned highly effective with imaginary visual and auditory solutions to fight-flight responses, which were created by visual and auditory memories and hallucinations. These techniques are from NLP, specifically as they are taught by Dr. Richard Bandler, which is about finding what people actually do to get over their problems and systematising them, so that we can do it ourselves.

The system being, changing how we think (visually and auditorily) changes how we feel (instinctively and emotionally) changes how we act (socially and cognitively). As with almost all activities, people get better, faster and more precise the more often they do the activity. Practice makes perfect and 'perfect' is just a lot of little things done well.

This next technique, whilst using the same NLP technology, is technique from an approach called *Neuro-Hypnotic Repatterning* (NHR), invented by Richard Bandler and is one of the most impactful and useful techniques. In this book, we shall use it, once more, to repair safety, in this case, your own.

Turning **Anxiety Around**[1]

> *"By reversing the spin of a negative emotion,*
> *you can transform it into a positive one"*
> **Richard Bandler**

Let's explore an approach to anxiety that takes us beyond merely acknowledging it and into the realm of actively engaging with how it feels in the body. Again, anxiety is an unpleasant feeling, so when you are practicing this technique, go all in so that you can learn the technique quickly and well.

Start by bringing to your mind something that makes you anxious or fearful. I can tell you, as a husband, father, brother and son, there are a number of things that could get me into a cold sweat in a heartbeat. So, if there is nothing making you anxious at present, make one up. As you focus on this, notice where the sensation of anxiety settles in your body. If you pay close attention, you'll find that it doesn't just sit still. In fact, anxiety often has a kind of spin to it, a movement that you can feel if you concentrate closely enough. This movement can take several forms.

For some, the anxiety might spin along the midline of the body, perhaps moving upward from the base of the torso, curving back down, and then repeating this upward and downward cycle. For others, it might move in the opposite direction, spinning downward, curving up, and then looping again. There's another possibility, where anxiety crosses from one side of the body to the other. It might rise up one side, cross over the midline at the top, descend the other side, and then come back up again. Or perhaps the motion starts lower, moving down one side, crossing at the bottom, and then rising again. Some people feel it more like a flat disc, spinning horizontally across the body, moving either left to right or right to left[2].

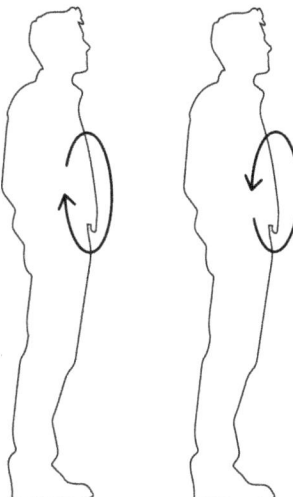

Spinning feeling coming up/ down the midline

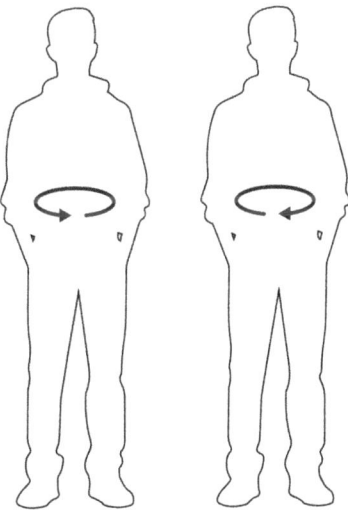

Spinning feeling like a flat disc, on/ crossing the midline

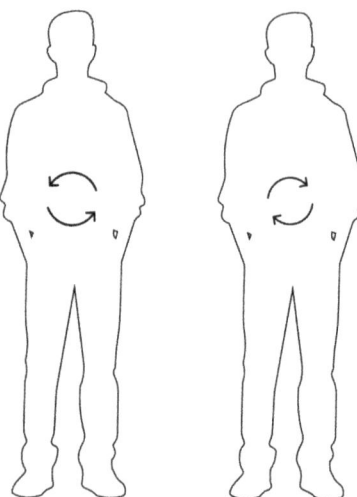

Spinning across the abdominal crossing the midline

Whichever way it moves for you, I want you to visualise it clearly. Imagine it as a red spinning energy, marking the direction of the movement. Once you've got this picture in your mind, here's the next step: speed it up. Double the speed of that red spinning motion, and as you do, you'll notice the anxiety intensifying. It's remarkable how easily we can make ourselves feel more anxious just by amplifying that sensation, by letting the spin accelerate. But here's the good news —just as you've sped it up, you can also slow it back down.

Gradually reduce the speed until the spin returns to its original pace. Already, you'll feel the anxiety settling. But let's take it further. Slow the spin even more—bring it down to half speed, then to a quarter. And then, stop it completely. Feel the stillness that follows when that anxious energy is absent.

Now, for the fun part: reverse the direction. Imagine that red spin turning green as it begins to rotate in the opposite direction. Let it start slowly, just as before—25%, then 50%, and finally back to full speed in the opposite direction. As it spins in this new way, notice how different you feel.

Keep thinking about the thing that used to make you anxious. The tension that was there earlier is dissipating. Where once there was anxiety, there is now something else and the opposite of anxiety is curiosity. And you can be curious about the sense of calm returning to the body. This is important because calm and curiosity are features of your safety repaired.

Now, bring to mind again the thing that was causing your anxiety. Look at it but notice how it's not the same as it was before. Something about the feeling has shifted, hasn't it? You've turned your fear around. Keep those green feeling spinning, reinforcing the new feeling of ease and control.

This technique isn't just about stopping anxiety—it's about expanding your understanding of what is possible in the *inner game*. You see, by engaging with the physical sensation of anxiety, by adjusting its speed and direction, you're showing yourself that this feeling is not as fixed or out of control at all. You *can* intervene. You are *able* alter it. You can speed it up, slow it down and put it into reverse. You have *agency*. You have *control!*

Now that you have the ability to think about things that used to scare you with complete impunity, I invite you to make a list of all of those things that once scared you. As you spin the green feeling, begin to grin as their effect on you floats out of you like vapour from a hot tub on a cool evening. The more you practice replacing unpleasant feelings with pleasant feelings the more you will, bit by bit, enjoy life to the fullest; which is the direction we are going now.

Let's explore these kinaesthetic submodalities in a technique designed to deepen the sense of calm inside you. The kind of inner calm that feels not only tranquil but also can be summoned at will—a practice I call *Wrapped in Serenity*. This technique not only helps to centre you in moments where you are under pressure but also teaches your body and mind to associate a simple gesture with profound peace. The beauty of this technique lies in its subtlety; the more you practice it, the more it becomes a natural part of your emotional toolkit, ready to be deployed whenever you need it.

Wrapped in Serenity

As you spin the green feeling, begin at the back of your mind, to remember a time when you felt completely calm and tranquil and serene. This is not just a casual glimpse of a memory—rather, I want you to truly immerse yourself in it. Maybe it was a time you were on holiday, watching the mesmerising sheen of sunlight glistening the sea. Or maybe it was a time when you were enjoying a lovely massage, and you found your mind drifting somewhere between being awake and in a dream. Whatever is your memory, remember a moment when calmness enveloped you, when the world seemed to align in peaceful harmony, and you felt entirely in control.

Close your eyes. And allow yourself to drift back into that experience. What do you see around you? What are the sounds that fill the air? Can you smell tranquil scents? Everyone is as unique as their own thumb print, so when you have a serene experience, savour it and file it away for later use. For me, the time that I go back to is my first time in India with my (to be) wife.

I was lazing on a hammock between two coconut trees on an island, which had palest sand I had ever seen. The island was off the coast of Goa and was idyllic. The sun was the colour of an egg yoke, which crowned the azure blue sky. The warmth of that sun was perfectly balanced by cool of the sea breeze. The hammock swayed in the breeze and, with the sound of the sea, I closed my eyes. I could hear children laughing in the distance, sea birds nearby and I drifted off into a revery. That was over twenty years ago and I can conjure it back effortlessly.

Whatever your memory you can bring to mind, the most important thing is to pick one gives a deep sense of peacefulness. When the feeling comes, how does it *feel* to be in that state of calm? If a specific memory doesn't come to mind, don't worry. Simply imagine a scene where you are as relaxed as you could ever wish to be, fully equipped with ease, comfort, and an unshakeable sense of self-control. Now start to spin that feeling of serenity into the green feeling.

Now, as you settle into that memory or imagined scene, let's take it a step further. I want you to *enhance* the experience—begin to manipulate and play with your submodalities. Make the colours softer and more gentle and more lovely. Make the sounds more soothing, more melodic, more entrancing. Spin all of these changes into the green feeling and say inside your mind, '*soften*', and say it softer. Softest.

Let yourself be completely absorbed by this serenity as it spread through your whole body. As you do this, gently press the thumb and middle finger of your right hand together. This is an important part of the technique, as it creates a physical link to this calm feeling: *things that are fired together are wired together*. By repeating this simple gesture while immersed in serenity, you're teaching your mind and body that this sensation of calm is always accessible. Do this a few times, each time deepening the peace you feel.

Now, let's solidify this connection. Reloop that moment of calm at least five more times. Each time you revisit it, spin the green feeling, press your thumb and middle finger together, reinforcing the bond between this gentle action and the serene emotions. You'll know the technique is taking effect when, simply by squeezing your thumb and finger, you start to feel a gentle wave of relaxation washing over you.

Next, we'll move on to a scenario that has caused you mild stress in the past. Think of a situation that, while not overwhelming, has triggered some level of tension or unease. As you bring that situation to mind, spinning the calm feeling, press your thumb and middle finger together once again. Let the calming sensation flow through you. Welcome that feeling. Now, see yourself carrying this calm into the stressful situation. As you spin the calm feeling, visualise everything unfolding smoothly, just as you would want it to. See the scene before you, hear the sounds, and feel what it is like to feel so safe, to remain calm and composed.

With that sense of calm fully restored, let's up the challenge. While continuing to press your thumb and finger together, think of the same scenario, but this time add a few extra challenges or obstacles. Perhaps the stakes are higher, or the demands on you are greater. But here's the key—spin the calming feeling, press your thumb and finger together, and see yourself handling it all with ease. Picture yourself moving through the scene with the same serenity as before. Hear the sounds, feel the sensations, and enjoy the satisfaction of knowing that no matter what arises, you remain in control.

Now, take a moment of quiet reflection. Notice the change in how you feel about what used to be stressful situation. It is no longer daunting, is it? Practice is an important feature of this ability. These things are never 'one and done'. Repeat the exercise regularly so that, should you be blindsided by an event or a moment, you'll know how to restore a sense of calm both consciously and unconsciously. With each repetition, you'll find that spinning feelings of calm becomes easier and more immediate. The control is at your fingertips.

Through this practice, you are not only building a reliable way to reduce stress; you are training your mind and body to work together, creating a sense of calm that you can summon whenever you need it most. This is the power of *Wrapped in Serenity*—simple, subtle, and yet deeply transformative.

As we conclude our exploration of instinct in leadership, remember that developing instinctual intelligence and effective stress management is an ongoing journey. It requires consistent practice, reflection, and a willingness to learn from both successes and failures. By mastering their *inner game*, leaders can navigate the complexities of business with greater confidence, agility, and effectiveness, while also creating more resilient and psychologically safe work environments.

SECTION TWO SUMMARY

*I can be changed by what happens to me.
But I refuse to be reduced by it*
Maya Angelou

The Personal Resilience Skills section serves as the foundation for mastering *neuro-resilience*, equipping leaders with the tools to navigate stress, regulate emotions, and enhance their decision-making. By delving into the interplay between instinct, physiology, and cognition, this section provides a practical framework for understanding and transforming unconscious responses into conscious, productive behaviours.

The journey begins with Core Skills in Chapter 4, where readers are introduced to the fundamental concept of instinct mapping. Drawing parallels between the instinctive responses of humans and animals, such as a gazelle's fight-or-flight reactions, the chapter explores how these primal patterns manifest in the workplace. Leaders learn that their body often chooses its responses—mobilisation, immobilisation, or social engagement—before the conscious mind even registers the situation[1]. Through techniques like Instinct Mapping and Finding Home, readers gain the ability to uncover their unique sensory patterns and regulate stress responses, setting the stage for more intentional and informed actions.

In Chapter 5, Intermediate Skills expands on these foundations, equipping readers with methods to manage more complex and emotionally charged situations. Leaders learn to maintain balance and perspective, even under significant pressure, by recognising the physiological and emotional triggers that can derail their effectiveness. Techniques such as Stepping Out of Fear, Taming Vicious Memories, and Silencing the Storm help leaders reframe their experiences, transforming overwhelming emotions into manageable challenges. Silencing the Storm, in particular, teaches leaders to dismantle internal narratives of self-doubt and worry, replacing them with constructive inner dialogues that restore emotional balance.

Finally, Advanced Skills in Chapter 6 takes readers to the next level of neuro-resilience mastery, introducing techniques to fine-tune emotional regulation and deepen instinctual intelligence. Leaders learn to move beyond instinct awareness into instinct acuity and intelligence, developing the ability to not only recognise but also manipulate and transform their emotional states. Techniques like Turning Anxiety Around and Wrapped in Serenity empower leaders to proactively reshape negative emotions, using them as opportunities for growth and self-mastery. This chapter also introduces the concept of layering calmness into even the most challenging situations, creating a reservoir of resilience that leaders can draw upon whenever needed.

Across all three chapters, the emphasis is on practice, reflection, and refinement. Leaders are encouraged to embrace these tools as lifelong skills, essential not only for personal growth but also for creating resilient, psychologically safe environments for their teams. By the end of this section, readers will have gained a robust toolkit for navigating the complexities of leadership with confidence, clarity, and calm.

Techniques Introduced in the Section[2]:

1. **Instinct Mapping** – Identify sensory patterns of primal responses.
2. **Finding Home** – Reset emotional balance to return to a state of calm.
3. **Stepping Out of Fear** – Create distance and clarity from overwhelming thoughts.
4. **Taming Vicious Memories** – Reframe emotionally charged past experiences.
5. **Silencing the Storm** – Dial down the negative internal dialogue.
6. **Turning Anxiety Around** – Reverse the physical sensations of anxiety.
7. **Wrapped in Serenity** – Anchor sweet calmness through kinaesthetic.

These techniques collectively form the foundation of personal resilience, enabling leaders to transform their instinctual responses into tools for success and wellbeing.

Autoregulation Exercises

Instinct Mapping

<u>Step 1: Choose Two Instincts to Explore</u>

Think of one "move towards" instinctual response that are pleasure seeking (such as desire, lust, or ambition) and one "move away from" response that you strongly dislike (such as disgust, fear, or rage). Write them down ahead of time.

<u>Step 2: Recreate the Positive Instinct</u>

Close your eyes and summon a vivid memory of a time when you felt the "move towards" instinct deeply, like a strong desire or lust. Bring the memory to life by seeing what you saw, hearing what you heard, and feeling what you felt.

<u>Step 3: Record the Negative Submodalities</u>

Using the 'Experience 1' column in the *Submodality Comparisons* sheet below, itemise the characteristics and qualities for each sensory modality.

<u>Step 4: Recreate the Positive Instinct</u>

Next, bring up a memory of the "move away from" instinct. Recreate the strong negative feeling, whether it was fear, disgust, or anger, and re-live it fully, with the same intensity as you experienced in the moment.

<u>Step 5: Record the Negative Submodalities</u>

Using the 'Experience 2' column in the *Submodality Comparisons* sheet below, itemise the characteristics and qualities for each sensory modality.

<u>Step 6: Compare the Differences</u>

Now compare the submodalities of your two instincts. What are the main differences between how you experienced the "move towards" and the "move away from" responses?

As Richard Bandler states, "It's the differences that make the difference". So, look for differences, not what's similar. That way you can easily calibrate to how your brain codes the positive versus the negative instinct.

Submodality Comparisons

	Experience 1	Experience 2
VISUAL		
Number of images		
Motion/still		
Colour/black and white		
Bright/dim		
Focused/unfocused		
Bordered/panoramic		
Associated/dissociated		
Centre-weighted/wide angle		
Size (relative to life)		
Shape		
Three-dimensional/flat		
Close/distant		
Location in space		
AUDITORY		
Number of sounds/sources		
Volume		
Tone		
Tempo		
Pitch		
Pace		
Timber		
Duration		
Intensity		
Direction		
Intensity		
Direction		
Rhythm		
Harmony		
More in one ear than another		
KINESTHETIC		
Location in body		
Breathing rate		
Pulse rate		
Skin temperature		
Weight		
Pressure		
Intensity		
Tactile sensations		
OLFACTORY & GUSTATORY		
Sweet		
Sour		
Salt		
Bitter		
Aroma		
Fragrance		
Essences		
Pungency		

Finding Home

Goal: To manage stress through a calm and controlled mindset.

1. Take a moment to think about the five biggest sources of stress in your life right now.

- Write them down. Naming your stressors makes them easier to handle.

2. Choose one stressor from your list to focus on for this exercise.

3. Activate Your *Finding Home Again* anchor

- Use a physical gesture (such as pressing your thumb and finger together) to signal calmness.
- Take a deep, steady breath while doing this to centre yourself.

4. Bring the stressful situation to mind but imagine yourself handling it with complete calmness.

- Picture yourself moving through the situation smoothly and effortlessly.
- See what you'll see, hear the sounds around you, and feel the calm in your body.

5. Now, imagine the situation with some challenges or setbacks.

- Visualise yourself calmly handling these challenges with the same ease and control.

- Keep your physical anchor gesture active to maintain your calm state.

6. Pause and check in with yourself. How do you feel about that stressor now?

- Notice if your body feels more relaxed or if the stressor feels less intense.

7. Move on to the other stressors on your list, repeating steps 2 to 6 for each one.

- Take your time, allowing the calm feeling to settle in after each round.

8. Build Long-Term Calm

- With practice, your mind will learn to handle stress from a place of calm and resilience.
- Over time, your unconscious mind will make this state your new default, helping you handle future stress more easily.

Practice this exercise regularly to make calmness a natural part of your response to life's challenges.

Stepping out of Fear

1. Identify the Stressor

   - Recall the stressful situation-past, present, or future.
   - Picture it clearly, either as a still image or a short video.

2. Step Out of the Scene

   - Imagine watching yourself in the scene, as if it's a film.
   - Visualise floating back until you can see the back of your own head.
   - Keep moving away until the scene is about three metres distant.

3. Create Emotional Distance

   - Turn the image black and white-this dulls its intensity.
   - Shrink the image to a tenth of its original size, making it feel smaller.
   - Make it transparent - let it fade until it's barely there.

4. Observe the Shift

   - Notice how the emotional weight has lightened.
   - You can now see the situation with greater calmness and objectivity.
   - This method helps disengage from overwhelming emotions, allowing you to regain clarity and control.

With the emotional intensity reduced, ask yourself if there are any decisions you need to make regarding the situation. If so, make those decisions from this calmer, more detached viewpoint.

Taming Vicious Memories

1. Sit in a cozy, relaxing space where you feel safe and comfortable. Imagine you're sitting in a peaceful cinema, ready to watch a movie.
2. Picture yourself in a comfy chair, with the lights dimmed, and everything quiet. You're fully relaxed, about to watch a film.
3. Imagine you gently float out of your seat and rise towards the projection booth above. From there, you can see yourself below, seated comfortably, watching the screen.
4. Think of a troubling memory. Identify two key moments:
    - The **Before Moment** (just before the difficult event happened).
    - The **After Moment** (right after the event has passed, when you're safe).
5. From your safe spot in the projection booth, see yourself in the cinema, watching the **Before Moment** projected on the screen.
6. Watch the memory unfold on the screen, moving from the **Before Moment** to the **After Moment**. Once it ends, freeze the scene at the **After Moment**, where you're safe.
7. Now, in your mind, rewind the memory quickly, from the end back to the start. Watch it all unravel in reverse. Repeat this step **three times**.
8. Each time you rewind the memory, observe how its emotional intensity lessens. The memory will start to feel more distant, like watching a movie instead of reliving it.
9. After the process, recall the memory. If you can remember it without the strong emotional charge, the exercise has been effective.
10. To further reduce any lingering discomfort, engage in

regular relaxation practices, like listening to calming music or a guided meditation. This helps reinforce the change.

By regularly practicing this exercise, you can reframe difficult memories, reducing their emotional weight and gaining clarity and peace.

Wrapped In Serenity

1. **Recall a Calm Memory**
   - Close your eyes.
   - Think of a time when you felt completely serene and at peace.
   - Imagine what you saw, heard, and felt in that moment of calm.
   - If no specific memory comes to mind, create a peaceful scene in your imagination where you feel totally relaxed.

2. **Deepen the Experience**
   - Enhance that memory or imagined scene: make the colours brighter, the sounds clearer, and the feelings stronger.
   - As you do this, gently press your thumb and middle finger together on your right hand. This will create a physical connection to the feeling of calm.

3. **Repeat to Reinforce**
   - Replay the calm memory or scene in your mind at least five times.
   - Each time, press your thumb and middle finger together again, strengthening the link between the gesture and the feeling of serenity.
   - Over time, this gesture will help trigger calmness more easily.

4. **Apply to a Mildly Stressful Situation**
   - Think of a situation that caused you mild stress in the past.
   - As you recall it, press your thumb and middle finger together.

- Imagine yourself feeling calm and in control during that situation, just as you did in your serene memory. Visualise it unfolding smoothly.

5. **Add Challenges**
    - Now think of the same stressful situation but add a few more challenges to it—perhaps the stakes are higher, or the pressure is greater.
    - While pressing your thumb and middle finger together, imagine yourself handling these new challenges with the same serenity and control.

6. **Reflect and Repeat**
    - Take a moment to reflect. Do you feel calmer and in control about the stressful situation?
    - If not, repeat the exercise until accessing your sense of calm becomes easier and more immediate.

This technique will help you build a reliable, calming tool to reduce stress and maintain control in challenging situations

SECTION THREE
REPAIR & PREVENT TRAUMA

I have been impressed with the urgency of doing.
Knowing is not enough; we must apply.
Being willing is not enough; we must do.
Leonardo da Vinci

The aim of *Section Two* was to lay the foundations for understanding the particulars of your own human stress responses, their evolutionary origins, and the neuro-resilient techniques that equip individuals to navigate life's challenges. In this section, we move from foundational principles to practical application, exploring how neuro-resilience manifests in real-world contexts—particularly when the stakes are high, emotions run deep, and safety is ruptured.

This section is not merely theoretical; it delves into the complexities of human experience, addressing what happens when safety—both psychological and emotional—is compromised. The chapters present practical strategies to address these challenges, repair the damage, and prevent future occurrences. As you engage with these chapters, you'll find yourself stepping into vivid scenarios and transformative dialogues, learning techniques that can be applied to your own life and leadership.

In Chapter 7: *When Safety is Ruptured*, we witness Jerry's breakdown in a high-pressure mining operation. His story illustrates the profound impact of unmanaged stress on both individuals and teams. Through Jerry's "frozen" state, we see how modern stressors—though vastly different from the dangers of our evolutionary past—trigger the same primal responses, leading to immobilisation, disconnection, and eventual collapse. Jerry's experience highlights the urgency for leaders to recognise and intervene before stress spirals into trauma. This chapter explores the nature of psychological safety, its fragility, and the critical role of neuro-resilient practices in recovery and repair.

Moving forward, Chapter 8: *Rupture Repair Coaching* provides a detailed, immersive look into the repair process. Through a masterfully facilitated coaching session, Paul helps Jerry regain his sense of calm and control. The session is a testament to the power of rapport, humour, and neuro-resilient techniques such as *Turning Anxiety Around* and *Wrapped in Serenity* techniques. It demonstrates how a skilled practitioner can guide an individual from distress to empowerment, equipping them with lasting tools for emotional regulation. This chapter is a practical guide for coaches, leaders, and anyone seeking to support others through periods of acute stress or trauma.

Finally, Chapter 9: *Rupture Prevention Practices* shifts focus to the preventative measures that can fortify individuals against the accumulation of stress. This chapter champions the adage, "An ounce of prevention is worth a pound of cure," emphasising the importance of daily autoregulation routines and mindful rituals. Whether through morning practices that energise and ground or nighttime routines that invite restorative sleep, readers will learn how to proactively cultivate resilience. The techniques discussed here are simple yet profound, encouraging consistency and intentionality to prevent safety ruptures from occurring in the first place.

Throughout this section, the emphasis is clear: neuro-resilience is not just about recovery; it is about creating environments—both internal and external—that foster safety, connection, and sustainable well-being. Whether you are leading a team, coaching an individual, or striving for personal growth, the lessons and techniques in these chapters will equip you to meet life's challenges with composure, creativity, and confidence.

As you read, consider how the scenarios and solutions resonate with your own experiences. Reflect on the ways safety has been compromised in your life or work and how the techniques presented here might help you rebuild or reinforce it. These are advanced skills for a reason—they go beyond basic stress management to address the deeper layers of human resilience, enabling not just survival, but flourishing. By the end of this section, you will not only understand these skills but be ready to apply them, transforming your approach to stress, safety, and success.

SEVEN
WHEN SAFETY IS RUPTURED

*When the heart is agitated and angry,
it is difficult for it to see clearly*
Zhuangzi

RED DESERT DISTRESS: Picture a mining operation in the middle of Australia. The landscape is both bleak and beautiful, dominated by red-hued earth, towering piles of processed ore, and large earth-moving vehicles steadily working in the heat. Despite the scorching sun, the workers wear hard hats, thick leather gloves, Hi-Viz vests, and reinforced boots. The operation runs like clockwork, with workers flying in and out on a tight schedule. This is routine.

Then suddenly, a crack appears in that routine. Jerry, the *Head of Engineering*, is meant to catch the flight out at the end of his shift, but instead, he refuses to leave. His colleagues buzz with curiosity and mild amusement as they board the plane without him, but the site *General Manager*, Douglas, senses something deeper is wrong.

Walking into Jerry's office, Douglas finds him frozen in place, eyes wide, teeth clenched in a terrified grimace, sweat dripping down his face, gripping his desk as though it's the only thing tethering him to reality.

Jerry has hit a breaking point, but this isn't just a moment of frustration or anger. It's a profound loss of psychological safety—a sudden stress response known as *freeze*[1]. In that moment, Jerry is incapable of social engagement or rational decision-making. His nervous system, unable to reconcile the pressures he's been facing, has shut down. To understand what's happening to Jerry, we need to delve deeper into the human stress response—an ancient mechanism that once ensured our ancestors' survival but can now wreak havoc in contemporary workplaces.

Jerry's frozen state, marked by a blend of heightened metabolism and immobilised action, is a natural, if not entirely helpful, response to overwhelming stress. In evolutionary terms, it's the same instinct that would have caused our ancestors to freeze at the sight of a predator lurking in the shadows, hoping to remain unnoticed and thus avoid danger.

Today, however, the perceived threats aren't sabre-toothed tigers but professional failures, economic insecurity, or the looming possibility of job loss. Yet to Jerry's reptilian brain, the distinction is irrelevant[2]. It reacts as though his survival is at stake, flooding his body with cortisol, freezing his muscles, and shutting down his capacity for social interaction.

As we've already explored in earlier chapters, the human stress response isn't limited to *fight* or *flight*—it also includes *freeze* and *shutdown*. When Jerry's body reaches the tipping point of stress, it defaults to freeze, paralysing his decision-making and social faculties. This could have been mitigated if Jerry had practised techniques like *Finding Home*, a neuro-resilience method designed to help individuals reset their emotional and physiological balance before reaching a breaking point. By regularly recalibrating his nervous system, Jerry could have prevented the slow build-up of stress that eventually led to this collapse.

EVOLUTIONARY ORIGINS

Stress is like fire.
It can keep you warm, or it can burn you.
It's all about how you handle it.
Richard Bandler

To understand how Jerry's modern-day crisis mirrors ancient survival instincts, we need to take a step back and consider how the stress response evolved. Picture our ancestors huddled around a fire, hyper-aware of the dangers lurking in the wilderness. A sudden snap of a twig in the distance would send hearts racing and minds scrambling, preparing the group for either confrontation or escape. This acute stress response was essential for survival.

Fast forward to today, and while the dangers have changed, the brain's response has not. The human brain, particularly the limbic system, is hardwired to detect threats to our safety—whether physical, social, or psychological. In the modern workplace, threats to job security, status, or professional reputation can trigger the same neurobiological reactions as life-or-death situations. When leaders and employees lack the skills to recognise and manage these responses, chronic stress can quickly take over, leading to burnout, disengagement, or, in Jerry's case, trauma.

In earlier chapters, we discussed *Instinct Mapping*, a method leaders can use to identify stress triggers in themselves and their teams. Douglas, the site manager, could have employed this technique to become more aware of Jerry's rising stress levels before they reached a critical point. Recognising the warning signs—such as irritability, reduced focus, and increasing withdrawal—could have prompted an earlier intervention, giving Jerry the support he needed to regulate his stress.

Workplace Wellbeing

> *Your brain has a fantastic capacity for stress, but it's equally capable of creating calm and joy. Choose your focus.*[3]
> **Richard Bandler**

CHRONIC STRESS IS NOT only debilitating for the individual; it creates ripple effects throughout a team or organisation. In Jerry's case, his stress-induced breakdown doesn't just affect his own performance; it influences everyone around him. His irritability, poor focus, and declining problem-solving abilities are felt by his colleagues, increasing their own stress levels and disrupting the flow of work.

In organisations where safety is fragile or non-existent, stress spreads like a virus. As Jerry's condition deteriorates, he begins micromanaging his team, driven by a hypervigilant need to regain control. This, in turn, stifles his colleagues' creativity and autonomy. Tasks are delayed, tensions rise, and eventually, the entire team's productivity suffers. This is the cost of unmanaged stress.

This is where techniques like *Stepping Out of Fear*, which we covered in Chapter 5, become crucial. Leaders like Douglas can learn to confront their own fears about difficult conversations or performance failures, allowing them to better address the stress in their teams. By stepping out of fear, leaders can prevent small issues from spiralling into full-blown crises, much like the one Jerry is experiencing.

Occupational Trauma

> *People aren't broken.*
> *They just have strategies that aren't working,*
> *causing them unnecessary distress.*
> **Richard Bandler**

As the site manager, Douglas plays a pivotal role in either exacerbating or alleviating Jerry's stress. His response in the office, when he finds Jerry frozen in fear, is critical. In Chapter 8, we introduced the concept of *co-regulation*, where individuals in a group unconsciously regulate their emotional states based on the signals they receive from others. In this case, if Douglas approaches Jerry with calm, open body language, and a regulated emotional state, he can help Jerry down-regulate his own stress response.

Had Douglas been more in tune with his own emotional regulation, he might have been able to guide Jerry back to a state of psychological safety. In earlier chapters, we discussed the importance of *Taming Vicious Memories*, a technique that helps individuals prevent past fears or failures from influencing their present state.

This technique, applied both by leaders and their teams, can prevent past mistakes or challenges from escalating into debilitating stress. If Jerry and Douglas had worked through previous project setbacks with this mindset, the situation might have played out differently.

Psychological safety, once ruptured, can be challenging to repair. The good news is that skilled practitioners using the right techniques can repair trauma quickly. After Jerry's breakdown, Douglas must take deliberate steps to restore trust and safety within the team. First, he arranges Jerry to meet with a coach to restore his lost safety, the transcript of which we cover in the next chapter.

Second, he brought the whole of site team together to address the matter, which we cover in *Section 6* to begin a new phase for the mine site. This includes dialogues where team members can express their concerns without fear of judgement, structured feedback sessions, or even team-building activities designed to reconnect the group.

By implementing regular check-ins, debriefs, or shared relaxation practices, Douglas helps his team re-establish a sense of safety and cohesion. These rituals allow team members to process their stress collectively, reducing the likelihood of future breakdowns.

Leaders must also practice *Active Hearing*, ensuring that team members feel heard and valued, especially after a stressful event. When team members see that their concerns are taken seriously and acted upon, they're more likely to trust the process of rebuilding psychological safety.

Jerry's breakdown serves as a cautionary tale, not just about the dangers of unmanaged stress but about the importance of proactive, neuro-resilient leadership. Leaders like Douglas must be equipped with the skills to recognise the signs of stress in themselves and their teams and to intervene before it's too late. By practising neuro-resilient techniques, such as *Instinct Mapping*, *Stepping Out of Fear*, and *Taming Vicious Memories*, leaders can help create environments where stress is managed, and psychological safety is maintained.

Rebuilding safety after a breakdown takes some effort, but it can be done well. By focusing on co-regulation, empathetic communication, and team rituals, leaders can help their teams bounce back stronger and more resilient than before. In the end, it's the leader's ability to navigate stress—both their own and their team's—that determines the success or failure of the entire organisation.

Chronic stress doesn't just stay at the level of unease or discomfort—it can spiral into something far more destructive: occupational trauma.

This is where we begin to encounter the long-term effects of unmanaged stress, particularly in fast-paced, high-stakes environments.

Occupational trauma isn't limited to catastrophic events like accidents or violence in the workplace. It also emerges from a series of small, insidious stressors—deadlines that never seem to relent, public criticism, and the looming fear of job loss or failure. These everyday stressors accumulate, chipping away at the individual's resilience until they face total collapse.

Let's return to the 'Jerry Moment': his immobilisation in the office wasn't an isolated incident; it was the product of months, perhaps even years, of eroded safety and unchecked stress. Like a cliff gradually eroded by unrelenting waves, Jerry's capacity to cope was worn thin by the constant barrage of work pressures. At some point, the weight of the stress became too much, and the collapse happened. As Angus had been "caught in the middle of the madness", he had been disoriented too, just like Jerry, and part of the all pain the entire mine site was feeling.

This phenomenon is echoed in the brain's neuroplasticity, where repetitive exposure to stress strengthens neural pathways associated with fear and anxiety. This rewiring makes individuals more susceptible to triggering stress reactions, and over time, they lose access to their higher-order thinking, decision-making, and emotional regulation abilities. It's as though the brain itself becomes trapped in survival mode, perpetuating a cycle of stress responses.

When high alert becomes chronic, it leads to a state of near-constant mobilisation. Once the human body is shunted into flight-or-flight, the human brain loses a load of cognitive heft. By some measures, that can be as much as 35%. This heightened fight-or-flight state becomes more dangerous the longer it is sustained, transforming what was once an adaptive survival response into something destructive—burnout, anxiety disorders, and even depression.

Now, we see a new side of the survival response. What happens when someone like Jerry is unable to escape their work environment? The constant stress means that the brain's mobilisation response is no longer enough to handle the strain, and the nervous system turns to immobilisation. This is the classic *freeze* response—the body goes rigid, physically unable to engage with the situation anymore.

The issue with chronic mobilisation and immobilisation is that these responses shut down creativity, engagement, and communication—core elements of any successful team. As Jerry becomes more disconnected and anxious, the more isolated he becomes from his peers, his family, and even himself. What happens next? Depression, anxiety, and withdrawal.

Trauma-Informed Leading

A frozen leader can't lead, and a frozen team can't perform. This is how chronic stress can not only destroy the individual but corrode the culture of an entire organisation.

Here's where the role of leadership becomes crucial. Trauma-informed leadership is not a new management theory—it's an approach that recognises the reality of occupational trauma. Leaders in this position need to become adept at spotting the subtle signs of chronic stress before it tips into trauma, and they need to know how to foster an environment that heals rather than exacerbates these stresses.

Key principles of trauma-informed leadership include:

1. *Normalising Conversations on Mental Health*: Rather than treating stress or emotional strain as isolated issues, normalise discussions around them, encouraging employees to seek help when needed.

2. *Recognising Stress in Real-Time:* Leaders should be trained to detect early warning signs—tension in the room, short tempers, silence during meetings—and intervene before stress spirals out of control.
3. *Preventing Burnout with Boundaries:* Create systems that allow people to recharge. This includes work-life balance policies, adequate leave, and encouraging employees to step back when they need to.
4. *Modelling Emotional Regulation:* Leaders themselves should be emotionally aware and demonstrate emotional resilience, helping to co-regulate the emotional states of their teams.

This type of leadership isn't just about managing crises; it's about proactively cultivating resilience in the workplace and ensuring that chronic stress doesn't lead to occupational trauma.

But what happens if this culture of psychological safety is lost? What if chronic stress has already taken root in your organisation? As we transition to Section Three, we will delve into the steps leaders can take to *repair* this damage.

The next chapter will begin by demonstrating *PACE Protocol* and *Safety Priming*, advanced co-regulation skillset that supports coaches and leaders can use to ruptured safety.

EIGHT
RUPTURE REPAIR COACHING

If you can't laugh at your past, you'll never get free of it. So it's time to start laughing, even if it's artificial laughter at first[1].
Richard Bandler

JERRY'S TRAUMA from his workplace challenges and the toll it took on his mental and emotional well-being, was explored in Chapter 7. His struggles were compounded by a cycle of anxiety and self-doubt, often triggered by specific work-related scenarios.

Now, in Chapter 8, we delve deeper into the process of recovery, focusing on practical coaching methods to repair emotional ruptures and restore a sense of personal agency. Below is a transcript of a coaching session I had with Jerry, during which he was grappling with the aftermath of his 'freeze' moment.

Helping people recover from trauma requires guiding their subjective experiences to produce a measurable effect on their biology—specifically, their metabolism. When people are in a state of trauma, their metabolism becomes misaligned with their environment. Therefore, the primary goal is clear:

Resynchronise their metabolism with their actual environment.

Practitioners achieve this through Safety Priming and coaching participants to regulate their own subjective experiences. By understanding how external and internal stimuli impact the brain and body, we can more effectively navigate their emotional landscape.

This process is similar to how a chef crafts a culinary masterpiece. A chef combines various temperatures, cooking times, and ingredients in precise ways to transform raw elements into an extraordinary meal. Understanding the science behind how heat and chemistry interact with ingredients allows the chef to create dishes that not only taste exceptional but also evoke specific physiological responses in their patrons[2].

A chef deliberately crafts a multisensory experience designed to produce measurable effects on a customer's biology:

- **Heightened Sensory Stimulation:** Vivid presentation, rich aromas, and complex textures intensely activate the limbic system, boosting dopamine, deepening anticipation, and priming the body for digestion.
- **Enhanced Pleasure & Reward:** Unique flavours and gourmet ingredients provoke stronger dopamine and endorphin release, intensifying satisfaction. Spices and umami-rich foods amplify pleasure and emotional fulfilment.
- **Optimised Satiety & Metabolism:** High-quality fats and proteins trigger more cholecystokinin (CCK) and leptin, deepening satiety, increasing thermogenesis, and boosting metabolism.
- **Deep Relaxation & Elevated Mood:** Post-meal, elevated serotonin and oxytocin promote calm energy and emotional well-being.

In sum, a chef's masterpiece transforms eating into a full-body experience of sensory pleasure, metabolic balance, and emotional fulfilment. Similarly, Neuro-Linguistic Programming (NLP) techniques aim to influence a person's subjective experience to produce measurable effects on their objective biology. Once this synchronisation is achieved, the participant naturally shifts their mental and physical behaviour.

For leaders and coaches, the 'ingredients and seasoning' are delivered through vocal prosody, sensory acuity, somatic awareness, wordplay, humour, and other co-regulatory techniques—each carefully calibrated to build trust, safety, and resilient change. By doing so, leaders use their neurology and skills as resources to help people move from a disconnected state to a grounded calm and optimistic one.

The PACE Protocol

From the earliest days of my NLP journey, I found myself working with leaders at every level, helping them navigate ruptured safety within their organisations. These weren't therapy sessions, nor were they meant to be. They were leadership and coaching conversations —designed to sharpen focus, strengthen decision-making, and build resilience.

But here's the problem. The more senior the client, the more circuitous the conversations became. Not because of intellectual difficulties—leaders are more than capable of juggling different perspectives, strategies, and persuasion techniques. No, the real reason these conversations meandered was avoidance. Beneath the surface-level discussions of tactics and execution lay deeper, unspoken tensions— anger, anxiety, and, in some cases, apathy.

I would sometimes catch myself thinking,

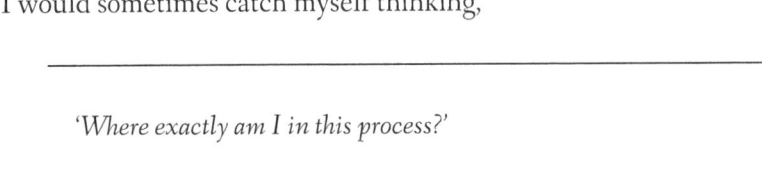

'Where exactly am I in this process?'

Richard Bandler never seemed to have this problem. I'd spent hours training with him and watching his demonstrations—both live and on video. Of course, our contexts were different. He had the advantage of a controlled setting, a primed audience, and a chosen demonstration subject. Meanwhile, I worked with whoever walked in, with whatever baggage they brought.

And yet, despite all the tangents, the storytelling, the unexpected detours—Bandler never lost track of where he was, nor where he was going. His demonstration subjects had no idea where he was leading them, yet they followed.

So I shifted my focus. Instead of asking, *'What is he doing now?'*—because he was doing a lot simultaneously, and trying to track every move was like *unscrambling a scrambled egg*—I began looking for the underlying structure that kept everything cohesive.

It wasn't about deconstructing each movement, just as you can't unmix an omelette back into its individual eggs. It was about recognising *the rhythm that held it all together*. Or, to put it another way, watching Bandler work was like listening to a master jazz musician. On the surface, it was all improvisation—unexpected notes, unpredictable shifts, playful deviations[3].

But jazz isn't just noise. Beneath the apparent chaos, there's a *hidden structure—a time signature, a harmonic foundation, a sense of progression* that holds everything in place. The real skill isn't in following each note but in sensing the *invisible thread that pulls the whole piece forward*.

Once I started listening for that thread instead of trying to decode every individual moment, I realised something: it wasn't about tracking *what* he was doing; it was about tracking where he was leading them and what route he was taking.

So, I decided to ask a more straightforward questions:

'To where is he leading them?'

'Where is he going next?'

That shift in perspective led me to a simple but invaluable framework—one that provided structure without rigidity, direction without force. I called it the *PACE Protocol,* named after the 'pacing' technique from NLP.

At its core, *PACE* provides a map and compass for coaching conversations—particularly those involving safety ruptures, resistance, or deep-seated emotional blocks. It ensures that, no matter how unpredictable or circuitous the dialogue becomes, I always know which *direction I am moving towards*. More importantly, it allows me to stay fully present—attuned to the client's words, tone, and body language—without becoming lost in the complexity of the moment.

The PACE Protocol unfolds in four natural phases:

1. **Prime & Probe** – This is where trust is built, tension is defused, and the client feels safe enough to engage. I use a blend of observational, conversational, and behavioural NLP techniques, which I explore in detail in Chapter 12. Once trust is established, I begin testing for psychological permission—probing through teasing, humour, confronting questions, and other approaches.
2. **Agency Over Instinct** – The client already has control; they just don't realise it yet. My role is to surface that latent control, guiding them to shift from reactionary patterns to deliberate action, reasserting their cognitive agency.
3. **Connect & Socialise** – As they regulate emotionally, their body and mind transition from protection to connection patterns. The telltale sign? Their humour returns. Playful back-and-forth banter signals safety—not just with me, but within themselves.
4. **Embed New Strategies & Meanings** – Change must extend beyond the session; the client needs to feel safe *anywhere* and with *anyone*. Through future pacing, they vividly envision and explain how they will apply their new patterns in real-world situations, ensuring lasting transformation.

These phases are not rigid steps but a dynamic flow, allowing for flexibility while maintaining direction. If a conversation takes an unexpected turn, the framework acts as a signpost rather than a constraint.

The beauty of this approach is that it allows *freedom within a framework*. It enables me to play with storytelling, analogies, and tangents, without ever losing track of the underlying trajectory. The coaching process remains fluid and responsive yet steadily progresses towards genuine change.

For leaders and coaches, this structured yet adaptive method offers a powerful tool—one that helps individuals reconnect with their inner resilience and take ownership of their own transformation.

Little Things Done Well

> *'Perfection' is just a lot of little things done well*
> **Chef Marco Pierre White**

How can leaders repair safety ruptures as thoughtfully as a master chef crafts a perfect meal? Just as Marco Pierre White suggests, achieving excellence is about consistently getting the small things right. The same principle applies to developing neuro-resilience skills—perfection is simply the result of many small, well-executed actions.

In the session, pay close attention to vocal tone, humour, pacing, and attentive listening. These elements gently surround Jerry's neuroception with cues of safety. The message to his unconscious mind—his body—is clear: "You are safe here with me."

Once Jerry senses enough safety cues, his body naturally shifts into an 'approach and connect' mode. This involuntary transition unlocks his social engagement behaviours, allowing him to fully participate in the coaching session.

I introduce Jerry to a series of simple, progressive exercises. Each builds on the last, giving him the agency to recognise and manage his 'patterns of protection' and transition into 'patterns of connection.' These exercises equip him with practical techniques for self-regulation, even in challenging situations.

Throughout this session, you'll witness the power of a well-paced NLP coaching dynamic. The coach carefully balances compassion, humour, and challenge, maintaining steady momentum and progress. As NLP expert Michael Breen of MBNLP describes, effective coaching is about "pushing without being pushy." Notice that I don't provide Jerry with solutions. Instead, I support him in thinking and feeling differently, helping him rediscover his personal agency over his emotional state.

By the end of this chapter, you'll gain valuable insights into why establishing emotional safety is the foundation for meaningful coaching in the workplace. You'll also see how practical NLP techniques—rooted in neuro-resilience principles—can help team members overcome anxiety, navigate complex emotions, and build a resilient mindset that promotes long-term well-being.

To illustrate how these techniques extend beyond one-on-one coaching and into everyday leadership practices, let's turn to Steve, an in-house coach and trainer. Steve has been tasked with equipping leaders in his organisation with practical tools to support their teams during high-pressure situations. In the next section, you'll see how Steve uses the recorded session between Jerry and me as a teaching tool in a leadership development programme.

By breaking down the strategies and techniques used in Jerry's session, Steve guides leaders to understand how they can create emotionally safe environments for their own teams. This approach not only fosters trust and engagement but also empowers employees to manage stress effectively and build resilience in the face of workplace challenges.

As we step into the training room with Steve, reflect on how you might apply these insights to foster emotional safety and resilience within your own team. Let's observe how Steve bridges theory and practice, turning individual coaching insights into actionable leadership skills.

Coach Training Session

Steve: "Good afternoon, everyone, and thank you for joining us today.

Before we begin, I want you to recall the *PACE Protocol*—a guiding structure designed to help you stay oriented throughout a neuro-resilience coaching session. Especially when working with individuals dealing with stress, trauma, or deeply rooted emotional challenges, coaches must heighten their awareness to remain fully attuned to the participant's verbal and non-verbal cues.

No two conversations are ever the same. Coaching sessions are fluid by nature and can drift in unexpected directions. This fluidity can make it easy to lose track of where the session is heading. The simplicity of the PACE structure keeps the coach grounded because each phase serves a distinct purpose. A helpful orienting question to ask yourself is:

"What goal am I pursuing now, and next?"

An early component of the *'Prime & Probe'* phase is what we call *safety priming*. Now, while this term is often mentioned, let's unpack its true significance. As coaches, leaders, or facilitators, we know that no meaningful progress can be made unless our clients feel genuinely safe. This sense of safety extends far beyond physical comfort—it's about generating enough cues of safety that the participant's neuroception shifts into a more connected and open state. As this connection deepens, the client naturally gives us permission to challenge them and help them make meaningful changes.

Safety priming involves subtle but deliberate verbal and non-verbal cues that signal to the participant that it is safe to approach, engage, and connect. As we receive signals of readiness, we continue to gently press and test for permission to guide the session forward.

In today's session, you'll observe Paul O'Neill, founder of *Neuro-Elevation Skills*, working within the *PACE Protocol* framework, applying a range of strategies and techniques to help the participant move naturally from one phase to the next. This willingness to transition to the next phase is a key indicator of the participant granting permission.

As you watch, pay close attention to how Paul engages with Jerry to address the lingering effects of workplace trauma—not through one-size-fits-all solutions but through a deliberate, structured process. This approach allows Jerry's instinctive responses to settle into emotional safety while his cognitive awareness begins to reaffirm his personal agency.

Notice how Paul transmits cues of safety using attentive listening, reframing, voice tone, and humour to prime Jerry's nervous system for deeper engagement. This intentional strategy helps Jerry gradually shift from anxiety and disconnection to a grounded state of calm and control.

This session underscores the importance of amplifying safety throughout the priming process. Paul's gentle questioning and subtle interventions steadily strengthen Jerry's sense of control over his emotions. By the end of this initial phase, Jerry isn't just calmer—he's primed for deeper, more transformative work.

As you observe, focus on the delicate balance between pressing forward and easing back, the ebb and flow of guiding the session, and the nuanced art of *probing for permission*. By following this structure, you'll see how neuro-resilient coaching moves beyond surface-level fixes to create lasting, meaningful change.

As I play the video, notice that safety priming begins from the moment of first contact. I'll signal to you as we transition through the remaining three phases of the *PACE Protocol*".

Video Session

Paul: *"Nice to see you, Jerry. How can I help you today?"*

Jerry: (*Looking tense*) *"I've been going through a bit of a rough patch."*

Paul: (*Softly*) *"A rough patch. What makes it that way?"*

Jerry: (*Pauses, looking down*) *"It feels like I'm drowning. Work's just been... relentless. Every time I think I'm getting a handle on things, something else comes at me."*

Paul: (*Nods*) *"Drowning... just trying to keep your head above water?"*

Jerry: (*Breathes out sharply*) *"Exactly. It's like... just when I come up for air, something else pulls me under. It's exhausting."*

Paul: *"It sounds exhausting."*

Jerry: (*Nods*) *"Yeah... and I'm not sure how much longer I can keep doing this."*

Paul: (*Slight smile*) *"Drowning isn't something you can do forever, right?"*

Jerry: (*Faint smile, still tense*) *"No, it's not. I'm tired. I'm weary."*

Paul: (*Playfully*) *"Well, unless you decide to develop gills, we're going to have to figure something else out, eh?"*

Jerry: (*Chuckles softly*) *"No gills, I'm afraid."*

Paul: (*Leaning back, giving him space*) *"Alright, well, good to know. No gills, no superpowers. So, here's a question, how do you know when it's time to be pulled down exactly?"*

Jerry: (*Looks straight at Paul*) *"I don't know what you mean."*

Paul: "Well, the drowning thing is a metaphor for how it feels, right?"

Jerry: "Right."

Paul: (Nodding) "So, what I'm asking is, 'How do you know that it's the right time to feel like you're being pulled down and drowning?'"

Jerry: (Eyebrows furrowed) "I'm not actually making that decision."

Paul: (Nodding in agreement) "Sure, not consciously, but something inside you is making that decision, isn't it? I mean, it's not your office desk or your computer, is it?"

It's just like water always boils at the same temperature. At whatever height above sea level it is, water always knows when to start boiling. At sea level, it knows to boil at 100°C and at the top of Mount Everest, it always boils at 68°C.

It's the same with your body, once something happens in a certain situation, your body always knows that it is time to feel like it's drowning.

Jerry: (Looking incredulous) "I'm not picking and choosing, Paul. I've got a condition!"

Paul: (In complete agreement) "Yes... exactly! That's my point: it's conditional. Your feelings of being pulled under is conditional on something happening on the outside, in some particular circumstances, that leads to you feeling like drowning. Yeah?"

Jerry: (Nodding as though following along) "OK"

Paul: "So, what I want to know is 1) what's the situation and 2) what's the thing that leads to the bad feeling? For example, do you get the bad feeling at home, at work, on holiday?"

Jerry: "Mostly at work. Sometimes at home."

Paul: "Right. Mostly at work and sometimes at home. Let's start at home. When does it usually happen?"

Jerry: "It depends on my shift pattern. I fly in and out of a mine site. Typically, it's building for two or three days before I take the flight back to work. But it really kicks in on the evening before."

Paul: "And this is the typical pattern?"

Jerry: "Yes."

Paul: "OK. So, it is conditional. Just like the water, you begin warming up for a couple of days before going back to work; and then you're at full boiling point the night before. Give yourself a crappy night's sleep. Then get yourself to work, both cranked up and tired. Ready for the fortnight ahead. Right?"

Jerry: (Nodding. Looking down.) "Pretty much."

Paul: "And, let me guess, you maintain this tension constantly just waiting for something to go wrong. And as nothing ever goes perfectly, something will always go wrong. And that's what pushes you over the edge. Or, rather, pulls you under and you feel like you're drowning."

Jerry: (Nodding. Looking down.) "Exactly."

Paul: (In a reflective tone) "Hmmm... well, that would do it. But have you ever thought of not doing this. I mean there has to be an easier way. I mean, how about you just feel nice and calm all the way through and then freak out only when something imperfect happens. That way at least you're calmer almost all of the time. Better still, why don't you stay pumped up and joyful all the time and, if something goes wrong, you put it right without any freaking out. Have you thought about doing it that way?"

Jerry: (Frowning. Shaking his head) "That would be great but it's not like I have that choice. It's like I'm locked into this tension and anxiety all the time".

Paul: (In an upbeat tone and demeanour) "You're locked into these bad feelings? I think we need to get you locked out from them. Don't you? Wouldn't that be better?"

Jerry: (Still looking unconvinced) "Of course."

Paul: (Inquisitively) "So, back to the two to three days before your about to fly into work. How do you know, two days out, it's time to make yourself feel bad."

Jerry: (Looking exasperated) "What?"

Paul: (Conversationally) "Well, my guess is that you start to make nasty pictures inside your mind of the kind of crappy imperfection that could lead to you feeling pulled under. That's my guess but it's your brain. So, what happens?"

Jerry: (Looking pensive) "Yes. I run scenarios that I am likely to be facing when I get back on site."

Paul: (Eyebrows up and smiling) "Happy scenarios where you are like a superhero, things go wrong, and you swoop in and put them right? Or maybe it's something a bit more horrible?"

Jerry: (Looking pensive) "I think about the things that could go wrong. The kind of things that would make me look bad."

Paul: (Sardonically) "Ah, yes. Just to get you in the mood! And to whom are you going to be looking bad?"

Jerry: (Slight smile) "The boss. I'm a bit intimidated by him."

Paul: (Inquisitively) "A bit? You're a lot intimidated by him! But why? Is he a gangster or tyrant or something? Is he likely to have you publicly flogged? What do you imagine is going to happen, exactly?"

Jerry: (Smiling a little. Eyes looking up. Pauses.) "I don't really know. I jolt myself out of the thought before I get to that part. I just picture his eyes, and I'm snapped out of it."

Paul: (*In mock amazement*) "But you're missing the best part — the finale! At least if you watch a scary movie all the way to the end, you at least get to the end... and then it's over! What you're doing is pausing the movie right at the cliffhanger, it's never over. You start the whole crappy thing again, all the way up to the cliffhanger and stop it again. It's like a loop that runs and runs and you never get to the end and see the final credits! You've really learned to stress yourself out like a pro. When are you flying back on site?"

Jerry: (*Looks bemused.*) "Three days."

Paul: (*Enthused*) So, the bad feeling is pretty much due! Cool. Well, that makes things a lot easier. What I want you to do is stop, backup and... [Paul blinks] close your eyes.

Jerry: (*Closes his eyes*)

[*Video pauses*]

Steve: Notice that Jerry complied immediately with the request to close his eyes. This is evidence that he had given Paul permission to progress.

Paul moves to the new goal of proving to Jerry that he has personal agency and control over his emotions.

[*Video resumes*]

Paul: (*Vocal prosody*) "That's right. Just go deep inside and begin to imagine all the scenarios that you know you are about to run through now. See what you will see. Hear what you will hear and begin to bring back all that anxiety. Have you got it?"

Jerry: (*Slight nod*)

Paul: "I want you to make the picture vivid and bright, sharp and clear. Can you hear sounds?"

Jerry: (Slight nod) "Yes."

Paul: "OK. Make those sounds crisper and richer. And really feel that feeling strongly now. Have you got that?"

Jerry: (Flat expression. Looking Paler) "Yes."

Paul: (Gentle tones. Downward vocal commands) "Ok. Where is the bad feeling in your body? Show me. Touch it with your hand."

Jerry: (Touches his upper chest)

Paul: (Prosodic tones) "Now, the feeling needs to keep moving to keep the feeling going. Still using your hand, show me where it moves to."

Jerry: (Pauses. Moves his hand to his stomach): "It moves here."

Paul: (Prosodic tones) "Excellent. Now the feeling isn't just going to sit there. It still has to move to sustain itself. Typically, it will move in a circle. It could feel like its rolling inside of you. Show me the direction and speed with your hand now. That's right, just like that."

Jerry: (Begins to move his hand clockwise over his stomach): "It's going this way."

Paul: (Prosodic tones) "Now. I'm going to get you to do a couple of things. At first, it will feel a bit worse, but it will come to a fun conclusion. Alright, now, give me a colour for this feeling."

Jerry: "Black."

Paul: "Spin the black feeling faster. I want an honest, complete doubling of the black feeling. You can keep using your hand if that helps. Let me know when you're there."

Jerry: (hand moving faster) "I'm there."

Paul: "Are you feeling better or worse?"

Jerry: "Worse."

Paul: (*Enthusiastic tones*) *"Perfect! Now bring it back down to its original speed... are you there?"*

Jerry: (*Slows his hand down. Nods*).

Paul: *"Now, down to 50%. Let me know."*

Jerry: (*Hand slows further. Slight nod*).

Paul: *"Now, 25%.... and stop it dead... now begin to reverse it... take it to 50% speed."*

Jerry: (*Hand begins to move anticlockwise*).

[*Video pauses*]

Steve: Jerry has demonstrated that he can dial up and down his negative emotion. This is personal agency and control. This is a strong counter example to Jerry's earlier assertion, when he said, "I'm not actually making that decision".

With these criteria satisfied, Paul now begins to assist Jerry into generating positive feeling.

[*Video resumes*]

Paul: *"Give me a new colour"*

Jerry: (*Shoulders relaxing*) *"Bright yellow"*

Paul: *"Now double the good feeling. A complete, honest full doubling"*

Jerry: (*Continuing to relax. Breathing Abdominally. Slight nod.*)

Paul: *"Now keep this good feeling spinning and look at the scenarios that used to scare you. How do you feel about them now"*

Jerry: (*Colour returning to his face*) *"I feel better."*

Paul: *"Out of ten, where one is the crappy feeling and ten is the most relaxed and carefree you've ever been, where are you?"*

Jerry: *"I'm at five."*

Paul: (Prosodic voice) *"Wonderful. For the rest of the session, the most important thing that I want you to do is to keep this good feeling spinning. Round and round and round. If you are visualising it on the outside, pull the yellow feeling in, so the full relaxing intensity is inside your body. That's right – just like that."*

Jerry: (Rolls his head up. Mouth opening slightly).

Paul: (Prosodic voice) *"Now spin this feeling up to the top of your head. Down to the tips of your toes. Let this lovely yellow feeling just wash all over you. Bathe every cell in your skin, ever sinew of muscle, every synapse in your brain with this feeling of deep, deeper, deepest relaxation.*

And, as you do so, just let your mind begin to sense your whole body go flippy and floppy. And I want you to think back to a time when you felt truly calm and serene. Maybe it was a time when you were on a peaceful holiday, or perhaps just a quiet moment at home where everything felt just right. Can you bring that to mind?"

Jerry: (Pauses, a small smile creeping onto his face) *"Yeah... I'm thinking of a time at the beach. Just sitting by the water, listening to the waves."*

Paul: *"Perfect. Now I want you to step back into that memory. See what you saw, hear what you heard, and most importantly, feel what you felt. Let yourself be there, at the beach, completely calm and safe."*

(Jerry's shoulders visibly relax even more, his breathing slow and steady.)

Paul: (Rhythmic and prosodic vocal patterns) *"As you feel that calm... calmer... calmer... calmest still. I want you to pour and spin it into* *your good feeling. Let it sparkle and let it shine. Let bliss spread inside your mind. Imagine it growing, spreading through your body. Feel the relaxation softening your body. Soft... softer... softest... ever so gently, ever so softly. How does that feel?"*

Jerry: *"It feels... good... Really peaceful."*

[Video pauses]

Steve: "Really peaceful" is a wonderful place to have assisted a traumatised colleague or client. It is as far away from trauma as a frog is from feathers. In doing so, the third criteria-set as been met.

Paul is now able to continue to the fourth goal: integrating new learnings and establishing new skills. We call these 'autoregulation strategies'.

[Video resumes]

Paul: *"Good. Now, I want you to keep that feeling with you by building a button that is a better button, probably the best button of your life. By pressing your thumb and middle finger together, gently.*

Now, some people wonder whether the button is on the finger, being pressed by the thumb. Others think that it's on the thumb and is being pushed by the finger. But the truth is there's a button on both your thumb and your finger. And because you've got two buttons on you, it's going to work doubly well for you.

From this day on and for the rest of your life, you are going to be able to become more relaxed than you've ever been now."

(Jerry presses his thumb and middle finger together, and you can see his body fully relax.)

Paul: *"Keep spinning the good feeling and say, just at the back of your* mind, the lovely word 'soften' and feel your whole body deepen its relaxation, bliss and peacefulness."

(Jerry's face shows visible relaxation, a soft smile on his lips.)

Paul: "Now, I want you to imagine it's the morning that you're heading back to work. Picture yourself waking up. Maybe you're still in bed, maybe you're brushing your teeth—whatever part of your morning routine you want to imagine. But this time, you're carrying that sense of deep relaxation with you. How do you see yourself starting the day?"

Jerry: (Pauses, closing his eyes) "I see myself... calm. I've slept well. I'm not rushing around like I usually do. I'm just... taking my time."

Paul: "Great. Now, keep the good feeling spinning inside of you. And once you double it, press your thumb and middle finger together. How does it feel to start your day like this?"

Jerry: (Smiling slightly) "It feels... easy. Like I'm in control."

Paul: "Perfect. Now, let's move forward a bit. You're stepping off the flight and walking onto site. Picture yourself walking in, your usual route, seeing your colleagues, getting to your office, seeing your desk. How does that feel?"

Jerry: (Nods) "It feels good. I'm walking in like... I'm not worried about anything. I know I can handle whatever comes my way."

Paul: "That's exactly what we want. Now, imagine you've got a challenge waiting for you—a difficult meeting or a tight deadline. But this time, your body is ready, and your mind is prepared. You're feeling calm, confident, and wrapped in a deep sense of wellbeing. See yourself going into that situation. How does it play out?"

Jerry: (Pauses, his expression softening) "It's different. I'm not tense. I'm listening more, and I'm speaking up when I need to. I'm not second-guessing myself."

Paul: *"Wonderful. And when the meeting's over, how do you feel?"*

Jerry: *"Relieved. But not just relieved—happy, like I handled it, and I'm proud of how I did."*

Paul: (Smiling warmly) *"That's it! That's what this is all about. Open your eyes and keep the good feeling spinning. How are you feeling?"*

Jerry: (Smiling) *"I'm still calm. I'm just so relaxed."*

Paul: *"Exactly. You've turned your anxiety around."*

Jerry: *"It's amazing how different I feel. I never thought I could change how I felt like this."*

Paul: *"Out of ten, how does this new sense of calm feel compare to where you were at the beginning of our session?"*

Jerry: (Pausing, smiling) *"It's a ten. It feels... lighter. Like a weight's been lifted. I feel like... I can handle whatever comes my way now."*

Paul: *"And isn't that exactly what we were aiming for? You've done incredibly well, Jerry, and I want you to remember this sense of calm, and keep spinning the good feeling because, the truth is, you have always held inside you the capacity to feel good despite all the challenges, you just needed to be shown how to tap into it. Now you know that control is always within you. Anytime you need it, just spin that good feeling and press your thumb and finger together. It's all yours."*

Jerry: (Nods, smiling) *"Thank you, Paul. This has been... life-changing."*

Paul: *"You did all the hard work, Jerry. Now, just keep practicing for the rest of the session, and you'll find that this calm becomes second nature. And because you're in control of how your body can feel now, we can move on and do something that will help you over the coming days."*

[Video paused]

Coach's Wrap-Up

Steve: "OK. I'll pause it there. What we've just seen is a very fluent application of the *PACE Protocol* in real-time. Each phase naturally flows on the last. This structure ensures that the participant is shifted from stress to calm to optimism. There's no need to rush, the PACE Protocol allows you to immerse yourself in the moment, without losing track. Just focus on doing each of the thousand little jobs well.

So, when you're in your next session, ask yourself:

'Which phase of PACE am I in now, and what's the next goal criteria?'

As leaders, our role isn't to eliminate pressure – that's impossible. Rather it is to equip our people with tools that prevent negative stressors from disconnecting and overwhelming them. It's to give them the ability to manage their stressors beyond this session: *safe from the skin in.*

This is the essence of neuro-resilience coaching: helping people feel safe from the inside out. It is *personal enhancement* to provide them the tools to make permanent changes.

Let's open the floor for any questions."

Q&A Session

Question 1: "*How do you know when someone is ready to move on from safety priming to something else?*"

Steve: "*Nice question. It really comes down to paying attention to the client's responses, both their verbal and non-verbal. When Jerry started to smile more, laugh a little, and his body was becoming more relaxed, and his breathing was becoming more abdominal. Whilst not definitive, they were indicative that Jerry's body was feeling safe enough to move forward.*

These indicators don't have to be unambiguous "green-to-go" signals: just get them from red to amber, then prime and probe. There's no need to rush, just be alert for the cues in: even if the door's ajar, it's open, so step right in.

Paul also used humour to press and test for permission—we call this 'probing'—if the client smiles or laughs or sees the funny side of their own predicament, even in part or somewhat, it's a cue they're body is ready to move on. It's about building safety and trust incrementally, but consistently; and testing gently, and taking the safety cues from the client."

QUESTION 2: "HOW DOES THE 'SPINNING' technique actually work to reduce anxiety?"

Steve: "This is a terrific technique. It's another great example of changing someone's subjective reality, changes their objective reality. Spinning is a way of tapping into the body's natural kinaesthetic responses to emotions. Anxiety has a particular movement—a particular direction and speed.

But everyone is slightly different, which means you've got to take the time to uncover it. Sometimes the process is quicker with some people than others. By tracking and tracing this movement and then deliberately changing its speed – faster and slower – the person begins to understand that they have agency over that unpleasant emotion: they can make it more intense, then less intense.

When they reverse the direction of the spin, they change the feeling to something else. They begin to gain control over multiple feelings. It's a terrific piece of submodality work, where the sensory qualities of an experience are altered to change how we feel about it. As such, by learning to manipulate their own subjective experience, they are learning to change their metabolism. Their biology."

. . .

QUESTION 3: *"What if the person doesn't have a strong memory of feeling calm, for the 'Wrapped in Serenity' technique?"*

Steve: *"That's actually more common than you might think, especially with people dealing with trauma or long-term stress. However, most people get tired and exhausted enough to fall asleep. You can tap into that feeling and amplify it.*

Even then, if a specific memory doesn't come to mind, we can use hypnosis and guided meditation to create an experience of calm. Then amplify that. The key is to make it really relaxing by using the individual's particular submodalities across all the senses to imagine the colours, sounds, and sensations of a peaceful scene.

Don't make the mistake that visual submodalities always need to be bright and vivid. Sometimes a person will associate better with more subdued submodalities. It is important to pace them. By helping people to uncover the visual and auditory qualities that works best for them, the more effective coaching will be. It's about giving each individual an experience of calm, even if it's one they're creating for the first time."

QUESTION 4: *"How does future pacing help solidify the change?"*

Steve: *"Future pacing is about getting people to imagine themselves successfully practicing their new exercises in real-life situations. In Jerry's case, Paul asked him to visualise himself at work the next day, handling stress with calm and control. By doing this, Jerry starts to associate the calm feeling with future events.*

This not only weakens or collapses the old anchors at his place of work, but it's also more likely that Jerry will actually use the techniques when the things that used to trigger him pop up. It's a way of mentally rehearsing success, making the new behaviours feel more natural and automatic when the time comes.

. . .

WELL, it looks like we've covered everything for now. I hope this session has given you valuable insights into safety priming in neuro-resilience coaching and how to support people who are navigating a disconnected state.

Remember, the key isn't to rush in with solutions but to build trust and create emotional safety at a pace that each individual can handle. Everyone is different, so continue to push gently, probe thoughtfully, and always test for permission. Once that foundation is solid, the rest becomes so much easier.

But the most important takeaway today is this: people aren't broken—they're simply running protective strategies that no longer serve them. Our role as leaders and coaches isn't to fix them but to offer better choices—choices that empower them to build stronger, more resilient versions of themselves.

So, take what you've learned today and begin integrating these tools into your leadership approach. Every moment you invest in creating safety and trust is a step toward a more resilient, engaged, and high-performing team.

Thank you all for your participation and questions!"

NINE
RUPTURE PREVENTION

We are what we repeatedly do.
Excellence, then, is not an act, but a habit
Aristotle

HOW TO REPAIR SAFETY RUPTURES, after they've occurred, was explored in Chapter Eight. This chapter shifts focus to prevention. After all, what's better than recovery? Never needing it in the first place. By integrating simple yet effective practices into daily routines, leaders can fortify themselves against the pressures that trigger breakdowns like Jerry's, safeguarding not only their well-being but also that of their teams and organisations.

In this chapter, we will explore the importance of daily autoregulation routines, along with ad hoc practices for managing moments when things don't go as planned. As Benjamin Franklin wisely said, *"An ounce of prevention is worth a pound of cure."* With that advice in mind, let's examine the practices that have helped many people I've worked with over the years—bearing in mind two important caveats:

1. **Everyone is Different.** Different techniques work better for different people. Most individuals discover that it's not a single practice but a particular combination of routines that best supports their well-being. Part of your journey is to experiment and identify what works best for your unique needs.
2. **Consistency is Key.** Once you find the techniques that truly work for you—keep doing them! You might be surprised how often people abandon their routines once they start feeling good, only to find themselves stressed again. The smarter approach is to commit to your bespoke autoregulation routine for life, refining it as needed. After all, perfection isn't some vague ideal; it's the disciplined practice of doing many small things exceptionally well. In the world of NLP, this means continuously fine-tuning and adjusting your sensory submodalities to optimise your state.

Preventing emotional ruptures begins with mastering your own internal state. One of the most effective ways to build this internal resilience is by integrating the PACE Protocol—not just as a tool for recovery, but as a proactive daily practice. Let's explore how PACE can become the foundation of your emotional resilience.

PACE Yourself

The PACE Protocol isn't just a tool for repairing safety ruptures—it's even more powerful in preventing them. When you make PACE part of your daily life, you don't just recover from stress—you create a mindset where stress struggles to take hold in the first place. Its strength lies in building emotional resilience and safeguarding your psychological safety. Before you can effectively lead others, you must first command your own internal state. Leadership begins within.

When you weave the four phases of the PACE Protocol into your daily life, you create an unshakable foundation. This isn't about scrambling to recover after stress strikes; it's about building a mental and emotional terrain where stress can't take root. Resilience isn't a reaction—it's a proactive stance. Let's explore how each step of the PACE Protocol fortifies your personal resilience.

Prime & Probe is the gateway to intentional leadership. Too often, we drift into our day, half-engaged and mentally unprepared. Granting yourself permission isn't passive—it's a deliberate choice to step forward with purpose and confidence. It's about silencing self-doubt and reclaiming your authority over the day ahead. Before diving into your tasks, ask yourself:

> *"Have I given myself full permission today to lead with presence and confidence?"*

This small but powerful check-in transforms you from a bystander in your own life to an active, intentional leader.

Whilst you can't control everything when 'shit happens' but you can choose how you respond. Instinct wants you to react. Resilience gives you response choices. This is where *Agency Over Instincts* comes in. Pausing to notice whether your actions stem from instinct or thoughtful choice gives you back control. Consider this question before acting:

> *"How much of my next action is driven by instinct and how much by cognition?"*

This moment of reflection interrupts automatic reactions and opens the door for better decisions.

Connect and Socialise is where leadership truly breathes. Leading isn't about control—it's about connection. It's about meeting people where they are, having tough conversations, celebrating wins, and challenging your team to grow. But you can't engage others if you're stuck in a disconnected survival mode. Leadership flourishes when you're grounded, calm, and open. Pause and ask yourself:

> *"Do I have full access to my social engagement behaviours?"*

If the answer is no, it's time to reset. Your ability to inspire others depends on your ability to connect.

Finally, *Embed New Strategies*. Resilience isn't a one-off effort—it must be embedded into how you operate. This is about turning resilience into habit, so it becomes as natural as breathing. Mental rehearsal is key here. Elite athletes don't wait for the game to start practicing—they prepare mentally and physically. Leaders must do the same. Ask yourself:

> *"Which situations can I pre-live or pre-frame to handle better?"*

By visualising and planning ahead, you train your mind to navigate challenges with agility.

PACE Yourself is about consistent, conscious engagement with how you lead yourself. Neuro-resilience is built primarily through simple, consistent habits. So, let's turn our focus to practical daily routines that can seamlessly support you—starting and ending your day on the right note.

Bliss List

When was the last time you felt completely at ease, filled with joy and energy? Stressors are all around us. They are constantly attempting to pulls us towards stress and negativity. Reclaiming those moments can transform your resilience. A powerful way to cultivate positive emotional states is through a *Bliss List*—a personalised collection of joyful memories and sensory experiences that spark calm, energy, and vitality. Our brains naturally gravitate toward negative experiences, a survival instinct that once protected us but can overwhelm us in today's world. The Bliss List serves as a strategic countermeasure, guiding your mind to amplify positivity and build lasting emotional resilience.

Crafting a Bliss List is more than recalling random happy moments—it's about intentionally selecting diverse experiences that evoke different kinds of positivity: excitement, serenity, satisfaction, and connection. Include significant milestones, like achieving a career goal, alongside small, everyday pleasures, such as feeling the warmth of sunlight on your face. Balance active joys, like dancing or hiking, with passive comforts, like listening to soothing music or sipping a quiet cup of tea.

To deepen its impact, fully engage all five senses. When revisiting these moments, make the colours more vibrant, the sounds richer, and the sensations more vivid. Imagine the steady rhythm of your footsteps on a forest path, the cool air brushing your skin, or the sound of laughter echoing with friends. This sensory richness intensifies the emotional effect, priming your nervous system for calm and confidence.

Tailor your Bliss List to fit your emotional needs. On sluggish mornings, revisit energising memories—a thrilling adventure, a hard-won success, or spontaneous laughter. When anxiety creeps in, focus on grounding experiences like the steady rhythm of your footsteps on a forest path or quiet moments of reflection. In moments of self-doubt, recall achievements that reaffirm your competence and strength.

Building and maintaining your Bliss List is an evolving practice. Reflect regularly on past joys, imagine future delights, and enrich your memories with sensory detail. Over time, this simple yet profound tool becomes a reliable resource for emotional balance, helping you navigate daily stressors with strength and composure.

Start now. Write down three moments that light you up inside. This is more than a list—it's your foundation for resilience, calm, and boundless energy.

For example, Sarah, a marketing executive, starts her day by revisiting the memory of hiking a mountain trail, feeling the cool breeze and hearing the crunch of leaves underfoot. This simple act energises her for the challenges ahead.

Research in positive psychology shows that intentionally recalling joyful experiences can rewire the brain for resilience and well-being (Fredrickson, 2001). Let your Bliss List be your guide to harnessing that power.

Easy Daily Practices

For most of my clients and trainees, just a ten-minute morning and/or nighttime routine is enough to make a significant difference. If the first thing you do upon waking is to feel safe, energised, and connected, you're off to a great start. Similarly, if the last thing you do before drifting into sleep is to feel calm, safe, and grounded, you're far more likely to enjoy restful and restorative sleep.

Even with solid routines in place, life's unexpected disruptions can throw you off balance. To stay resilient, it's essential to clear emotional clutter before it builds up. This next section introduces powerful techniques to release lingering stress and prevent small setbacks from becoming major disruptions.

Bosses, spouses, kids, colleagues, and clients are abundant sources of disruption to even the most contented mind. Beyond interpersonal triggers, the world itself offers its share of challenges: bad weather, traffic delays, minor illnesses, and, more seriously, life-altering events like job loss, breakups, or bereavement.

We'll address how to navigate significant disruptions shortly. But first, let's focus on foundational morning and nighttime routines designed to strengthen your emotional resilience and keep you centred—regardless of what the day brings.

"Rise & Shine" Patterns

To create an effective *Rise & Shine* routine, start by identifying activities that make you feel truly energised. This can be done by making a short 'Bliss List' of sensory-rich experiences—things you are naturally drawn to when you see, hear, touch, smell, or taste them. These should be moments or ideas that evoke positive energy and motivation.

If You Wake Up Groggy…

If you, like me, are a bit groggy in the morning, make sure what you put on that list are the kinds of things that get you bouncing out of bed in the morning. Before I knew that there were more pleasant alternatives, I used to motivate myself out of bed by hearing my father's booming (slightly threatening) voice, yelling, "Move!". The jolt of adrenaline worked a treat in getting me up, out and to the gym. But I've found more pleasant ways that work even better.

One of the simplest and most effective techniques is breath control. Starting with box breathing—inhaling for four counts, holding for four, and exhaling for four—helps balance oxygen flow and energises the body. This breathing method activates the parasympathetic nervous system, which helps regulate energy levels and prepare the body for action. After three or so rounds, turn your focus to your Bliss List.

Recall energising experiences: socialising with great friends, laughing at something really funny, making love with energy and passion, or cheering for your favourite sports team as they win the championship, engaging in a competitive activity like skiing, debating or riding a roller-coaster.

Whatever gets you thrilled, get it on your list and get into your morning: replay it in your mind vividly... relive it convincingly, just like the song, *"Right here! Right now!"*.

See what you saw and hear what you heard. Make the colours brighter and the images bigger. Make the sounds crisper, richer and louder. Begin to feel the energy running through your whole body. And begin to grin as the thrill builds. Then, at the back of your mind, with a voice like rolling thunder, say:

"This day is <u>mine</u>!"

IF YOU WAKE UP ANXIOUS...

On the other hand, if you are apt to wake up in the morning feeling slightly apprehensive or, perhaps, worrying about the day; that's OK, it's only your body has shifted into a 'pattern of protection'. Just take this as a sign that your body is running this strategy because it needs to begin to *feel safe and connected*.

Again, breathing is an easy first step, so you might begin with some *4-7-8 breathing*. To address this, start with 4-7-8 breathing—inhale for four counts, hold for seven, and exhale for eight. This breathing technique helps slow the heart rate and engages the vagus nerve, calming the nervous system and reducing anxiety.

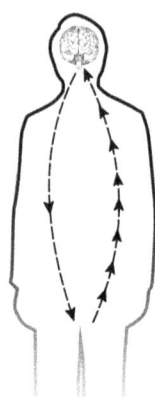

Vagus Nerve:
Information Superhighway

80%
of the vagus nerve fibers communicate from the body to the brain

20%
communicate from the brain to the body

ONCE YOU BEGIN to feel calmer, think about activities where you feel competent and at ease. This maybe a hobby, such as golf or badminton or playing poker. It could be a skill in which you have achieved excellence over the years, such as woodwork or painting or cooking. Or it may be something that, soon after beginning the activity, you go into a heightened state of focus, such as dancing, running, playing an instrument, gardening, walking in nature or writing.

Whatever it is that gives you that grounded feeling of certainty, replay it in your mind. Again, do it as though you are reliving it "right here, right now". See what you saw and hear what you heard. Make the colours brighter and bolder. Then push the images away from you and, as you do so, make them grow bigger; so they become as large as a giant *Imax* screen.

Make the sounds crisp, clear and resonant. Begin to feel a deep sense of grounded surety running through every vein and oozing from every pore. Feel that sense of *'in the moment'* focus and calm resolve spreading through your whole body. And, at the back of your mind with a deep sense of absolute truth, say:

"Today... belongs... to me!"

THE POWER of Conviction

Remember, the purpose of doing these practices is to prime your body with the right metabolic state for a terrific day ahead. Therefore, it's got to be convincing! If you say, *"today belongs to me"* in a weak, wimpy, wishy-washy, zero-conviction voice... you're not going change your state!

However, if you are fully committed, and say it and hear it with the rich, rhythmic and resonant voice of Morgan Freeman, you will feel more calm, more grounded and more confident.

Own it. Let this powerful start carry you through your day.

GET RID of It

Things can trigger us because we are alive, and our body wants to keep it that way. In doing so, we can get angry to the point of seething; scared to the point of being petrified; saddened to the point of total deflation. With a close associate, I refer to this phenomenon as, the *Wobble*. Every two to three months, she experiences a mini 'Jerry Moment'. Like the straws on the proverbial camel's back, things build up... then the back breaks.

Of course, it is not the sheer quantity of unpleasant experiences she has amassed between wobbles that causes the next wobble. Rather, like all of us, her brain is compelled to revisit these unfortunate moments again and again. Yet, each revisiting is itself a bad experience; therefore, she generates the majority of the straws herself until... 'Wobble'!

This going back and picking through bad times is known as *rumination*, which is another pattern of protection. Interestingly, like cows and sheep, camels also ruminate as they chew their cud (fun fact: camels are *pseudoruminants*). Our bodies revisit snippets of snarky comments, hushed tones, ambiguous gestures, fleeting glances or a verbal faux pas. They seek to yield some protective insight to what is going on, *right here, right now*.

"The threats and dangers of the future are hidden inside our prior bad experiences": that is a basic program within our survival instinct, and it's gotten our species to where we are today. As a consequence, our bodies are constantly raking and sifting through the worse of our history. A relentless search for parallels and patterns to solve the problem of evading life-threatening moments in the future.

The price of this life-extending program is to diminish the quality of the very life the program has extended. Put simply, revisiting a bad memory in the brain means vividly reliving it in the body. Because each time we recall these bad memories, our adrenaline and cortisol levels begin to climb. We become fearful, angry and depressed. We become disconnected from others. But disconnected leader is no leader at all. A tyrant, a distraction or a burden, but not a leader.

Leaders face constant challenges—some predictable, others entirely unexpected. Without regular mental and emotional upkeep, these stressors can quietly accumulate. Much like physical hygiene, leaders must develop 'mental hygiene' practices to stay emotionally clear and effective:

- If you are in a leadership role where lots of things can and do go wrong, there's a lot of opportunity to become triggered.
- If you are in an executive role where there is a lot of ambiguity, uncertainty and complexity, you will be subject to shocks and surprises.
- If you're working in an aggressively competitive, unforgiving or toxic environment, where your integrity, intelligence and credibility can be called into question with scant evidential grounds, you will be subject to unfair criticism and cheap shots.

In all of these scenarios, you will fare better if you are able to sustain a calm, confident and connected state. If not, your likelihood of having a 'Jerry moment' is high and rising.

Leadership Hygiene Practice

Think of it like washing your dishes after a meal. The alternative? Eating off the same dirty plate again and again. Or consider taking the rubbish out when the kitchen bin is full. The alternative is letting waste pile up and rot in your home. Gross, right?

Yet many leaders don't "clean their neurology" after a stressful day or week. Like Jerry, they let disconnecting moments of disappointment, frustration, regret, embarrassment, fright and upset pile up. Then they go to bed and relive them all again. They fail to understand that *disconnection* is the denial of the body to heal itself – because human connection is the biological imperative to emotional safety and health. They forget two scientific truths:

1. *Disconnection* suppresses the body's natural ability to heal itself
2. *Connection* is a biological imperative for emotional safety and health.

So, let's wash away the mental clutter.

Bring to your mind a memory of a bad experience on which you have been ruminating. Start to adjust and noodle with the submodalities. Pause the movie and flicker it black and white quickly for a count of five. Then push the picture away from you so that it becomes tiny. Repeat this five times quickly. Then go to the end of the memory and begin to rewind it so that people talk backwards and walk backwards. Play the memory backwards all the way to the beginning of the memory, so it stops just before the bad experience happened.

Begin to spin the same green feeling that you created in *Turning Anxiety Around* from Chapter 6 and rewind the movie faster. Do these three more times rewinding the memory faster and faster each time. As mentioned earlier, practice makes perfect and perfection is just about doing a lot of tiny things well. So, keep practicing this at the end of each difficult day.

This combination of techniques created by Richard Bandler has been widely used to help individuals manage negative emotions. In my view, they are a true gift to humanity. The formula is easy to remember:

- Flicker the picture black and white for a five-count.
- Shrink the picture, five times fast.
- Then play the sights, sounds and sensations backwards, five times fast.
- Done!

GET to Sleep

When it comes to getting to sleep, your body needs to feel safe and calm. However, people go to bed stressing about something silly or embarrassing or upsetting that happened during the day. Hopefully, we've taken care of that problem above. Make sure you practice the '*Get Rid of It*' exercise as soon as you practically can – there's no reason to hold onto a bad experience.

Once you've cleared the day's emotional clutter, the next step is ensuring a restful night's sleep. Sleep is your body's most powerful tool for restoration, but it's often compromised by unresolved stress. People go to bed worrying about and fretting over a meeting or encounter or some event that is going to happen the following day.

They run and loop convincing disaster scenarios, thereby ensuring their adrenaline and cortisol levels are elevated right before bedtime.

Inevitably, they lie in bed 'determined' to get to sleep but, all the time, they are stressing about their upsetting hallucination. Convinced by their brain's scary scenario-playing, their body pumps more and more adrenaline into their system to mobilise them out of their bed and away from the imagined danger. Even more 'determined' to get to sleep, they roll over, punch their pillow, yank their covers back over themselves and go back to dwelling on and mulling over their scary thoughts.

Of course, this lack of fleeing from what their body interprets as "clear and present danger" induces it to pump even more adrenalin into their system. And so, this battle continues with the person's cognition simultaneously keeping themselves in a vulnerable position in bed as well as generating scary thoughts to which their body responds with increased escalation. With practice, their body learns that going to bed is very unsafe and perfects its stress response every night.

I ask such people what they would think if I recommended that they drink a couple of cans of Red Bull before going to bed. They always say that would be a stupid thing to do because it would keep them awake. And I am forced to agree with them. Then I say, *"But at least the Red Bull won't scare you. So, what is more stupid, taking the Red Bull or scaring yourself every night into persistent or chronic insomnia?"*

Of course, they claim that they don't have a choice, that it is out of their control and that it just keeps happening. This is all complete nonsense, of course, but they are convinced of it. So, for all the people out there that either can't get to sleep or, if they wake up in the middle of the night, can't get back to sleep, let's explore how to transition smoothly into deep, restorative rest.

RUPTURE PREVENTION

The first of which is to have a short mental list of things that, when you did them, you felt deep satisfaction and gentle joy. As a clue, bungy-jumping, rollercoasters and theme parks are not what I have in mind. I'm thinking more along the lines of listening to soothing music, getting a gentle massage, lazing in the sun, a cool glass of water on a hot day, children giggling, slowly completing a jigsaw puzzle, feeling satiated after a big meal, a beautiful smile.

Whatever should be on your *'Bliss List'*, write it down. Look at the completed list itself. Make a picture of it in your mind. Check that you have commit it to memory by recalling the remembered picture of the list. Test yourself by reading each line in your mind with a soft and sleepy inner voice. This is important because, as I joke with my clients, the word 'relax' is called re-lax because you have to do it several times. Otherwise, it would just have been called… 'lax'!

So, we are going to begin to relax several times in several ways. And, once more, begin with your breath. Just notice from where it is you are breathing – is it high in the chest or low in the abdomen? If it is high in the chest, begin to move it lower with every passing breath. As you do so, begin to breathe slower. When you breathe in, notice how much your lungs inflate. Calibrate to this level and, when you breathe out, count to two before breathing in to the same level. Breathe out, hold for two, and breathe in. Repeat and on the third intake of breath, *take twice as long to fill your lungs half as much.*

Now, use the *Connect with Yourself* technique and turn on your 'light of joy', which is just one inch below your bellybutton. Feel the light moving as you breathe in and out, and how it stays still for a count of two after you have exhaled. Picture your *Bliss List* and read the first line in that soft and sleepy voice and then relive that peaceful relaxing moment in your life. Let your body go all flippy and floppy, so that every patch of your skin, every fold and every follicle just softens completely. Keep the 'count for two' breath pattern going and, at each count of two, let a gentle wave of relaxation bathe every cell, every sinew and every synapse in *softened bliss*.

Keeping your mind reliving the first item on your list and, even as you do, allow yourself to go to other lovely, related times. If your brain goes to something less pleasant, that's OK, it just means that it's time to go to the second item on your list. And, as you do, turn up your joy light and let it begin to spread through your whole body. Picture your list and read the next line in that soft sleepy voice and fall into the memory completely. Relive the sumptuous sights, sounds and sensations just as you lived them. Feel your body soften completely and, during the count of two, feel a wave of bliss and peacefulness wash over your body.

Sometimes you can wake up in the middle of the night; perhaps from a 'call of nature' or from an upset child. When you get back to bed, settle down and get comfortable. Then, ever so slowly, softly and gently, just curl your toes up a little bit and let a sleepy smile move through your body. Let it come up to your mouth, up and into your mind. Turn your joy light on and return to the next line on the Bliss List. Remember, relaxation is re-laxation and, each time you re-lax, soften your body from the top of your head to the tips of your toes. As you are doing so, you are training your body to drift off to sleep, deeper and deeper still.

Conclusion

The proverb "*An apple a day keeps the doctor away*" reflects a 19th-century belief in the health benefits of fresh fruits and vegetables—wisdom grounded in experience long before science explained why it worked. Similarly, the practices in this chapter are more than routines; they are *strategic investments* in your well-being, resilience, and leadership capacity.

Prevention is the highest and most effective form of resilience. Small, consistent actions—like integrating the *PACE Protocol* and curating a deeply personal *Bliss List*—aren't fleeting techniques. They are essential habits that form the bedrock of sustained leadership excellence.

When leaders commit to *daily autoregulation*, they don't just shield themselves from burnout and emotional ruptures—they set a powerful example. This proactive approach cultivates psychological safety, emotional stability, and collective confidence. It fosters a culture where teams feel secure, valued, and emboldened to innovate and collaborate, even in the face of adversity.

Consider this: every small moment of self-discipline compounds over time. Every intentional breath, every mental reset after a setback, and every conscious return to joy strengthens your capacity to lead with presence, clarity, and authenticity. These practices don't just prevent breakdowns—they unlock your potential to lead with greater influence and purpose.

Leading demands more than reacting well under pressure—it demands preventing stress and overwhelm from ever taking hold. In times of galloping complexity and relentless change, resilient leaders are those who actively fortify their inner world to remain steady, grounded, and adaptable.

Remember:

- *Permission* allows you to lead with presence and purpose.
- *Agency* empowers you to override impulsive reactions.
- *Connection* serves as a buffer against daily stressors.
- *Embedded new strategies* give you clarity, calm, and grounded confidence.

Neuro-resilience is a daily discipline. The world doesn't wait for you to feel ready—and neither should you. Let me offer a twist on an old saying:

"A practice a day keeps the Wobble away"

Begin now. Practise consistently. Refine relentlessly.

As these habits take root, you'll not only witness your personal resilience grow but also see a profound, positive shift ripple through your team and organisation.

SECTION THREE SUMMARY

This final section of 'The Inner Game' brings home the principles and importance of neuro-resilience to life. By focusing on the practical application of these techniques in high stakes, emotionally charged situation undergone by a real flesh-and-blood manager. Through compelling narratives and step-by-step guidance, it highlights how leaders and individuals can tackle ruptures in psychological safety, repair the damage caused by acute stress or trauma, and establish daily practices to prevent future breakdowns.

In Chapter 7: *When Safety is Ruptured*, we meet Jerry, a senior engineer in a remote mining operation whose mounting stress finally overwhelms him, leading to a complete shutdown. His "freeze" state, marked by rigidity, panic and disconnection, reveals the profound consequences of chronic stress when left unaddressed. Drawing on evolutionary biology, the chapter explains how modern day stressors activate ancient survival responses that, left to their own devices, are maladaptive in the workplace. It also explores the ripple effects of psychological safety breaches, showing how an individual's breakdown can destabilise an entire team. The chapter underscores the importance of recognising early warning signs and implementing neuro-resilience techniques to recalibrate the nervous system before stress becomes overwhelming.

Chapter 8: *Repair & Prevent Trauma* builds on Jerry's story, offering a detailed account of how a skilled practitioner can help someone recover from acute stress. Through Paul's coaching session with Jerry, readers witness the power of rapport-building, humour, and neuro-resilient techniques. The session illustrates how safety priming—creating a secure emotional environment—lays the groundwork for deeper interventions. Techniques like Turning Anxiety Around and The Serenity Technique are used to reframe Jerry's internal experience, helping him transition from distress to calm, confidence, and control. The chapter demonstrates that effective coaching doesn't just resolve immediate problems but equips individuals with tools for sustained emotional self-regulation.

In Chapter 9: *Rupture Prevention Practices*, the focus shifts from repair to prevention. Drawing on the maxim, *"An ounce of prevention is worth a pound of cure"*, the chapter explores the importance of integrating neuro-resilient routines into daily life. By adopting morning and nighttime practices, individuals can prime their bodies for calm, focus, and emotional strength while cleansing their neurology of accumulated stress. The chapter also introduces ad hoc techniques for managing difficult moments during the day and reflective rituals to address lingering negativity. These habits empower individuals to maintain psychological safety proactively, reducing the likelihood of stress spiralling into trauma.

Taken together, the chapters in this section emphasise that neuro-resilience is a dynamic process of controlling stress, recovering from disruptions, and preventing future ruptures. Leaders are shown how to create environments where psychological safety is a priority, enabling individuals and teams to thrive under pressure. Through vivid examples and actionable techniques, Elite Skills in Action

SECTION THREE SUMMARY

provides a roadmap for transforming stress into resilience, enabling not just recovery but sustained growth and well-being.

Part 1 Personal Resilience: Wrap Up

As you draw breath at the close of Part 1, I invite you to consider not only what you've learned but also how you've learned it. This section of the book was not an arbitrary collection of insights and techniques, but a deliberately structured journey—a progression designed to mirror the very framework it seeks to teach: the PACE Protocol. From the outset, you have not merely read about *Permission, Agency, Connection* and *Embedding*; you have experienced them. The PACE Protocol has quietly guided you, not only through the content but also through the structure of the narrative itself.

Let us step back for a moment and examine this journey through the lens of the triune brain. If our brains are a layered hierarchy of evolution—reptilian at the base, mammalian in the middle, and primate (or rational) at the top—then this book has spoken to all three, engaging each in turn. At its heart, the PACE Protocol has been a tool for integration, giving each layer of the brain the opportunity to play its role in building resilience.

We began with the *reptilian brain*, the ancient and vigilant sentinel of survival. This part of your brain, attuned to fight, flight, and freeze, craves safety above all else. It does not ask questions or deliberate; it reacts. To soothe this primal guardian, you were offered techniques designed to bring safety into the body. Practices like the Tension Releasor and Body Scanning whispered to the reptilian brain that the world need not always be a battlefield. The phase of *Permission* was, in many ways, a conversation with this part of you—an assurance that it could lay down its weapons, that it was, in fact, safe to explore.

From there, we ascended to the *mammalian brain*, home to emotion and connection. This is the brain that seeks the warmth of belonging, the comfort of co-regulation, and the vitality of social engagement.

SECTION THREE SUMMARY

Here, Agency came into play. With the reptilian instincts dialled down, the mammalian brain could turn outward, embracing connection with the self and, by extension, others. Techniques like Wrapped in Serenity encouraged this brain to anchor itself in trust and connection, quieting the inner storms that make collaboration difficult. It was here that you began to sense not only a diminishment of survival-driven instincts but an emergence of something far greater: an increasing capacity for engagement and openness.

Finally, we spoke to the *primate brain*, that great architect of reason and reflection. This is the brain that delights in understanding, that seeks meaning and coherence in the patterns of life. It was engaged through logical progressions, scientific insights, and structured techniques. Decision-Journalling, for instance, allowed this part of your mind to step into the driver's seat, crafting intentional actions out of instinct and emotion. In this phase, *Connection* and *Embedding* were not abstract ideas but tangible practices, bringing the rational brain into alignment with its instinctual and emotional counterparts.

In Section Three, these ideas culminated in a focus on practical application. Through compelling narratives like Jerry's journey in a remote mining operation, we saw the profound consequences of unchecked stress and the transformative power of neuro-resilience techniques. Jerry's "freeze" state illustrated the reptilian brain in action, overwhelmed by chronic stress, and the steps taken to recover highlighted how safety priming and rapport-building could guide him toward calm and control. Paul's coaching session with Jerry brought the PACE Protocol to life, showing how Permission, Agency, Connection, and Embedding translate into real-world leadership scenarios.

What is remarkable is that the PACE Protocol is not limited to the inner game. What you have experienced internally, as a sequence of regulation and repair, will soon expand outward, shaping your interactions with others and the teams you lead. The Permission you gave

SECTION THREE SUMMARY

yourself to explore will become the permission you extend to others to bring their whole selves to the table. The Agency you cultivated within your instincts and emotions will mirror the agency you foster within your teams. The Connection you cultivated within your nervous system will reflect in the trust and collaboration you create among colleagues. And the Embedded new strategies and insights, which you have installed within yourself, will inspire action and momentum in the groups you guide.

This is why the PACE Protocol is not just a method; it is a philosophy. It bridges the personal and the interpersonal, the subjective and the collective, the instinctual and the intellectual. By the time you've reached this point, you have not only learned about the PACE Protocol; you have lived it. You have given your reptilian brain safety, your mammalian brain connection, and your primate brain understanding. You have aligned your inner world in preparation for the outer work that lies ahead.

As we transition to Part 2, remember this alignment. The work you've done to calm your instincts, connect with your emotions, and engage your rational mind has laid the foundation for a new kind of leadership. What began as a personal journey to conquer stress and foster resilience will now extend outward, transforming how you lead others.

In Part 2, you will learn to apply the PACE Protocol to the dynamics of teams and organisations. You'll see how the emotional trust and safety you've cultivated within yourself can ripple outward, fostering a culture of resilience, adaptability, and connection within your teams. You will explore how to create environments of trust, foster meaningful connections, and align groups toward shared goals. Just as you've experienced the power of Permission, Agency, Connection, and Embedding new strategies within yourself, you will now see how these practices build resilient, unflappable teams that thrive under pressure and adapt to challenges with agility and grace.

Explored in Section Three to repair and prevent trauma:

1. **PACE Yourself** – The same structure applied to autoregulation.
2. **The Bliss List** – A curated list positive experiences prepared as mental resources
3. **Rise & Shine** – strategies for getting the day off to a terrific start
4. **Get Rid of It** – Leadership hygiene techniques for clearing out stress.
5. **Get to Sleep** – Strategies for calmness and relaxation for restorative sleep

Introduced and to be fully explored in Part 2, The Outer Game:

6. **The PACE Protocol** – A four-phase structure for tracking coaching sessions.
7. **Safety Priming** – Advanced co-regulation skills.
8. **Co-Regulating Humour** – Tactical use of humour and reframing to foster safety.
9. **Anchoring States** – Wiring positive emotions to physical/ mental triggers.
10. **Future Pacing** – Pre-living and pre-framing desirable future outcomes.

CONCLUSION TO PART ONE
OWNING YOUR INNER GAME

Pause for a moment. Breathe in slowly through your nose, hold for a beat, and exhale gently. Feel the weight of your body in your chair, the tension—or lack of it—in your shoulders. Notice how your breath settles into a steady rhythm. Now, cast your mind back to the first pages of this book. How much of this awareness was present then?

Most people think of resilience as a matter of sheer willpower—a mental discipline that can be summoned when needed. But this is an illusion. Resilience is not just about how you think; it is about how your body responds under pressure. It is the difference between recognising stress and being trapped inside it.

True resilience is older than thought itself. It is not just about what you know—it is about what your body does when stress rises, when uncertainty looms, when pressure mounts. It is the difference between noticing fear and being ruled by it, between recognising instinct and being enslaved by it.

At the heart of this transformation lies your nervous system. More than anything else, this book has been an act of retraining, a slow, deliberate rewiring of the patterns that dictate your reactions to the world. It has guided you through the biology of your survival instincts, showing you not just how to regulate them, but how to harness them, refine them, and integrate them into something greater—*instinctual intelligence*.

To understand what has changed, we must look at how your nervous system has learned to shift between *Patterns of Protection* and *Patterns of Connection*. The distinction is crucial: in Patterns of Protection, your body is primed for survival—mobilised into fight or flight or immobilised into withdrawal and shutdown. Metabolically, behaviourally, and cognitively, you are in a state of defence.

But in Patterns of Connection, something else happens. The threat subsides, the nervous system signals safety, and the body shifts into an entirely different mode—one optimised for engagement, creativity, and complex thinking.

Everyone begins their neuro-resilience journey at the mercy of their nervous system—stress triggers the body, and the mind scrambles to keep up. But now, the equation has reversed. You no longer just experience stress—you shape your response to it. You are no longer a passenger; you are the driver.

Every technique, every shift, every realisation has been part of a greater biological process—one that has not only freed you from reactive survival but has given you the capacity to thrive within stress, not just endure it.

But how exactly does this rewiring occur? To see it clearly, we must turn to the three primary neural networks within your brain: the Reptilian, Mammalian, and Primate brains. As stated in Chapter 2, neuroscience confirms that the brain is far more interconnected than the Triune Brain model suggests.

Yet, like Newtonian physics, the Triune Brain model remains a simple but powerful tool. It may not capture every nuance of neural complexity, but for leaders, it offers one of the clearest ways to understand how instinct, emotion, and reason interact in real-time. It helps coaches, decision-makers, and strategists grasp the forces that drive behaviour—both in themselves and in those they lead.

To be clear, the Triune Brain Theory is a description of *neural networks*: ancient biological systems, each governing a distinct realm of experience. The fossil record shows the subtle but gradual shift from reptile to mammal to primate: so, we understand the lineage. This is confirmed by the neural networks that are present and absent in reptiles, mammals and primates today. It is certain that these three neural networks have always been present in humans.

By learning neuro-resilience skills, you have been training your three neural networks to *work together*. That means, learning to generate sufficient cues of safety to trigger a neuroception of safety within you. This is the key characteristic of a *flexible autonomic nervous system*.

The delivery mechanisms for this increased flexibility has been *Neuro-Linguistic Programming* (NLP), as I learned it from Dr. Richard Bandler and applied it as a leader and coach in commercial and non-commercial businesses for twenty-five years.

Patterns of Protection

At the base of your skull, nestled deep within the oldest structures of your brain, lies the *Reptilian Brain*. It does not care for nuance, nor for reasoned debate. It does not weigh up pros and cons, nor consider the long-term consequences of a poorly chosen word in a meeting or a rising heart rate before a difficult conversation. It is concerned with one thing alone: *survival*.

In this domain, cognition is an afterthought. When the Reptilian Brain perceives threat, it grabs the controls of your nervous system and overrides everything else. Your heartbeat quickens, your muscles tighten, and the blood drains from your frontal cortex—where higher reasoning lives—to the larger muscle groups, preparing you for fight, flight, or freeze. Your metabolism follows suit, prioritising fast-burning glucose over slower, more sustainable energy sources.

The Reptilian Brain does not plan for the future. It does not *strategise*. It does not care for connection, creativity, or even accuracy. It reacts. And yet, for all its crude simplicity, this part of your brain is also *a necessity*. Without it, you would not be here. It has saved you more times than you can count. The problem is not the existence of the Reptilian Brain—it is how often we allow it to run the show.

At the beginning of this book, much of your instinctual behaviour was governed unconsciously by these survival responses. Stressors—whether physical, emotional, or social—triggered mobilisation or immobilisation before you even had time to think. In other words, your body was responding before your mind could intervene.

You now know how to change that. Through the structured progression of techniques, you have taught your nervous system to pause, to assess, and to regulate itself before automatically defaulting to protection.

At first, this work was simple, physical, and immediate. You began with '*Somatic Honing*', learning to feel your stress responses without judgment. You used '*Tension Releasor*' and '*4-7-8 Breathing*' to signal to your body that it could exit survival mode. These were not trivial exercises; they were interventions in the very mechanics of your autonomic nervous system, ensuring *that fight, flight, and shutdown no longer dictated your experience of the world.*

And then the real shift began. You did not just *calm* the Reptilian Brain—you *trained it*. You learned to recognise its signals before they took over, mapping its sensory patterns through '*Instinct Mapping*' and building internal safety through '*Finding Home*'. Where once you were merely a passenger to its reflexes, now you are the pilot, guiding it back from mobilisation before it takes hold.

CONCLUSION TO PART ONE

This transformation is not just psychological; it is metabolic. When you live in *chronic mobilisation*, your body burns through energy reserves faster, increasing fatigue, heightening inflammation, and impairing long-term cognitive function. Every technique you have learned has not just *relieved stress—it has optimised your body for resilience.* Your *metabolism now works with you, not against you.*

But most importantly, *your cognition has returned.* When the Reptilian Brain is in charge, deep thinking is impossible. The higher brain—the Primate Brain—receives little oxygen and less attention. If you have ever felt that stress made you 'stupid', this is why: your body quite literally redirected your mental resources elsewhere.

The change is undeniable. Now, when the Reptilian Brain activates, you *notice*. You intervene. You regulate. The survival response no longer dictates your behaviour—*it informs it.*

You are no longer merely reactive. You are responsive.

And because of this, something new has become possible. You are now capable of inhabiting the next level of resilience—the realm of connection.

Patterns of Connection

If the Reptilian Brain is the body's emergency response system, then the Mammalian Brain—the limbic system—is its emotional compass. This is where the world is no longer a question of survival, but of meaning, memory, and connection. It is here that stress ceases to be merely metabolic and becomes something personal.

For the Mammalian Brain, safety is not just the absence of threat—it is *the presence of trust, warmth, and social belonging.* And yet, when the body is locked in survival mode, these things feel distant, if not impossible. A nervous system trapped in a *Pattern of Protection* cannot fully engage in *Patterns of Connection*. It cannot think freely, love freely, or lead freely. It remains on edge, mistaking colleagues for competitors, mistakes for disasters, challenges for threats. It is not the external world that has changed—*only the internal conditions of the nervous system.*

Throughout this book, you have gradually shifted these internal conditions. At first, the Mammalian Brain, conditioned by past experiences, resisted the idea that safety could be created rather than passively experienced. Emotional states, after all, had long felt like something that happened to you, rather than something you could shape. But as your Reptilian Brain became regulated, your Mammalian Brain became free to do something it could not before: experience safety fully.

This was not a matter of wishful thinking, nor of mere emotional management. It was biological. Through *'Finding Home'*, you built neural associations between calmness and stability, rather than calmness and waiting for the next disaster. With *'Bliss List'*, you trained your nervous system to access joy on command, proving that positivity is not a passive state but an active skill. With *'Silencing the Storm'*, you rewired the circuits that once turned minor stressors into looping, inescapable ruminations.

But the greatest transformation was in how you now relate to others.

The limbic system is not designed for isolation. It is wired for co-regulation, meaning that its *default state is shaped not just by your own nervous system, but by those around you.* You now recognise this intuitively. You have seen how tension spreads through a room like electricity. You have felt the difference between a voice that soothes and a voice that sharpens. You have noticed that *safety is a social phenomenon, not just an individual one.*

The question, then, was never just whether you could regulate yourself, but whether you could *regulate others through your presence, your voice, and your leadership.*

CONCLUSION TO PART ONE

You read how I used *Safety Priming* and *Co-Regulating Humour* could be used in the process of repairing trauma. You will learn about these explicitly in Part 2, The Outer Game. Safety, you discovered, is not just a personal feeling, but an interaction your nervous system is having with the environment. You learned to soften stress in conversations before it took hold. You recognised that the way you present yourself—your tone, your facial expressions, your openness—actively dictates whether those around you remain in protection or shift into connection.

And this can change everything.

Leadership, decision-making, and problem-solving can all improve—not because you learned new intellectual skills, but because you have learned to keep yourself in the optimal state for thinking. What once was personal resilience is now something broader, something more fundamental: social fluency, the ability to lead not just with authority, but with presence, trust, and psychological safety.

The Mammalian Brain, once ruled by stress, is now ruled by awareness. You know how to recognise when your own nervous system is slipping into protection, and just as importantly, you now recognise it in others. You see when a colleague's frustration is really fear. You sense when a team member's withdrawal is not laziness, but immobilisation. And most importantly, you know what to do about it.

This is not just resilience—it is *leadership over the social nervous system.*

And because of this, a new possibility opens: not just controlling emotions, but controlling the conditions under which collective thinking flourishes.

To understand this final transformation, we must turn to the Primate Brain—the seat of logic, reason, and innovation. The place where cognition is either *trapped by stress or liberated by safety.*

Cognitive Overload

There is a persistent illusion, deeply embedded in contemporary thought, that reason operates separately from emotion—that clear, rational thinking is a purely intellectual exercise, rising above the turbulence of the body. But this is a fantasy. A mind in distress is a mind in disarray. The Primate Brain—the neocortex, our seat of logic, strategy, and foresight—is not an autonomous command centre. It is a dependent system, entirely contingent on the conditions of the nervous system beneath it.

No matter how intelligent a person is, when their body is locked in survival mode, higher reasoning is off the table. Stress hijacks cognition, diverting resources away from deep thought and long-term planning into immediate, reactive decision-making. The more the body perceives threat, the less the mind can engage in what we associate with true intelligence: creativity, strategic foresight, and the ability to weigh consequences beyond the immediate moment.

This is why what is often called 'poor decision-making' is, at its core, not a failure of intelligence—but a failure of state. It is not that people become irrational under pressure; it is that their cognitive bandwidth shrinks, compressed by the body's demand for survival. A leader caught in a state of stress does not simply think worse—they think differently, trapped in a survival triage: fight, flee, or freeze.

At the start of this book, your Primate Brain was often working against itself. When stress arose, it followed the path it had always followed: over-analysing, spiralling into worry, cycling through worst-case scenarios. It tried to solve emotions with logic—like attempting to put out a fire by reading about water. You knew you were 'overthinking', but knowing was not enough to stop it. You had no mechanism for interrupting the momentum of cognitive overload before it consumed you.

But cognition is not an isolated process—it is a state-dependent phenomenon. The quality of your thinking is not dictated by willpower or intellect, but by whether your nervous system is in a state where complex thought is possible.

This is the crucial shift. Instead of trying to fix thinking directly, you learned to shift the conditions under which clear thinking emerges.

At first, this involved simple but powerful interventions.

- *Dual-Mind Reflection* allowed your rational mind to engage with your instincts rather than dismiss them.
- *The Worry Solver* reframed stress into action, preventing rumination from spiralling into paralysis.
- *Stepping Out of Fear* allowed your neocortex the space to function without the weight of emotional overwhelm.

And then, as the Mammalian Brain settled into safety, something even more profound happened: thinking became effortless. No longer tangled in a constant battle against stress, your Primate Brain could return to its full capacity—fluid, agile, sharp.

This cannot be overstated: cognition is not just something to be improved—it is something to be transformed. It has already begun.

- You no longer waste mental energy on unnecessary overanalyses, because you now recognise the difference between useful thought and stress-driven mental noise.
- You no longer burn hours wrestling with decisions, because you trust your instincts to signal what requires attention and what does not.
- Most importantly, your nervous system has been rewired so that under pressure, your thinking does not degrade—it sharpens.

This is what instinctual intelligence truly means. It is not merely the ability to regulate emotions, nor is it simply the capacity to think clearly under stress. It is something greater: the full integration of survival, emotion, and intellect into a seamless whole—where instinct does not overpower thought, and thought does not ignore instinct.

It is the ability to move fluidly between mobilisation, connection, and cognition—to detect, understand, and shape the shifting patterns of your nervous system, so that in any given moment, you are operating from the most effective state possible.

For the first time:

- Your Reptilian Brain does not react blindly—it signals usefully.
- Your Mammalian Brain does not overwhelm you with emotion—it informs you.
- Your Primate Brain does not collapse under stress—it remains clear, sharp, and adaptive.

And this, ultimately, is the mark of true resilience.

Not merely the ability to withstand hardship, but the ability to navigate complexity with intelligence, presence, and control.

- Where once survival ruled, now modern humans can flourish.
- Where once protection dictated action, now connection and cognition can coexist.

This is not just a new way of managing stress.

This is a new way of *being*.

True Instinctual Intelligence

The mind does not work in isolation. The sharpest intellect in the world is useless when the nervous system is dysregulated. And yet, most leaders attempt to solve stress-driven thinking failures by thinking harder. They push through, unaware that they are battling their own biology.

True intelligence is not found in forcing reason to overcome instinct—it is found in integrating the two. This is where instinctual intelligence begins.

Neuro-resilience is not about willpower; it is about rewiring the nervous system. At the start of this journey, your mind and body were pulling in different directions.

- The Reptilian Brain, ever-vigilant, triggered fight, flight, or freeze at the first sign of stress, flooding your system with adrenaline before your conscious mind could even process what was happening.
- The Mammalian Brain, shaped by past experiences, reacted emotionally—sometimes protecting, sometimes connecting, but often reinforcing old habits of fear, withdrawal, or overstimulation.
- The Primate Brain, the grand architect of reason, tried to impose order, attempting to think its way out of stress while unknowingly making the situation worse.

This constant internal struggle—the overthinking, the emotional highs and lows, the inexplicable anxiety that rises unbidden—is what most people consider normal. The human condition. The exhaustion of a nervous system that never seems fully at ease. No wonder so many live in a perpetual state of mental and emotional depletion, their bodies locked in Patterns of Protection long after the threats have passed.

But now, the conflict has begun to resolve. Something fundamental has shifted.

When your three brains move out of sync, you now have the ability to realign them.

- Where once your instincts hijacked you, they now act as early-warning signals—alerting you to stress without overwhelming you.
- Where once your emotions dictated your behaviour, they now serve as tools for insight, motivation, and connection.
- And where once your rational mind fought against stress, it is now free to think, plan, and lead with clarity.

This is instinctual intelligence—a state where all parts of the system work together, where protection no longer overrides connection, and cognition is no longer derailed by emotion.

But what, exactly, has changed?

At a physiological level, you have built flexibility into your autonomic nervous system. Your body, once primed for habitual stress responses, now knows how to shift into a state of regulation deliberately. What was once disruptive—fight, flight, freeze—has now become adaptive, a response that is chosen rather than imposed. This means that under pressure, instead of collapsing into a survival state, your system remains fluid and responsive. You do not lose yourself in stress—you remain present.

At an emotional level, you have learned to trust the signals of your body rather than fear them. What once felt like chaos—anxiety, uncertainty, physiological discomfort—is now understood as information, a message from your nervous system rather than an enemy to be fought. And this trust has allowed you to access a new kind of control—not the rigid suppression of emotions, but the fluid, dynamic control of mastery. And cognitively? The greatest transformation of all.

You have discovered what few ever do: that the brain works best when it is not at war with itself. That intelligence is not just about knowledge, but about state—the ability to maintain the conditions in which thinking is sharpest, creativity is at its peak, and decisions are made not from fear, but from clarity.

This is not just a different way of processing stress. It is a different way of being. From this moment forward, resilience is not something you do. It is something you are. It is woven into the structure of your nervous system, embedded in your responses, present in the very way you hold yourself, breathe, speak, and lead. Your body knows safety. Your mind knows control. Your instincts, once erratic, now serve you. You have, at last, become fully integrated.

And from here, anything is possible.

The Wind Beneath the Wings

If this journey has felt fluid, if each step seemed to unfold naturally from the last, if the transformation you have begun to experience has felt unforced and inevitable—it is because Part 1 was more than just a collection of scientific theories and fact combined with a series of matching NLP insights and strategies. Rather, it was a carefully structured process.

Every chapter, every exercise, every realisation was selected to follow the same rhythm that governs all successful change: first, creating trust and safety, then cultivating personal control, then deepening social fluency, and finally installing strategies and meanings for the long-term. This is not coincidence—it is the structure that allows resilience to move from theory into instinct, from knowledge into lived intelligence.

The PACE Protocol is not just a framework that was presented and explained to you. It is the method that was applied to the structure of Part 1 to support your cognitive, emotional and instinctual journey of learning. It was the unseen framework that has made everything feel more intuitive and more digestible towards being, more lasting.

You will not have just surfed atop of the process—you will have experienced it with the *Primate, Mammalian* and *Reptile* brains. This is to say that you have been learning both consciously (slow-thinking) and unconsciously (fast-thinking). The same structure that had begun to rewire your nervous system over these pages is now an embedded learning within you.

With continued practice, which builds up the unconscious competence of the fast-thinking system, resilience will begin to feel like 'a part of who you are and just do', rather than something you must 'remember to apply'. That is why it's 'neuro-resilience' and what who have been practicing are 'neuro-resilience skills'. So, let's now touch on some practice.

Neuro-Resilience is Practiced Skills

Resilience is not an achievement. It is not a trophy to be placed on a shelf, nor a finish line to be crossed with a sigh of relief. It is a set of skills that must be practiced. Resilience is not a one-time achievement. It is an ongoing interaction between your nervous system and your environment. Without continued engagement, even the sharpest instincts dull.

The mistake many make is assuming that transformation is permanent simply because it has been experienced once. They assume that because they have felt clarity, they will always think clearly. Because they have found calm, they will always remain calm. But the nervous system is not a machine—it does not retain new habits through willpower alone. It is an adaptive, living system, shaped by what it is repeatedly exposed to.

CONCLUSION TO PART ONE

What you reinforce is what remains.

That is why the work does not end here.

The skills you have gained, the instincts you have rewired, the clarity you now possess—these are *not fixed traits but cultivated conditions.* They exist because you have trained them into being. And they will remain, not because you understand them, but because you *continue to practise them.*

Neuro-Resilience Daily Routine

These three daily practices are not rigid formulas but adaptable frameworks that evolve as you refine what works best for you. As with any skill, leadership resilience is built through *purposeful practice*—tweaking, testing, and noodling with different approaches until they become second nature. Over time, you'll learn to *do the little things better and really well*, making these habits more fluid and effective. What follows is a great place to start that pursuit of *perfect practice.*

1. 'Rise & Shine'

Start your day ready to be the best version of yourself. Mornings set the stage for the entire day, so the *Rise & Shine* practice ensures you begin with energy, clarity, and intention. Start with controlled *breathing*—if you need an energy boost, use *Box Breathing* (inhale for four, hold for four, exhale for four). If you wake up anxious, try *4-7-8 Breathing* to regulate your nervous system.

Next, engage with your *Bliss List*—whether you need an *energiser* (vividly reliving triumphant, joyful, or playful moments) or a *calmer* (recalling serene, grounding experiences). Use sensory detail to make the memory immersive. Once you've primed your state, move into *PACE Yourself*:

- *Prime & Probe* – Have you permitted yourself to lead well confidently?
- *Agency Over Instincts* – Are your actions the best blends of reason and instinct?
- *Connect and Socialise* – Are you spinning a good feeling and socially engaged?
- *Embed New Strategies* – Have you pre-lived and pre-framed any challenges ahead?

By the time you've finished this process, you've already won the morning—you are stepping into the day as the best leader you can be.

2. 'Get Rid of It'

Throughout the day, stress, frustrations, peeves and, in the modern vernacular, 'micro-aggressions' can and do build up. If left unchecked, these accumulate, leading to disengagement, irritability, or exhaustion.

The *Get Rid of It* practice is about *taking out the garbage*—processing and releasing emotional tension before it festers. Start by mentally scanning your day for any unresolved stressors.

Then, use a structured *leadership hygiene practice* to clear them:

- *Flicker the Image* – Take any stressful memory, make it black and white, and flicker it rapidly for five counts.
- *Shrink the Image* – Push it away until it becomes tiny. Repeat five times.
- *Rewind the Memory* – Play the experience backward with all the sounds and movements reversed.

By shifting these VAK *submodalities*, you break the emotional grip of the stressor, allowing your body to reset. Just as you wouldn't let dirty dishes pile up in the sink, don't let stress accumulate in your mind—

clear it daily to stay sharp, connected, and adaptable. Practice makes perfect and perfection is lots of little things done well.

In NLP, those 'little things' almost always involve ways to shift submodalities.

3. 'Get to Sleep'

The *Get to Sleep* practice ensures that you don't carry the day's stress into the night. Sleep is your body's most powerful recovery tool, but poor mental habits—such as replaying anxieties or running worst-case scenarios—can sabotage it. Begin with *breathing* to shift into relaxation mode. If your mind is racing, return to *4-7-8 breathing* or a slow, deep diaphragmatic rhythm. Then, engage with your *Bliss List*, selecting calming experiences that bring you into a state of gentle joy —soothing music, a warm breeze, the sound of laughter. Immerse yourself in these memories using soft internal dialogue to deepen relaxation. If sleep disruptions occur, don't fight them—gently return to your *Bliss List* and re-lax multiple times, allowing your body to associate bedtime with peace and safety.

Sleep is the ultimate integration process. Guard it fiercely.

Integrated Intelligence for Life

You began this journey reacting. You end it responding proactively. You began ruled by instincts operating below your conscious control. Now you can end in command of it.

But resilience is not something you hold onto—it is something you practise, something you embody, something that is *only as strong as the habits that sustain it.*

This is your work now. To maintain what you have built. To sharpen what you have cultivated. To carry this not just as knowledge, but as a way of being.

And if ever you find yourself slipping, losing clarity, feeling the return of old patterns, that's your body telling you it is sensing something. Maybe it's receiving a true signal. Maybe it's wrongly sensing noise. Remember:

- If your body's survival mode reflects your environment, in that you are in real and imminent danger or life threat, immediately take the necessary action to get physically safe. Emotional safety will return once your body senses it is safe.

- If your body is out of sync with your environment, in that you are *not* in actual danger: hey, shit happens! We're not infallible and we have to live in this uncertain and ambiguous reality. You've just been blown off course, but you've got the skillset. Get your body's metabolism back in sync with your actual environment.

How do you do that? Tune your cognition back into your instincts—do the *Worry Solver*, the *Dual-Mind Reflection*, *Stepping Out of Fear*, *Turn Anxiety Around*, *Get Rid of It* and get *Wrapped in Serenity*.

You have already rewired your nervous system. The intelligence, the control, the instinctive ability—they are all still there. You need only return to them. This is your path now.

Resilience is not theory. Resilience is practice. Resilience is a state of activation—the more you engage with it, the stronger it becomes. This is more than just everyday resilience—it is full command over the conditions of your intelligence. The future no longer dictates your course—you shape it, moment by moment.

This is *neuro-resilience*.

PART TWO
THE OUTER GAME

SECTION FOUR
GROUP RESILIENCE SKILLS

*Our biological imperative is to connect with others.
Humans are not able to flourish without connection.*
Dr. Stephen Porges

The Leadership Imperative

Humans do not thrive in isolation; we think, create, and adapt in groups. From ancient hunting bands to modern corporations, success has never been about individual brilliance but about the intelligence of the collective. Yet, groups can be either extraordinarily adaptive or catastrophically dysfunctional. The factor that determines which path they take is not talent or strategy—it is *psychological safety*.

Without it, groups default to self-protection, stifling creativity and adaptability. Psychological safety is both a goal to be achieved and a fragile condition that must be constantly maintained, shaped by countless micro-signals that dictate what is permissible and what is not.

A leader's role is not to control individuals but to curate the conditions in which people feel safe enough to contribute fully. This requires an understanding that psychological safety is neither static nor self-sustaining. It must be cultivated, protected, and—when necessary—repaired.

The problem for many leaders is that psychological safety is not purely rational. It is not simply about policy or team values; it is embedded in the moment-to-moment signals that people exchange with one another. A dismissive glance, a slight hesitation before someone speaks, a defensive shift in tone—these seemingly trivial cues accumulate into a shared perception of what is permissible and what is not.

This is where most leaders fail—not because they do not value psychological safety, but because they misunderstand how it is created and maintained. It cannot be dictated from above or enforced through a single intervention. It must be embedded into the very structure of group interactions. And this requires a dual approach:

- *Safety-Embedded Structures*: The deliberate, methodical process of creating systems and rituals that align cognition, our intellectual slow-thinking system, to establish shared learnings and understanding. Through these structures, interpersonal trust is built and reinforce over time. This approach is managerial in nature and fosters and supports psychological safety indirectly from the outside-in.
- *Safety Priming*: The visceral, unconscious signals that regulate social interactions in real-time—the verbal and non-verbal cues that shape creates a sense of emotional safety, within each person, which then allows their social engagements behaviours and autonomic invitations to signal safety between people, before rational thought even takes place. This approach is flesh-and-blood leadership in nature

and induces psychological safety directly from the inside-out.

To achieve, sustain and repair psychological safety, organisations need both the structured impersonal managerial practices and the fluid interpersonal leadership psychological capabilities. Structured safety ensures that trust is reinforced over time, while instant safety prevents that trust from being lost in critical moments and can repair it rapidly should it be lost.

Psychological safety is not an individual experience—it is a collective phenomenon. A single person may feel confident in their abilities, but if the group as a whole signals caution, hesitation, or defensiveness, even the most courageous will adapt accordingly. Safety is not something individuals bring with them into a room; it is something they find—or fail to find—when they arrive. And that is where the Hive Mind takes over.

Chapter 10: The Hive Mind, we explore how a group of minds is not simply the sum of its parts. It becomes its own entity: a living, emergent system, shaped by unspoken rules, emotional undercurrents and collective behaviour patterns. Before leaders can achieve and sustain psychological safety, they must first recognise that they are not just managing individuals—they are shaping a dynamic network of interdependent minds through *influence*.

Consider a murmuration of starlings. Thousands of birds move as one, shifting direction in breathtaking synchrony. There is no centralised command, no explicit agreement among the birds—only an emergent intelligence that arises as each bird responds to the micro-movements of those closest to it. The result is an adaptive system that reacts to external threats faster than any single bird could on its own.

Like starlings, human groups operate as emergent systems, where individual behaviours are shaped by collective cues. Psychological safety stabilises this system, enabling adaptive intelligence rather than defensive paralysis. These are patterns of connection and protection, often elusive and unseen, but at the group level.

We take our cues from those around us, often unconsciously through our neuroception. Who speaks and who remains silent? Which opinions gain traction, and which are ignored? These patterns are not determined solely by logic or expertise but by a complex interplay of mimicry, emotional contagion and social signalling.

A team does not need explicit rules to suppress dissent—witnessing the subtle punishment of those who challenge authority is enough. Once a negative dynamic sets in, a team's intelligence collapses into defensiveness, and the Hive Mind turns from a connective pattern of adaptive intelligence into patterns of protection for oneself and one's clique.

This is why psychological safety is not just an individual experience but a property of the group itself. A single person may be courageous, but if the Hive Mind leans towards caution and self-preservation, their courage will be constrained by the surrounding atmosphere. In the face of this context, neuro-resilience training enables people to sustain a robust sense of safety.

However, for most people, their safety sense not robust. Indeed, even if explicit danger and threat cues are not detected, an absence of safety cues will often trigger an aversive neuroception. *Nothingness is somethingness* when it comes to our evolved neurology; because those predecessors whose bodies assumed safety, and not danger, were removed from the gene pool.

When the Hive Mind is functional, it enables adaptive intelligence—a state in which the group remains flexible, able to integrate new ideas, and unafraid of complexity. When dysfunctional, it collapses into rigidity, conformity, and defensive self-preservation.

Leaders who fail to recognise this focus too much on individual performance and too little on the system in which that performance occurs. They assume low engagement is a motivation problem rather than an environmental one. They misdiagnose symptoms as causes.

The solution is not to order people to "speak up" or "be more engaged" or "have fun". The solution is to change the terrain, not the traveller—to create the conditions within which people feel safe enough to contribute fully. This requires structured interventions that ensure the Hive Mind does not drift into dysfunction but remains aligned, adaptable, and psychologically secure.

Because, while psychological safety feels natural when it is present, it does not emerge naturally: the 'nothingness is somethingness' phenomenon will suppress it. It must be elicited and repaired by sufficient cues of safety, both neurologically systemically.

In Chapter 11: Safety-Embedded Structures, we consider psychological safety and what kinds of management structures can help. Consider a scenario familiar to anyone who has worked in a team. A high-stakes meeting is underway. The issue at hand is complex, requiring decisions that will have lasting consequences. Around the table sit capable, intelligent professionals—each with something valuable to contribute. And yet, the discussion is oddly muted.

Some people speak, but cautiously. Others remain silent, even when their expertise is directly relevant. Those who do contribute hedge their statements, wrapping their points in careful qualifications: *"I might be wrong, but..."*, or *"Just playing devil's advocate here..."*. No one outright disagrees, but nor does anyone push bold, creative, or unconventional ideas.

What has gone wrong? The leader of this meeting might assume the team lacks confidence or engagement. But the issue is rarely about motivation. More often, it is about psychological safety—or the absence of it.

Psychological safety does not mean agreeableness or harmoniousness; it means *the presence of interpersonal safety.* In an unsafe environment, people do not openly disagree, challenge, or propose risky ideas—not because they lack opinions, but because the cost of speaking up feels too high. The issue is not competence; it is an unspoken social calculus, made in real time, about what is socially and professionally permissible.

Leaders must understand the limits of management practices that foster and encourage psychological safety. It cannot be expected or requested any more than it can be imposed within a group. It is something nonlinear in its nature and what works for one team might not be sufficient for another team. However, it can be enabled and made more likely through reliable, repeatable processes that support alignment and group function.

One of the greatest but least visible threats to team effectiveness is *cognitive misalignment*—subtle, unspoken differences in how individuals interpret expectations, priorities, and boundaries. People assume they are working from the same shared understanding, but these assumptions often diverge in ways that remain invisible until conflict arises.

One person believes candour is valued; another believes hierarchy dictates truth. One assumes mistakes will be treated as learning opportunities; another fears failure will be remembered long after it is corrected. These misalignments, if left unaddressed, create fault lines in trust and cohesion.

Structured safety ensures that misalignment is surfaced and corrected before it hardens into disengagement. Knowing 'the rules of the game' creates predictability, making it clear to team members what is expected, what is encouraged, and what will be met with resistance. This structured approach ensures that psychological safety is not left to personal confidence but is embedded into the way the group thinks and functions.

One of the most effective ways to do this is through *structured group reflection*. *After-Action Reviews* (AARs) depersonalise failure, turning mistakes into shared learning opportunities. Similarly, *Crumple & Toss* allows teams to surface tensions anonymously, fostering open dialogue without individual risk.

Also, strength-based analysis techniques—such as *Gold Seam Mining*—shift attention away from risk aversion and towards reinforcing competence. When people see their contributions recognised and valued, they feel *less need for self-protection and more willingness to engage*.

Structured safety is effective because it *removes ambiguity*. In the absence of clarity, people default to defensive strategies—withholding ideas, softening language, filtering out potential risks before they are even spoken aloud. Structured interventions counteract this tendency by making expectations explicit, predictable, and repeatable.

But structured safety, for all its necessity, has a big limitation: it takes time. It is a gradual process, working through deliberate reasoning, repeated interaction, and ongoing reinforcement. It is an excellent long-term regulator of trust, but it does not account for the real-time nature of human interaction.

There are moments—high-pressure meetings, unexpected conflicts, interpersonal tensions, external shocks—where trust is not built but tested. In these moments, people do not stop to assess whether they feel psychologically safe. They react instinctively, based on immediate cues. If those cues suggest threat, no amount of structured safety will prevent the group from slipping into defensive behaviours.

This is why leaders must also learn *safety priming*—the ability to regulate trust at a neurological level, in real time.

In Chapter 12: Safety Priming Skills, we delve in to how leaders can generate psychological safety rapidly. Trust is often spoken about as something that develops gradually—through repeated positive interactions, shared experience, and reinforcement over time. While this is true, it is only half the story. Trust is something we feel instinctively and emotionally before we understand it cognitively.

See yourself walking into a room where two people have just had an argument. No one tells you what happened. No words are exchanged. And yet, you *feel* it—an unease in the air, a stiffness in posture, a subtle but unmistakable shift in the way people hold themselves. This is not intuition; it is neuroception, our unconscious assessment of whether an environment is safe or threatening. And here is the key insight:

The body tells the brain whether it is safe, not the other way around.

This is why safety priming operates *from the inside out*. While structured safety reinforces trust over time, safety priming is *rapid co-regulation*, preventing small ruptures from escalating into defensive postures and disengagement.

The best leaders do not rely solely on structured processes to maintain trust; they *regulate it in real time*, through subtle but powerful non-verbal and verbal cues that shape group behaviour before anyone consciously processes what is happening.

One of the most powerful mechanisms for instant safety is *vocal prosody*—the modulation of tone, rhythm, and cadence in speech. People process vocal tone before they process words, and a leader's voice can either escalate stress or regulate it. A slow, warm, steady voice signals reassurance. A clipped, abrupt tone signals urgency, or worse, hostility. This is why tone matters as much as content—not because people are overly sensitive, but because the Reptilian and Mammalian Brains respond to sound before the Primate Brain responds to reason.

Equally important is *non-verbal acuity*—the ability to detect and adjust the micro-signals of interaction before they become problems. A slight narrowing of the eyes, a tightening of the jaw, a sudden stiffness in posture—these are all read instinctively by others, influencing how safe they feel to engage. Leaders who can sense and recalibrate these cues prevent small signals of uncertainty from cascading into group-wide disengagement.

Another critical skill is *pacing and leading*—the ability to match the group's current emotional state before shifting it towards greater openness and trust. If a team is on edge, an overly optimistic leader will seem detached from reality, even disingenuous. But a leader who first acknowledges the tension, mirrors it briefly, and then gently moves the energy towards calmness creates a natural shift that the group follows unconsciously.

And then there is *Co-Regulating Humour*—one of the fastest, most effective ways to break cycles of tension and reinforce social safety. Laughter, used wisely, is not just an expression of amusement; it is a neurological reset, activating the social engagement system and signalling that the environment is non-threatening. A well-placed joke, a moment of shared levity—these are not just mood boosters; they are strategic interventions in group trust regulation.

These techniques work because they bypass the need for conscious reasoning. They clear the pathway for structured safety to function more effectively, ensuring that people do not just *know* they are safe but feel it, instinctively and immediately.

This is why the most effective leaders do not choose between structured and instant safety. They use structured processes to ensure long-term trust formation and instant safety techniques to maintain engagement in the moment.

The leader who understands both does not just create high-functioning teams.

They create teams that stay engaged, adaptive, and resilient—even under pressure.

The Emotional Steward

The real test of leadership is not in moments of stability, where trust is high and collaboration flows easily. It is in moments of uncertainty, disruption, and stress—when pressure mounts, mistakes happen, and tensions rise. Under these conditions, a well-structured organisation absorbs disruption without fracturing. A weakly structured one buckles, psychological safety erodes, and the group shifts from adaptive intelligence to defensive self-preservation—where silence is safer than contribution and interpersonal risk feels too costly.

Resilience is not about avoiding stress but about maintaining cohesion and clarity within it. Psychological safety, when embedded as a self-sustaining system, allows groups to recover, adapt, and grow stronger rather than retreat into fear. But this only happens when safety is engineered into the culture, not reliant on the leader's presence.

The best leaders do not control behaviour; they regulate the conditions for trust and resilience. They ensure that psychological safety is not just an idea but a self-sustaining force *within the group*. When safety is embedded into the groups unconscious presuppositions—when it is no longer dependent on the leader but reinforced by the system itself—teams do not just function.

They can become *unflappable*.

TEN
THE HIVE MIND

The things we fear most in organizations—fluctuations, disturbances, imbalances—are the primary sources of creativity.
Margaret J. Wheatley

THE HIVE MIND, in the natural world, exemplifies the breathtaking coordination and intelligence that can arise from collective effort. Picture a bustling beehive: thousands of individual insects working in perfect harmony to sustain their colony. Each bee, though seemingly insignificant on its own, contributes to a larger system of breathtaking efficiency and adaptability. This synergy is not directed by any central authority but emerges organically, driven by shared goals and instinctual cues. The result is a self-organising system capable of remarkable feats—a living example of collective intelligence in action.

This phenomenon is not limited to bees. We see echoes of the Hive Mind in other species—from ant colonies to flocks of birds that wheel and dive as if guided by a single mind. These natural systems inspire awe because they seem to defy the chaos that often defines human attempts at collaboration. But what if the principles underpinning the Hive Mind could be applied to human organisations? What if we could harness this collective intelligence to create workplaces that are more innovative, adaptable, and resilient?

The concept of the Hive Mind in human organisations is not new. It manifests whenever individuals come together to achieve a shared purpose, whether in a start-up brainstorming session, a surgical team performing a complex operation, or a disaster response unit coordinating under pressure. Yet, the Hive Mind is not without its challenges. While it has the potential to drive creativity and efficiency, it also harbours vulnerabilities. Groupthink, emotional contagion, and resistance to change are just some of the pitfalls that can derail even the most well-intentioned teams.

This essay explores the dual nature of the Hive Mind in organisational settings. On one hand, it is a powerful engine for innovation, capable of synthesising diverse perspectives into groundbreaking solutions. On the other hand, it can spiral into dysfunction when safety and trust are compromised. The key to unlocking the Hive Mind's potential lies in understanding its mechanics and guiding it with thoughtful leadership strategies.

Throughout this exploration, we will draw parallels between natural systems and organisational dynamics, delve into the evolutionary roots of collective behaviour, and examine the role of psychological safety as a foundation for collaboration. We will also introduce narrative framing as a critical leadership tool for steering the Hive Mind, showcasing how effective storytelling can align teams, diffuse tensions, and inspire action.

Consider the story of a major technology company navigating the chaos of rapid growth. Its small, tight-knit team expanded into a sprawling workforce within months, bringing together individuals from vastly different backgrounds and expertise. At first, the Hive

Mind flourished, generating bold ideas and driving exponential growth. But as the organisation scaled, cracks began to appear. Misaligned goals, eroding trust, and poorly managed emotional dynamics led to a breakdown in collaboration. It wasn't until leadership prioritised psychological safety and implemented deliberate strategies to rebuild trust that the team regained its collective strength.

This narrative underscores a crucial point: the Hive Mind is not a static state but a dynamic process. It thrives in environments where individuals feel safe to contribute, challenge, and innovate. It falters when fear, mistrust, or rigidity take hold. The role of the leader, therefore, is not merely to direct but to curate the conditions in which the Hive Mind can flourish.

As we embark on this journey, we will consider the Hive Mind through multiple lenses: biological, psychological, and organisational. We will explore how evolutionary instincts like tribalism and neuroception influence group behaviour, and how these instincts can be harnessed rather than hindered. We will examine real-world examples of both triumphs and failures to understand what distinguishes effective collective intelligence from chaotic group dynamics.

Ultimately, this essay is a call to action for leaders. In an era defined by complexity and uncertainty, the ability to cultivate and guide collective intelligence is no longer optional; it is essential. Whether you are managing a team of five or leading a multinational corporation, the principles of the Hive Mind offer valuable insights for building organisations that are not only effective but also resilient and humane.

By the end of this chapter, you will understand the mechanics of collective intelligence, setting you up to employ the frameworks, models, tools, techniques and practical strategies described in the rest of this book. In doing so, we shall unlock the full potential of our *human hives* and shape a future where collaboration becomes our greatest strength.

Human Hives

The term *Hive Mind* often evokes images of insects working in perfect synchrony, but its applicability to human organisations is more nuanced. In its essence, the Hive Mind represents a form of collective intelligence—a system where the whole becomes greater than the sum of its parts. This phenomenon arises when individuals pool their knowledge, skills, and perspectives, creating an emergent property of group problem-solving and decision-making.

To understand the Hive Mind, we must first dissect its components:

1. *Shared Purpose:* In natural hives, survival drives the collective effort. For human organisations, this purpose could range from achieving a business objective to solving global challenges. A shared purpose aligns individual actions, creating a unifying force.
2. *Interdependence:* In a hive, every member contributes uniquely to the whole. Worker bees gather nectar, drones ensure reproduction, and the queen governs the hive's continuity. Similarly, human teams thrive on role clarity and mutual reliance.
3. *Dynamic Communication:* Communication is the lifeblood of any Hive Mind. Bees use pheromones and the "waggle dance" to convey critical information. Humans rely on language, non-verbal cues, and increasingly, digital tools. Effective communication channels are essential for coordinating efforts and avoiding missteps.
4. *Adaptive Behaviour:* The Hive Mind excels in adaptability. When resources dwindle, bees pivot their activities to ensure survival. Human organisations, too, must navigate

change by leveraging collective intelligence to adapt strategies and innovate solutions.

Human organisations mirror the Hive Mind in surprising ways. Consider the technology sector, where agile methodologies emphasise cross-functional teams working collaboratively toward iterative goals. Each "sprint" resembles the dynamic responsiveness of a hive, with members contributing their expertise to achieve incremental progress.

Another example lies in emergency response teams, where shared purpose and clear communication are paramount. These teams operate under immense pressure, often making life-or-death decisions. Their success hinges on the ability to synchronise individual expertise into cohesive action—a hallmark of the Hive Mind.

While the Hive Mind offers immense potential, it is not without its challenges. Its strength lies in its collective nature, but this very characteristic can lead to pitfalls:

- *Groupthink:* When dissent is discouraged, the Hive Mind can devolve into an echo chamber. Divergent perspectives are suppressed, leading to poor decision-making.
- *Emotional Contagion:* Emotions can ripple through a group, amplifying anxiety, anger, or fear. This can disrupt rational decision-making and create a volatile atmosphere.
- *Resistance to Change:* The Hive Mind can become rigid, adhering to established norms even when they are no longer effective. This inertia can stifle innovation and adaptability.

These vulnerabilities underscore the importance of skilled leadership. Leaders must create environments where the Hive Mind thrives without succumbing to its darker tendencies. This involves fostering psychological safety, encouraging constructive dissent, and guiding the group toward adaptability.

. . .

Technology in the Hive

In today's digital age, technology acts as both an enabler and a disruptor of the Hive Mind. Collaboration tools like Slack, Microsoft Teams, and Zoom facilitate seamless communication, mirroring the intricate signalling systems of natural hives. However, the over-reliance on digital platforms can also lead to "digital groupthink," where algorithms and echo chambers reinforce biases.

Artificial intelligence further complicates this terrain. AI systems can amplify collective intelligence by processing vast amounts of data and offering insights. Yet, they also introduce risks, such as the potential for automation to dehumanise decision-making or perpetuate systemic biases.

Case Story: NASA's Apollo Program

The Apollo program exemplifies the human Hive Mind at its best. Faced with the monumental task of landing a man on the moon, NASA brought together thousands of scientists, engineers, and administrators. Each played a specific role, contributing their expertise to a larger mission.

Key to the program's success was the alignment of purpose: every individual understood that their work was part of a shared endeavour. Communication channels were robust, with meticulous documentation and real-time collaboration. Most importantly, the leadership fostered an environment where innovation thrived, encouraging team members to challenge assumptions and propose bold solutions.

The result was a historic achievement that showcased the power of collective intelligence. Yet, the Apollo program also highlighted the fragility of the Hive Mind. Internal rivalries, bureaucratic inertia, and the high-pressure environment created moments of tension that required deliberate intervention to resolve.

To SUMMARISE, the Hive Mind in organisations can be defined as:

A self-organising system of collective intelligence, driven by shared purpose, interdependence, dynamic communication, and adaptive behaviour, which enables groups to achieve outcomes beyond individual capabilities.

To be effective, leaders must balance the strengths and vulnerabilities of the Hive Mind, ensuring that its emergent properties align with organisational goals.

The next section will delve into the evolutionary roots of collective behaviour, exploring how instincts like tribalism and neuroception shape the dynamics of the human Hive Mind. These insights will provide a deeper understanding of why we behave as we do in groups —and how leaders can harness these instincts to build stronger, more cohesive teams.

3. Evolutionary Roots of Group Behaviour

Understanding the Hive Mind in human organisations requires a closer look at its evolutionary origins. Throughout history, humans have relied on collective intelligence for survival. From hunting in coordinated groups to building intricate societies, the ability to pool resources, knowledge, and effort has been a defining feature of our species. At its core, the Hive Mind is not a recent innovation but an ancient survival mechanism.

Tribalism

Tribalism is one of the most deeply ingrained aspects of human social behaviour. In our evolutionary past, belonging to a tribe increased the chances of survival. Tribes provided safety from predators, a reliable food supply, and support during illness or injury. The need for belonging is so central to human psychology that exclusion or rejection often triggers a primal fear response.

In modern organisations, tribalism manifests in team dynamics, company cultures, and even interdepartmental rivalries. While tribalism can foster loyalty and cohesion, it also has a darker side. The same instincts that bind groups together can create "us versus them" mentalities, leading to silos, resistance to collaboration, and even outright conflict.

Key Characteristics

1. *In-Group Loyalty*: Employees often prioritise the interests of their immediate team or department over the broader organisation. While this loyalty can enhance group cohesion, it may also hinder cross-functional collaboration.
2. *Out-Group Suspicion*: Teams may perceive other groups as competitors or threats. This suspicion can lead to miscommunication, mistrust, and a reluctance to share resources or information.
3. *Cultural Echo Chambers*: Organisational cultures can become echo chambers where dissenting ideas are stifled. While this reinforces the tribe's identity, it limits innovation and adaptability.

The Science of Safety

The concept of *neuroception*, introduced in Chapter 3, sheds light on how humans assess safety and threats within groups. You will recall that neuroception is the brain's subconscious surveillance system which evaluates whether an environment or interaction is safe, dangerous, or life-threatening. This evaluation happens before we are even consciously aware of it.

In organisational contexts, neuroception plays a crucial role in shaping group dynamics. Employees constantly assess their psychological safety—whether they feel valued, respected, and free to express themselves without fear of retribution. When psychological safety is high, the Hive Mind thrives, as individuals feel empowered to contribute ideas and take risks. Conversely, when safety is compromised, employees may retreat into defensive behaviours such as silence, compliance, or resistance.

Threat Detection in Organisations

- *Fight*: Open conflict, confrontational behaviour, or aggressive responses to criticism.
- *Flight*: Avoidance of responsibilities, withdrawal from discussions, or reluctance to engage in decision-making.
- *Shutdown*: Buckling in the face of challenges, inability to take action, or excessive reliance on authority figures for guidance.

Leaders play a pivotal role in shaping the neuroceptive landscape of their teams. By fostering an environment of trust, empathy, and transparency, they can mitigate threat responses and create the conditions for collective intelligence to flourish.

Emotional Contagion

Emotional contagion—the tendency for emotions to spread rapidly within groups—is another evolutionary adaptation with profound implications for the Hive Mind. In early human societies, shared emotions helped coordinate group responses to threats. For example, a sense of fear could mobilise a group to flee from danger, while collective joy reinforced social bonds.

In organisations, emotional contagion remains a powerful but often overlooked force. Positive emotions such as enthusiasm and optimism can energise teams, driving creativity and collaboration. However, negative emotions like anxiety, anger, or frustration can quickly derail group dynamics, spreading like wildfire and undermining trust.

Managing Emotional Contagion

1. *Model Emotional Regulation:* Leaders set the tone for their teams. By managing their own emotions, they can influence the emotional climate of the group.
2. *Acknowledge and Address Negative Emotions:* Suppressing negative emotions often intensifies them. Instead, leaders should acknowledge challenges openly and provide constructive outlets for addressing concerns.
3. *Foster Positive Rituals:* Regularly celebrating successes, expressing gratitude, and recognising contributions can amplify positive emotions and strengthen the Hive Mind.

Another evolutionary trait that shapes the Hive Mind is *group polarisation*—the tendency for group discussions to lead to more extreme positions than individual members initially held. While this can drive bold decision-making and innovation, it also increases the risk of groupthink and entrenched biases. Contributing factors include:

1. *Reinforcement of Shared Beliefs:* Group members often validate each other's perspectives, amplifying consensus while sidelining dissenting views.
2. *Desire for Social Approval:* Individuals may conform to the group's dominant opinion to avoid conflict or gain acceptance.
3. *Echo Chambers:* Homogeneous groups are more prone to polarisation, as they lack diverse perspectives to challenge assumptions.

Three simple ways to avoid the adverse unintended consequences of group polarisation are:

- *Encourage Diverse Perspectives:* Actively seek out and value differing opinions to counterbalance the tendency toward consensus.
- *Appoint a "Devil's Advocate":* Designate a team member to challenge prevailing ideas, fostering critical thinking.
- *Promote Reflective Dialogue:* Encourage group members to revisit and critically evaluate their decisions before finalising them.

THE HIVE MIND is a powerful but delicate phenomenon. Its success hinges on the interplay between instinctive behaviours and deliberate leadership. While the evolutionary instincts that drive collective behaviour have served humanity well for millennia, their misapplication in modern organisational settings can lead to fragmentation, mistrust, and stagnation. Leaders who fail to recognise these dynamics risk creating silos or reinforcing biases that limit the potential of their teams.

Conversely, leaders who embrace the principles of the Hive Mind—who foster trust, champion adaptability, and prioritise psychological safety—can unlock extraordinary outcomes. These leaders transform instinct into innovation and tribalism into shared identity. They create cultures where individuals are not only aligned in purpose but also feel empowered to challenge, collaborate, and grow.

In environments defined by complexity, uncertainty, ambiguity, and rapid change, the lessons of the Hive Mind are more relevant than ever. Whether guiding a start-up, navigating corporate restructuring, or leading a multinational team, understanding and harnessing collective intelligence is essential. By aligning the mechanics of the Hive Mind with organisational goals, we can build teams that are not only more effective but also more humane. Let us strive to lead with insight, empathy, and resilience, shaping workplaces where collaboration becomes our greatest strength.

The Hive Mind's power lies in its ability to self-organise, adapt, and amplify intelligence. However, this same emergent nature also makes it fragile—left unchecked, it can spiral into groupthink, emotional contagion, or stagnation. The key to harnessing its full potential is not to control it, but to regulate the conditions in which it operates.

This is where formal safety structures and safety priming become essential—working together to stabilise the Hive Mind, ensuring that its collective intelligence remains an asset rather than a liability. Safety embedded structures provide the stability needed for collaboration to be sustained over time, while safety priming ensures that trust and openness are reinforced in every interaction. These elements act as the guardrails that keep the Hive Mind aligned with organisational goals, ensuring that its immense potential is fully realised.

With this in mind, the next chapters explore how leaders can create the conditions necessary for the Hive Mind to thrive—through both structured safety mechanisms and real-time safety priming techniques.

Chapter 11 examines how formal safety structures provide stability but must be actively reinforced through consistent leadership behaviours to sustain and repair psychological safety.

Chapter 12 expands this understanding by exploring how leaders can cultivate emotional and psychological safety through observational acuity, conversational nuance, and behavioural practices—embedding safety into the fabric of daily interactions.

Together, these chapters equip leaders with actionable strategies to not only harness the power of the Hive Mind but also ensure it flourishes under the pressures of modern organisational complexity.

ELEVEN
SAFETY-EMBEDDED STRUCTURES

The cycle of reciprocity, rupture, and repair
is the nature of healthy relationships
Deb Dana

PSYCHOLOGICAL SAFETY IS NOT *JUST* a trendy concept—it's the bedrock of high-performing, resilient teams. It is the felt sense of safety in expressing oneself without fear of adverse consequences. This directly impacts team dynamics, innovation, and performance in measurable ways.

Humans are inherently social, wired for group welfare. Psychological safety taps into this instinct, providing teams with the stability they need to excel. In this chapter, we'll explore what it is, how to cultivate it, and how to sustain it over time. Drawing on earlier discussions of primal instincts (Chapter 1) and emotional regulation (Chapter 4), we'll outline a framework for leaders to create environments where people feel secure, supported, and free to contribute.

Psychological safety cannot be mandated—it must emerge from the right conditions. Formal structures help by reducing ambiguity, aligning expectations, and ensuring that failure, risk-taking, and dissent aren't punished. But structure alone isn't enough. A leader may implement check-ins and reviews, yet if vulnerability is met with punishment, safety dissolves.

This is the paradox of formalised safety: it can create conditions for trust but cannot guarantee it. Psychological safety is not a compliance exercise—it is built through real interactions. Ultimately, leadership behaviour determines whether a safety structure fosters trust or merely exists on paper.

Personal Psychological Safety

There's a certain *lightness* in those who feel psychologically safe—a quiet confidence that allows them to *show up fully*, unguarded, without rehearsing every word before they speak. It's the freedom to admit a mistake without fearing a career-limiting consequence, to ask a question without bracing for a condescending response. It's the *absence of that internal, grinding hesitation*—the one that makes people second-guess whether to contribute, whether to disagree, whether to take the risk of being *seen*.

The best way to spot psychological safety in action? It's not just about the ease of speaking up—it's about the *willingness to listen*. Those who feel safe don't need to dominate conversations or protect their ideas at all costs. They stay open, *curious*, even when faced with contradiction. They don't collapse into defensiveness, because they trust that disagreement isn't an attack—it's an opportunity.

And that's where safety breeds innovation. When people feel secure enough to experiment, to take small intellectual risks, they begin *testing the edges* of what's possible. Mistakes become teachers rather than threats. Creativity flourishes, not because risk disappears, but because the *fear of retribution does*.

Group Psychological Safety

A truly safe group isn't just one where people *avoid conflict*—it's one where they *engage fully*, knowing that their voices matter. It's not just the absence of hostility but the *presence of something deeper*—a collective willingness to think together, challenge ideas without undermining trust, and *lean into discomfort* rather than retreat from it.

In a group with high psychological safety, ideas don't just bounce around—they *ignite*. Conversations flow with an energy that isn't about competing for dominance but about *co-creating something better*. Even disagreements take on a different tone—there's curiosity rather than contention, a search for understanding rather than a battle for position. The quietest person in the room feels just as entitled to speak as the most senior leader.

But the *real test* of psychological safety? How the group treats *mistakes*. In a fragile culture, errors trigger blame, shame, or silence. But in a *resilient* group, mistakes become stepping stones—an invitation to learn, to adapt, to improve. Risk-taking is no longer an individual burden but a *shared endeavour*—people dare to put forward bold, unpolished ideas because they trust the group to engage thoughtfully rather than dismissively.

At its core, group psychological safety is about *more than speaking up—it's about being heard*. And when that happens, collaboration shifts from being a process to being *a force*—one that makes teams not just *functional*, but *formidable*.

Building Blocks

Psychological safety isn't something you can *mandate*—it's something that *emerges*. You can install all the right structures—open-door policies, anonymous feedback systems, regular check-ins—but if the underlying culture contradicts them, they become *empty gestures*. A team won't speak freely just because there's a process for it; they'll speak freely because they *trust* that doing so is genuinely welcomed, not subtly punished.

Trust isn't built through policies—it's built through *patterns of behaviour*. A leader who *asks for input* but reacts defensively when challenged creates a contradiction that no framework can fix. If people sense that honesty comes with risk, they'll *default to silence*, regardless of how many times they're told to "bring their whole selves to work."

At the heart of this is neuroception—our unconscious ability to detect safety or threat. People don't just *listen* to what a leader says; they *read* their posture, their tone, their micro-expressions. Psychological safety depends on both Inner Game (autoregulation) and Outer Game (co-regulation). A leader who masters their *Inner Game* can project genuine confidence and calm, creating stability for the team.

Take Jill. She *wants* open dialogue and tells her team to "speak freely." But her body language—pursed lips, tightened shoulders, subtle frowns—signals discomfort. Her team reads her hesitancy before they hear her words, and instead of an open exchange, the room fills with *cautious calculation*.

Leaders like Jill don't need another policy—they need *awareness*. Without realising it, they're sending out *autonomic warnings*—subtle nervous system cues that say, *danger*. If a leader doesn't know how to manage their own stress, they *radiate instability*, and no one feels safe taking risks in that environment.

This is why *neuro-resilience* matters. Leaders who practice self-regulation techniques—like *Finding Home* (from Chapter 4)—don't just benefit themselves; they create a ripple effect of *safety and composure* that stabilises their teams. When a leader holds *their own ground*, they make it safe for others to do the same. And that's when psychological safety becomes *not just a concept, but a reality.*

. . .

How Safety is Lost

"The art of leadership is the ability to bring out the best in others while being willing to grow yourself"
Richard Bandler

Psychological safety is *fragile*—it takes time to build, but it can be shattered in an instant. Leaders don't always erode safety through dramatic failures; more often, it's lost through a series of small, subtle betrayals—inconsistencies, unspoken rules, and contradictions between *what's said* and *what's done.*

Take Davey, a boss I once had. He *believed* in brainstorming, but only if the ideas aligned with *his* thinking. He *invited engagement* but shut it down when it didn't suit him. One moment he'd *micromanage*, the next he'd be *completely absent*. Nobody knew which version of Davey they were getting on any given day, and that killed trust. The official structures said, *We value your input*, but reality said, *Watch your back.*

Psychological safety isn't just about having the right policies—it's about living them. When a leader's behaviour contradicts their words, even well-intended initiatives collapse. And once safety is lost, the cost isn't just silence—it's disengagement, passive resistance, and, ultimately, a weakened organisation. Here are the most common ways safety gets eroded:

1. Behavioural Inconsistency

Consistency between a leader's words and actions is crucial for trust. Davey often urged his managers to "pour a bit of treacle down their throats" — his way of saying, be nice to shopfloor workers, keep them motivated, and butter them up for when overtime was needed.

Yet, almost every Friday, he'd check productivity, find something amiss, and order the manager responsible to:

'Kick them to death!'

Unlike the Red Queen's, 'Off with their head!', demands in *Alice in Wonderland*, 'Kick them to death' was Davey-speak for reprimanding someone. One Friday, I questioned the wisdom of the instruction, given that we were going to need the same people to work over time.

Davey's timeless wisdom was, "OK. Once they've been kicked to death, pour some treacle back their throat and get each of the lazy bastards to work four hours overtime".

When overtime turnout was refused by the workforce, he fumed about 'ingrates' and warned, '...there will come a time!..

2. Public Criticism

Public criticism, however subtle, erodes psychological safety. When leaders correct team members in a group setting, it triggers fight, flight, or freeze responses, discouraging risk-taking and collaboration. As discussed in Chapter 5, punishing vulnerability teaches people to hide mistakes rather than learn from them. Even minor public criticism signals that mistakes are unacceptable, stifling growth and creativity.

For example, Davey gathered his senior team for a brainstorming session. Marker in hand, he announced, *"Right—I need some killer ideas to improve shopfloor productivity!"*

My colleague, Sean, offered: *"How about introducing industrially engineered standards attached to an incentive structure?"*

Davey replied, *"We tried something like that fifteen years ago! It was a pain in the arse to administer. Absolutely, fucking hopeless. I'm never going back there"*.

Sean said, *"Maybe we could do it better this time"*.

Davey rebuked, *"Is there something about 'I'm not going back there' you didn't understand, Sean?"*

After that, there were no other ideas put forward. Davey spent ten minutes rebuking us for a lack of imagination, expressing his disappointment, and saying that he knew it was going to be a waste of time.

3. **Inconsistent Follow-Through**

Leaders who request feedback but fail to act on it signal that input doesn't truly matter, fostering disengagement. To maintain psychological safety, they must follow through—either by taking action or explaining why they can't. Acknowledging input reinforces respect and inclusion.

In true Davey fashion, he impulsively promised a worker, Malky, that the factory would sponsor his son's football team. The donation was small, yet the cost of adding company-logo patches to the jerseys nearly matched it—a fact Davey grumbled about. Weeks passed, and Malky politely reminded him. Davey's enthusiasm had faded, but he stuck to his word. A month later, Malky, now visibly uncomfortable, informed him the patches and donation were overdue and urgently needed.

When the deadline passed, Malky, now desperate, followed up. Davey, in a frosty tone, snapped: *'Look, I didn't think it'd cost this much. Either you or your wife sew the patches, you pay for it, or I deduct it from the donation.'*

Along with a cheque and a bag of patches, Malky left with a bitter, angry expression.

4. **Favouritism**

FAIR TREATMENT UNDERPINS PSYCHOLOGICAL SAFETY. When leaders show favouritism, others may feel undervalued, discouraging risk-taking and open dialogue. A truly inclusive team culture requires consistent recognition of all contributions.

Davey's favourite was Sally—"Sal" for short—his finance manager and numerical lifesaver. She was his secret superpower, his crutch. In his eyes, she could do no wrong.

The numerically inclined shrugged off Sal's special treatment, seeing it as her reward for tolerating Davey. The rest resented her. What began as playful banter morphed into seething frustration.

Davey's jibes, from innuendos about *'spreadsheets and bedsheets'* to quips like:

- *"Are you working that sum out with a crayon or just colouring it in?"*
- *"Learn to count like Sal and you'll get out early on Fridays too."*

Whilst Davey's mockery might have begun as jovial banter. But what is banter when psychological safety is in place creates seething resentment, as well as other patterns of protection, when it is lost.

Leaders rarely set out to erode psychological safety, yet the pressures of high-stakes environments can drive subtle but corrosive behaviours. These missteps, though often unintentional, accumulate quickly, fraying trust, stifling open dialogue, and dulling a team's collective intelligence. Awareness is the first defence. A leader who understands the fragile architecture of safety is better equipped to protect it.

The sections ahead offer practical strategies to reinforce a culture of trust and resilience. Encouraging productive failure through After-Action Reviews helps normalise learning from mistakes. A strengths-based approach like *Gold Seam Mining* shifts focus towards what is working, fostering motivation and engagement. For teams where safety has been fractured, *Crumple & Toss* offers a structured way to restore open dialogue.

Psychological safety is neither an abstract ideal nor a passive state—it is an ongoing practice. Leaders who commit to sustaining it unlock higher levels of creativity, adaptability, and collaboration. The effort is continuous, but the payoff—a culture where individuals feel secure, valued, and empowered—is well worth it.

Strategies for Safety

Having formal safety structures in place is a necessary starting point, but it is not enough. For these systems to be truly effective, they must be reinforced through leadership behaviour that is predictable, consistent, and emotionally attuned to the team's needs.

The following strategies are designed to bridge the gap between formal safety structures and the real-time leadership actions that make them meaningful. By embedding these approaches into everyday leadership practice, psychological safety becomes not just a structural expectation but a lived experience within the team.

Having recognised the importance of psychological safety and the common pitfalls that can undermine it, we now turn to practical strategies leaders can employ to build and sustain this essential aspect of team culture. The following approaches offer structured, actionable methods to foster a psychologically safe environment where individuals feel empowered to take risks, contribute ideas, and work collaboratively without fear.

. . .

Productive Failure

In a neuro-resilient environment, failure is a teacher, not a threat. The way leaders respond to setbacks determines whether teams grow from them or retreat into self-protection.

One of the most effective ways to normalise learning from mistakes is the After-Action Review (AAR)—a framework developed by the US Army to enhance performance under uncertainty.

AARs don't analyse failure as an autopsy—they turn mistakes into stepping stones for mastery. The process revolves around three simple but powerful questions:

1. **What really happened?**

The first question helps teams build a shared understanding by integrating diverse perspectives, creating a fuller picture of events. Research by Varela and Maturana suggests up to 90% of perception is shaped by personal experiences, assumptions, and beliefs, making this alignment crucial.

2. **What insights did we gain?**

This is where real learning begins. The second question prompts reflection on what worked, what didn't, and why. Leaders should frame it as exploration, not blame, fostering curiosity, critical thinking, and openness to new insights.

3. **How can we improve next time?**

The third question shifts from reflection to action, enabling the team to turn insights into practical strategies for improvement.

The AAR is adaptable, ranging from quick 15-minute debriefs to in-depth reflections on complex projects. It supports two learning types:

behaviour-based (observing outcomes) and premise-based (examining underlying assumptions).

For example, after a high-pressure project, a team using AAR first establishes a shared narrative, integrating diverse perspectives. They then review successes and challenges without blame, extracting key insights for improvement. Finally, they define actionable steps, enhancing future performance.

By normalising failure as a growth opportunity, AAR fosters psychological safety, enabling resilience, adaptability, and innovation. In a neuro-resilient culture, failure becomes a bridge to progress, not a threat to avoid.

Bypass Self-Censoring

Psychological safety isn't just about permission to speak up—it's about making it easier to do so. In many teams, people censor themselves out of fear of judgment, rejection, or retribution. Even when leaders actively seek input, social dynamics can keep people silent—especially in larger groups where status, power, or past experiences make open discussion risky.

The Crumple & Toss technique is designed to bypass self-censoring by creating a low-risk, high-trust way for teams to surface honest concerns and insights anonymously:

1. Preparation
2. *The leader begins by distributing half-sheets of paper to each participant, asking them to respond to two key prompts:*
   - *"What concerns or issues are preventing you and the group from progressing?"*
   - *"What needs to happen for the group to start moving forward?"*

These questions prompt participants to consider both challenges and solutions, steering discussions toward constructive insights rather than complaints.

3. Crumple & Toss

Once participants have written their responses, they are instructed to crumple the paper into a ball. This symbolic act of crumpling the paper serves multiple purposes: it injects a playful, relaxed element into the process, it signals that there is no need to hold onto these thoughts personally, and it reinforces the anonymity of each contribution.

Participants toss their crumpled papers into the centre or a bucket. After a few exchanges, each picks up a random paper ball, ensuring anonymity and fostering honest contributions.

4. Reading Aloud

Each participant then reads the responses aloud to the group, following a strict rule of no commenting or analysing during the reading. This encourages the team to focus on the content of each response without personalising or critiquing the ideas.

The moment of listening creates a shared experience, allowing team members to hear one another's concerns without the usual filters of ego or fear of judgment.

5. Pattern Recognition

Once all responses have been read, the facilitator gathers the crumpled papers and lays them out for everyone to see. The team is then invited to look for recurring themes or patterns. What concerns are most frequently mentioned? Which issues appear most pressing?

This collective reflection builds a clearer picture of the team's underlying needs, giving everyone a chance to contribute without the pressure of direct ownership.

6. Solution-Focused Discussion

Finally, with the main issues identified, the team is ready to discuss potential solutions. The leaders guide the group through a collaborative discussion, focusing on concrete actions that address the surfaced concerns.

This stage transitions the team from hesitance to action, empowering members to take ownership of the solutions they develop together.

Crumple & Toss fosters psychological safety by enabling anonymous concerns, encouraging honesty, and ensuring issues are acknowledged. This strengthens team trust, belonging, and security.

SURFACING Stories

Stories aren't just words exchanged in meetings; they are the pulse of an organisation. A Hive Mind doesn't store knowledge in static reports—it breathes it in conversations, gestures, and quiet admissions over coffee. Yet, too often, leaders reduce this living intelligence to sterile data points, stripping away the humanity that gives them meaning. A 30% disengagement rate tells you nothing about the quiet engineer whose innovations go unnoticed or the frontline worker whose frustration is masked by polite compliance.

I was once captivated by Dave Snowden's *Anecdote Circles*, a deceptively simple practice that uncovers the raw, unfiltered narratives shaping workplace culture. Organisations don't fail because they lack information—they fail because they overlook the signals hidden in plain sight. The problem isn't missing data, it's missed intelligence.

But translating theory into practice was another story. Managers hesitated, uneasy about surfacing uncomfortable truths. Some found themselves lost in the sprawl of unscripted conversations, struggling to keep discussions on track. Others encountered silent resistance, where teams, wary of power dynamics, withheld the very stories that could spark change.

This is where *PACE Strengths* and *PACE Surfacing* stepped in—not as rigid methods but as subtle, invisible currents guiding the process. Anecdote Circles had the right goal, but the NLP approach embedded in PACE really made them work. Without forcing narratives or imposing rigid template of a structure, PACE creates the conditions for stories to emerge naturally—revealing patterns that no survey or review could ever expose.

Why Uncover Tacit Knowledge?

Traditional feedback methods—surveys, performance reviews, post-mortems—promise clarity but often deliver distortion. They take the messy, layered reality of human experience and flatten it into neat, digestible metrics. A 30% disengagement score looks precise, but it tells you nothing about the exhausted project lead who stays silent in meetings, or the ingenious workarounds devised by an overlooked team. Numbers capture outcomes, but they erase context.

The real problem? Feedback is rarely honest. Employees filter their words, dressing up their struggles in neutral, professional language. The higher the stakes, the more politeness replaces truth. And when organisations rely on these sanitised responses, they make decisions based on what people say in safe spaces, not on what's actually happening on the ground.

Most leadership models are reactive, detecting problems only when they've already spread—like diagnosing an illness after it's turned critical. By then, trust is frayed, resistance is entrenched, and valuable time is lost. What's needed isn't more measurement, but early detection—the ability to catch weak signals before they become full-blown failures.

This is where the power of surfaced stories comes in. Unlike imposed analysis, which dissects knowledge like a specimen under glass, stories self-organise. Insights don't need to be extracted—they emerge when the right conditions are set.

PACE Surfacing ensures this happens naturally. The framework is subtle, guiding conversations without stifling them. Participants don't feel like they're being audited or assessed; they feel like they're finally being heard. The result? A steady flow of authentic intelligence—unvarnished, actionable, and infinitely more valuable than any retrospective report.

PACE Strengths[1]

The best conversations aren't forced—they flow. And the most engaged teams don't need to be fixed; they need to be recognised. When I first experimented with an NLP-infused version of Anecdote Circles, I wasn't looking to solve problems. I was looking to surface what was already working.

It was a volatile time—constant pressure, shifting expectations, and managers exhausted by firefighting. The idea of open storytelling felt risky. What if people focused on grievances? What if tensions rose instead of trust? But that's exactly why I reframed the discussion. Instead of asking teams to expose weaknesses, I invited them to explore their strengths.

It was a simple but powerful shift. People rarely feel defensive about what already works. Unlike traditional retrospectives—where even constructive feedback can feel like a post-mortem—these sessions framed past challenges as stories of resilience, ingenuity, and growth.

And it worked.

The impact was immediate:

- Momentum replaced resistance. People leaned in, eager to share insights.
- Defences dropped. Teams felt safe enough to speak freely.
- Morale spiked. Recognising success wasn't just rewarding—it was energising.

The leaders facilitating these conversations didn't have to manage spiralling debates or awkward silences. PACE acted as an invisible guide, structuring the flow without rigid steps. The discussions felt organic, but they were anything but random. Every phase had purpose:

- *Safety Priming*: Sessions opened with recognition and permission-seeking, ensuring psychological safety from the outset.
- *Setting the Frame*: Subtle cues steered teams away from defensiveness. A well-placed phrase—'Success rarely happens without setbacks' or 'Rome wasn't built in a day'—allowed space for past struggles without turning them into failures.
- *Letting Stories Unfold*: Teams revisited their journeys, reliving key moments. Strengths that had gone unnoticed—ingenuity under pressure, seamless collaboration—surfaced naturally.
- *Embedding the Insights*: By the end, what had started as casual reflection crystallised into something greater—shared ownership of success. The conversation wasn't just an exercise; it became an ongoing mindset.

Unlike standard problem-solving tools, PACE Strengths isn't about repairing—it's about amplifying. Small wins compound into unstoppable momentum. Done right, it doesn't feel like a technique. It feels like an effortless conversation.

It's the difference between tossing a pebble into a pond and watching the ripples spread—or digging deep into the earth to mine gold. The first creates waves of engagement within a team; the second extracts and scales excellence across an entire organisation. That's where *Gold Seam Mining* comes in.

Gold Seam Mining

Great teams don't always realise how good they are. Strengths—real strengths—aren't always obvious from the inside. They feel natural, routine, almost unremarkable. A frontline team develops an instinctive rhythm, solving problems without second-guessing. A department adapts to pressure without needing a blueprint. Excellence, when truly embedded, looks effortless. The tragedy? Most organisations never notice it.

PACE Strengths worked because it kept improvement local, fast, and organic. The insights stayed where they belonged—with the teams who uncovered them. But what happens when you need to scale these strengths beyond a single unit? How do you transform local brilliance into an organisational advantage? That's where Gold Seam Mining begins.

Just as miners don't create gold but unearth it, leaders don't impose psychological safety—they reveal and amplify it. The process isn't about fixing problems; it's about finding the gold that's already there and refining it into something lasting.

Scattered to Consolidated Strength

In most companies, high performance is accidental. It happens in pockets—one high-functioning team, an innovative department—but it doesn't spread. Gold Seam Mining changes that. It extracts, refines, and circulates excellence across the organisation.

It's a structured process, but it doesn't feel like one. Done well, it mirrors the natural flow of discovery, ensuring that strengths aren't just recognised—they become repeatable, teachable, and scalable.

Phase 1: *Prospecting*—Natural Discovery of Strengths

Most organisations default to scanning for problems, assuming growth comes from fixing what's broken. But real, lasting improvement comes from a different kind of leadership—a shift in attention.

Instead of asking, *"Where are we struggling?"*, high-performing teams instinctively ask, *"What do we already do well, even under pressure?"* The change is subtle but transformative. When people focus on strengths instead of flaws, their thinking expands. Defensiveness fades, curiosity takes over, and suddenly, excellence that was once instinctive but invisible starts revealing itself.

In one session, I watched a team go through this shift in real-time. At first, their responses were cautious—half-joking remarks, a few polite nods. But as the conversation deepened, stories emerged. Someone recalled a moment when everything could have fallen apart but didn't—because of a quick decision made under pressure. Another remembered a time when an unexpected challenge forced them to improvise on the fly, turning a setback into an innovation.

None of these moments had been recorded. No metric had captured them. But here they were—surfacing in conversation, revealing a team's hidden formula for success.

That's how excellence is uncovered—not through structured assessment, but by creating the conditions where people can see, often for the first time, what they've been doing right all along.

Phase 2: *Excavation*—The Moment Strength Becomes Visible

At first, recognising strengths feels like an observation—*"Oh, that went well."* But the real shift happens when teams begin to break down why something worked.

In one case, a department known for handling high-pressure deadlines with ease had never actually discussed how they did it. When asked what made them so effective, their first instinct was to shrug —*"That's just how we work."*

But as the conversation unfolded, patterns emerged. They weren't just good under pressure—they had an unspoken set of behaviours that made last-minute pivots feel effortless. They automatically anticipated roadblocks. They trusted each other's judgment without micromanagement. They had an instinct for simplifying chaos.

For years, this was just "how things worked." But in that moment, the team saw it for what it was: a repeatable advantage that could be scaled and taught to others.

What had once been intuitive and unspoken was now something they could describe, replicate, and strengthen. That's the moment when a strength stops being an accident and starts becoming an asset.

Phase 3: *Refining*—Turning Strength into Strategy

Raw gold is valuable, but only when refined and forged into something lasting. Strengths, too, must be tempered, tested, and deliberately reinforced before they become enduring assets. The same applies to organisational strengths—recognition isn't enough; they must be sharpened into something lasting.

At this stage, the focus shifts from observation to deliberate application. A team might start by recognising that they handle crises well, but the real question is why? What behaviours make them resilient? What unspoken habits keep them steady under pressure?

For one team, the answer wasn't obvious at first. They assumed they simply had "the right people"—until they started retracing their steps. It wasn't luck; it was a hidden system. They had an instinct for spotting risks early, an unwritten rule of quick check-ins before major decisions, and a culture where asking for help wasn't seen as weakness, but as a shared responsibility.

Once a team recognises not just what works, but why, something fundamental changes. Suddenly, their strengths aren't just talent—they're transferrable knowledge. They can train others, embed these habits into daily work, and scale excellence without losing its essence.

And this is where the *Look Back and Laugh* effect kicks in. A moment that once felt like a near disaster becomes a turning point. Teams stop viewing retrospectives as post-mortems and start seeing them as fuel for mastery. The shift is unmistakable: when people laugh at past challenges instead of cringing at them, you know they've turned mistakes into stepping stones rather than scars.

Phase 4: *Distribution*—Turning Strength into Culture

Strength isn't an asset unless it spreads. What happens in one high-functioning team should be absorbed by others—not through formal policies, but through shared experience.

Some of the best organisations don't just recognise excellence—they circulate it. It happens informally at first—one team borrows an approach, a leader adapts a method, a new hire absorbs a habit just by watching how things are done.

But when these strengths are actively nurtured—when they become part of how new employees are trained, how teams collaborate, how leaders think—they shift from being isolated successes to organisational muscle memory.

In one case, a team's ability to handle unexpected changes in real time became the foundation for an entire company-wide training initiative. Not because leadership mandated it, but because other teams saw it working—and, like a fire catching in dry grass, they wanted to bring it into their own work.

That's how cultures evolve. Not by enforcing rules, but by making excellence so natural, so embedded, that it becomes second nature to everyone.

Gold Seam Mining vs. PACE Strengths?

PACE Strengths was really designed for small, immediate improvements. It keeps progress within a team, reinforcing trust, engagement, and cohesion on a local scale.

Gold Seam Mining plays a longer game. It takes the best of what works and embeds it across the organisation. Unlike quick wins, this process requires resources, leadership backing, and strategic follow-through.

Think of it like this:

- PACE Strengths is like tossing a pebble into a pond, near where you stand, creating ripples of local engagement.
- Gold Seam Mining is digging deep into the earth, uncovering, standardising and formalising strengths that can fuel an entire organisation.

For me, the momentum started with PACE Strengths, in a very low key, modest way but, as momentum built, the business wanted to take what was their intellectual property and scale it across their organisation. The lasting transformations came from Gold Seam Mining.

When To Use Which?

Scenario	PACE Strengths	Gold Seam Mining
Quick & cheap team engagement	✓ Best fit – simple and rapid impact	✗ Too complex and resource-intensive
Low budget, decentralised teams	✓ Easy single team implementation	✗ Requires resources and coordination
Organisation-wide initiative	✗ Not designed for scaling	✓ Ideal for codifying and standardising best practices
High Volatility & Defensiveness	✓ Works well due to focus on psychological safety	✗ Requires stability and structure
Continuous local improvement	✓ Teams own process & solutions	✗ Centralised process managed by organisational leads
Formalise & scale excellence	✗ Keeps improvements within the team	✓ Systematically extracts and spreads best practices

PACE Surfacing

Insightful leaders don't impose understanding. They create the conditions for it to emerge. Organisations try to bottle intelligence in surveys and reports, but knowledge resists being captured. It moves, shifts, and emerges in hallway conversations, passing remarks, and quiet admissions in moments of trust. By the time leaders see the numbers, the signals have already passed.

I learned this the hard way. After the successful use of PACE Strengths, I saw an opportunity. What if, instead of guiding teams within a defined strength-based frame, we removed the constraints altogether? What if we let stories surface naturally, without forcing structure?

The results were remarkable. When you create the right environment, people tell you exactly what you need to know—without realising they're doing it.

PACE Surfacing achieves this—not through rigid steps, but through imperceptible guidance, ensuring insights emerge instead of being extracted. It feels effortless, but beneath the surface, every phase is carefully designed to unlock deeper intelligence.

1. **Setting the Stage for Truth**

Truth doesn't emerge in unsafe spaces. Before people share openly, they scan the room for permission—consciously or not. The first few moments of a conversation determine everything. A single hesitant glance, a nervous shift in posture—these are the unspoken cues that tell a leader whether a team is guarded or ready to speak.

I've seen it happen in real time. A simple opening question—'Can you tell me about your experience with this project?'—isn't just a query; it's a test. The response isn't just words; it's body language, hesitation, the micro-second delay before someone decides whether to speak freely.

This is why the group itself acts as a collective participant. If one person shares candidly, it gives permission for the next. If humour enters the room—genuine, relaxed laughter, not the forced kind—the tension dissolves. It signals that the space is real, not performative.

The goal isn't to control the conversation. It's to build an environment where people naturally drop their guard.

2. Making Honesty Safe Again

Even in well-intentioned discussions, people censor themselves. They frame experiences in ways that sound acceptable, shaping their words to fit the expectations of their audience. The moment storytelling feels like a performance, it stops being useful.

PACE Surfacing shifts this dynamic. Instead of framing stories as explanations, it frames them as contributions—perspectives, not confessions.

A fundamental truth about memory: no one recalls events in a straight line. We reconstruct, we edit, we emphasise details that felt significant at the time. This isn't a flaw—it's the key to unlocking real insights.

So, instead of steering conversations toward "the right answer," a skilled leader guides without force:

- They let silence do the work. The space between words is where real thoughts emerge.
- They resist the urge to correct or clarify. The goal isn't accuracy—it's resonance.
- They encourage reflection, not just reporting. A simple phrase—*"Tell me more about that moment"*—draws out what was nearly left unsaid.

When people stop editing themselves, they start revealing what truly matters.

3. **The Story Beneath the Story**

Most discussions follow a predictable arc. Someone shares a perspective, others nod, a polite exchange follows. But the real insights aren't in what's said first—they're in what follows.

I once watched a routine debrief turn into something far more revealing. A team started discussing a high-stakes project that had almost failed. At first, the conversation stayed on safe ground—the tight deadlines, the external pressures. Then, someone mentioned a moment when everything could have unraveled—but didn't.

That was the spark.

Another team member chimed in, remembering how an unspoken trust between them had kept things from collapsing. Someone else recalled how a particular habit—checking in informally every morning—had prevented small issues from turning into crises.

What began as a post-mortem became a revelation. No one had ever formalised these behaviours as "best practices"—yet they were the very things that had saved the project.

This is why conversations must be allowed to unfold naturally. If they had stuck to the agenda, these insights would have remained buried. Instead, they surfaced organically—not through forced analysis, but through the space to reflect, connect, and recognise patterns.

4. Hearing What Isn't Being Said

Organisations track what people report—but the real signals are in what people don't say.

A single frustration, voiced once, might be dismissed as an outlier. But when the same tension echoes across multiple teams, it's a fault line forming beneath the surface.

I once sat in a session where people kept making offhand comments—light jokes about a process that "never quite worked," a half-serious remark about a policy "that no one really follows." At first blush, it sounded like casual chatter. But after the fourth or fifth mention, a pattern was clear—this wasn't humour, it was quiet resistance.

Silence isn't proof of harmony. Too often, leaders mistake the absence of complaints for the absence of problems. But the weakest signals are often the most important ones. They show up in repeated jokes, small hesitations, topics that shift quickly before they can be explored.

Savvy leaders don't just listen to words—they listen to patterns. What's left unsaid often speaks louder than what's voiced.

Why PACE Surfacing Matters

Traditional feedback models fail because they analyse too late and measure too narrowly. They mistake politeness for truth, metrics for meaning, data for intelligence.

PACE Surfacing fills this gap by ensuring:

Psychological safety enables truth. Fear distorts feedback. Safe spaces encourage honesty, not compliance.

Real-time awareness prevents resistance. Policies fail when leadership misreads reality. Engaging with frontline stories stops disengagement before it takes hold.

Adaptive learning becomes continuous. Knowledge isn't static—it evolves daily through shared interactions.

In complex environments, rigid strategies fail. The best leaders don't impose understanding—they cultivate the conditions for it to emerge.

PACE Surfacing equips them to do exactly that—to listen beyond words, to hear what isn't being said, and to guide strategy with intelligence that truly matters.

Summary

The difference between a high-performing team and a dysfunctional one often comes down to a single invisible factor: *psychological safety*. Without it, creativity withers, mistakes multiply, and disengagement takes root. Like oxygen in a room, its presence is barely noticed, but its absence is suffocating—choking collaboration, stifling risk-taking, and turning workplaces into arenas of silent compliance.

At its core, psychological safety is a paradox: it cannot be imposed, yet it must be deliberately cultivated. Leaders may establish formal structures—regular check-ins, open forums, feedback loops—but these mechanisms are meaningless if vulnerability is punished or dismissed. A system can encourage dialogue, but only consistent, trustworthy behaviour ensures that people actually speak. The moment a leader's body language betrays their words, or engagement is selectively rewarded, safety fractures.

When it's present, safety is felt rather than announced. Individuals display quiet confidence—the ability to speak freely without rehearsing, to ask questions without self-censorship, to treat mistakes as lessons rather than liabilities. Within teams, it translates into a culture where ideas spark, where disagreement fuels progress instead of conflict, and where failure is recognised as an opportunity to refine, not a reason to retreat. The strongest indicator of such an environment is not whether people talk, but how mistakes are handled—are they treated as moments for collective learning, or as ammunition for blame?

Yet safety, no matter how carefully built, is fragile. It takes time to establish but can be shattered in seconds. The fastest way to erode it? Inconsistency. Hypocrisy. Public humiliation. Favouritism. Consider Davey, a leader who preached openness but punished dissent, who championed engagement but wielded fear. His inconsistency poisoned the very structures he put in place, making participation a liability rather than an opportunity.

Or take the silent damage of public criticism. Picture offering an idea in a meeting, only for your manager to shoot it down in front of everyone. Your stomach knots, your pulse spikes, and suddenly, silence feels safer than risk-taking. This is how safety is lost—not through grand betrayals, but through small, repeated moments of learned helplessness. Just as damaging is the failure to follow through—when leaders invite feedback but fail to act, they teach people that contributions are performative rather than meaningful. Favouritism compounds the problem, dividing teams into insiders and outsiders, breeding quiet resentment where trust should be.

Restoring lost safety requires more than platitudes. It must be embedded in practice. After-Action Reviews (AARs) reframe failure as an opportunity for collective learning, ensuring that reflection leads to improvement rather than blame. The Crumple & Toss technique creates a structured space where honesty can thrive without fear of reprisal, allowing the unsaid to surface.

But safety isn't just about preventing harm—it's about amplifying strengths. Inspired by Dave Snowden's narrative methods, PACE Surfacing helps leaders uncover the hidden intelligence within teams. While organisations focus on data, they often overlook the tacit knowledge embedded in daily interactions. Stories—shared or withheld—reveal the true culture of an organisation. Leaders who create the right conditions for these stories to emerge don't just receive insights—they gain an unfiltered window into reality.

Successful executives don't just protect trust—they build enduring strength. PACE Strengths and Gold Seam Mining shift the focus from fixing deficiencies to amplifying what already works, creating a culture of excellence rather than mere damage control. Like a skilled miner, a leader must uncover hidden potential, refine insights, and distribute them across the organisation.

Psychological safety is not a static condition but a continuous practice. The best teams don't just survive uncertainty—they thrive in it.

The best leaders don't just prevent harm; they create cultures where people dare to think, speak, and build something greater than themselves.

TWELVE
SAFETY PRIMING SKILLS

> When people learn to laugh at what used to terrify them, they are free[1]
> **Richard Bandler**

THE SAFETY SENSE is a necessary but not sufficient condition for psychological permission. That's why, in the PACE Protocol, safety priming is the first priority—engaging observation, conversation, and behavioural aspects from the very first interaction.

Just like driving through a busy town centre, leadership requires constant awareness and real-time adjustments. Every interaction, every response, and every non-verbal cue determines whether the environment feels safe or uncertain. This chapter is about applying your inner and outer game skillsets to safety priming, equipping you with the tools to create, sustain, and repair psychological safety in real-time.

These techniques range from foundational skills—such as breath control and observational acuity—to more nuanced conversational and behavioural strategies. As you gain fluency, you will learn to experiment and refine these approaches, much like an artist blending colours to create a masterpiece.

While safety priming is an active, dynamic process, it does not replace formal safety structures. Formal safety provides *predictability and stability,* but only safety priming can create *immediate, real-time trust*—activating safety embedded structures and making them meaningful in practice. Without skilled safety priming, even safety embedded structures risk becoming hollow—policies exist, but psychological safety remains absent. The techniques in this chapter bridge that gap, ensuring that safety is not just an institutional goal but a lived experience within the team.

Stage 1: Observation

A leader's ability to prime safety begins with keen observation. Like a ship's captain steering his vessel through changing waters, the leader who reads subtle verbal and non-verbal cues is prepared to adjust their approach. Observational skills help you assess your team's current state, revealing when they're relaxed, tense, or in need of reassurance. Here, we introduce key observational techniques that empower you to sense and respond to the emotional undercurrents that impact team performance.

To attain heightened sensory acuity, you need to be in a grounded, alert state, where you focus is entirely externally oriented. For me, to support myself to be fully concentrated on what is going on around me, I fire two 'anchors' which turn on 1) a state of fascination and 2) keen awareness of my peripheral vision. Once these aspects are in play, my senses are alert, and I am in the moment.

Breathing Patterns

Breathing is more than a simple bodily function; it's a window into a person's emotional state. High, shallow breaths in the chest often signal stress or anxiety, while low, deep breaths in the abdomen indicate relaxation and control. As a leader, observing these breathing patterns in both you and your team can serve as an early indicator of emotional readiness. If you notice shallow, rapid breathing during a meeting, for instance, it may suggest heightened tension or unease—a cue that safety priming techniques could be beneficial.

Exercise: Practice observing your own breath before important interactions. Take a moment to lower your breathing to your abdomen, bringing calm to your body. As you interact with your team, observe their breathing, particularly during high-stress discussions, to gauge when a grounding exercise might be helpful. Also, see if you are able to identify a baseline for each of them: some people naturally breathe higher or lower. Calibrating this is useful because it's the change in their breathing pattern that is the meaningful cue.

Physical & Emotional Cues

Our bodies communicate continuously, often revealing emotions we may not verbalise. Recognising cues such as stiffness in shoulders, clenched fists, fidgeting and fleeting expressions of tension or discomfort can help you detect the team's underlying feelings. Facial expressions, posture, and vocal tone often change subtly in response to anxiety or comfort, giving you insight into whether your team feels psychologically safe or if they're operating under pressure. As with breathing, it's useful to calibrate a baseline for person – for example, when someone who fidgets a lot become still, that's what's important. Also calibrate a baseline for the group: being alert and noticing when baseline noise and activity levels shift is important.

Pro Tip: *Try noting body language patterns during a routine team meeting. Do you notice any changes as specific topics are discussed? A team member sitting back with arms crossed might suggest disengagement or defensiveness, while relaxed, open postures signal comfort and trust. Recognising these cues allows you to adjust your approach, promoting a more open and connected environment.*

. . .

Group Dynamics

In both coaching and team settings, the level of the group's cooperative accord, it's unity and cohesion, although distinct from, it is indicative of the group's safety level. Observing how team members respond to playful or probing comments can help you assess whether safety is strong or needs reinforcement. If your light-hearted question or comment is met with smiles and engagement, safety is likely intact; if team members appear uncomfortable or closed off, it may be time to refocus on priming safety.

Exercise: At your next team meeting, begin with a light-hearted question or brief personal story to gauge initial rapport. Observe reactions—smiles, laughter, or relaxed postures typically indicate strong rapport, while tension or silence may suggest areas for growth. Building rapport creates a foundation for safety priming, encouraging team members to engage more openly.

Co-Regulation

Co-regulation is the act of using shared neurological and emotional states to restore and maintain connection within the team. A leader who remains grounded in moments of stress can **actively regulate the team's collective emotional state**, reinforcing stability even under pressure.

The mechanism by which this occurs is subtle but powerful: the leader's composure sets the baseline for the group's neuroception, allowing team members to mirror and absorb their emotional steadiness.

As you practice safety priming techniques, observe how others' demeanours shift in response to your grounded, centred behaviour.

Co-regulation allows your team to *unconsciously synchronise with your emotional state,* which can reduce collective tension and enhance receptivity to guidance.

Pro Tip: *Next time you enter a high-stress meeting, focus on regulating your own emotions. Take a few deep breaths and maintain a relaxed posture. Observe whether others in the room also begin to relax, signalling that co-regulation is taking effect. This shared calmness can be a powerful tool, helping teams remain focused and connected even in challenging situations.*

Safety priming is only as effective as its consistency. Leaders who apply these techniques sporadically—exuding warmth one day but reacting defensively the next—create uncertainty rather than trust. Because the nervous system continuously scans for safety or threat, inconsistent leadership behaviour triggers hypervigilance, making team members hesitant to engage. Trust is built through predictability. The most effective safety primers are not just skilled communicators; they are dependable ones. Every interaction, every non-verbal cue, and every moment of engagement must send a clear, aligned message:

'This is a space where you are safe to contribute'

STAGE 2: **Conversation**

If the Hive Mind is the system through which psychological safety is shaped, then safety priming is the mechanism through which leaders regulate it in real time. Safety cannot be demanded, nor can it be enforced through policy alone. It must be cultivated at a physiological and social level, through every interaction, micro-cue, and exchange of trust.

The most immediate and continuous form of safety priming is conversation. A leader's voice—its tone, rhythm, and cadence—can either steady the nervous system or trigger defensiveness. Their choice of words can either invite participation or stifle engagement. Safety priming operates within this emergent system, using verbal and non-verbal signals to reinforce trust as rapidly as the group perceives safety or threat—before rational thought has even taken place.

Formalised safety structures provide stability and predictability over time, but they cannot, on their own, elicit psychological safety. Conversational skills are the real-time stabilisers that determine whether those structures feel meaningful or performative. A team may have policies that support trust, but without reinforcing interactions, those policies remain theoretical rather than lived experiences.

In leadership, how you speak matters as much as what you say. Conversational skills in safety priming rely on tone, humour, empathy, and clarity to create an environment where team members feel comfortable expressing themselves. Mastering these skills involves both content and delivery—each exchange, even the briefest comment, can either strengthen or undermine psychological safety. The following conversational techniques will equip you to foster trust, reduce defensiveness, and guide your team toward open, constructive dialogue.

Vocal Prosody

The voice has a profound influence on how people feel and react. When leaders adopt a calm, melodic, and rhythmic tone, they can ease anxiety, encourage trust, and promote a sense of security. Vocal prosody, or the modulation of pitch, tone, and rhythm, can subtly signal that everything is under control, helping to calm team members during stressful situations. Think of how a lullaby soothes a baby; similarly, a well-modulated voice can help your team relax and feel safe to contribute.

Exercise: Practice vocal modulation by recording yourself speaking about a challenging topic, focusing on maintaining a calm, downward-sloping vocal pattern. As you listen back, ask yourself whether your tone conveys reassurance and stability. Over time, this practice will help you naturally set a calm tone in real-time, especially useful in high-stakes or tense meetings.

Playfulness & Humour

Humour and playfulness are powerful tools in safety priming, helping to break down formal barriers and make people feel at ease. Playfulness triggers the brain's social engagement system, which reduces defensiveness and invites connection. By opening with a light-hearted question or sharing a funny, relatable anecdote, leaders can foster an atmosphere of openness and camaraderie. Playfulness also signals that it's safe to let one's guard down—a vital component in building safety.

Example: Start your next team meeting with an unexpected, light-hearted question, like "If you were a superhero, what would your power be?" or "If your workday was a movie genre, which one would it be today?" This simple act shifts the team's focus from task-oriented tension to something lighter, encouraging everyone to laugh and relax.

Pro Tip: *Notice the reactions. If people laugh or respond playfully, the team is likely in a good place rapport-wise. If they're hesitant, more work may be needed to build comfort and trust.*

Communication Style

In times of change or uncertainty, clear, transparent communication is essential to creating safety. When leaders communicate openly—acknowledging challenges honestly and explaining decisions without defensive posturing—they reduce team anxiety. Verbal empathy, in particular, goes beyond simply proving that you've been listening; it involves validating team members' feelings, showing that their experiences and perspectives have been heard and understood properly. This is received as a cue that they are being respected.

Pro Tip: *When introducing a difficult change, be direct but considerate. For example, instead of saying, "We have to cut the budget," try, "I know this is a challenging adjustment, and many of you may have concerns. Here's how we plan to work through this together." This approach combines honesty with empathy, allowing the team to feel seen, heard, and supported.*

Exercise: Practice verbal empathy by restating a team member's concerns in *their own words*. For instance, if someone says:

"I feel like I'm drowning... every time I get a breath; I keep getting dragged under".

Now, *active listening* advocates would have you listen to their words and respond with different words. That would be something like,

"It sounds like you're really struggling"

Certainly, if you were a third party watching the from the outside, such a response is empathetic, as far as it goes. However, if you're the person that feels like you are drowning, that level of understanding doesn't go far enough.

After all, 'really struggling' doesn't have the same degree of visceral intensity as 'near death by drowning', does it? And yet, 'near death by drowning' is how that person is representing their situation both to themselves and to you.

However, if you say, "Drowning... just trying to keep your head above water?", you are engaging with them, and showing that you understand them, in *their* terms... not yours. When you do that, they will feel safer faster and will give you their permission sooner: the primary goal of "Prime & Probe" phase.

. . .

DEEPER ENGAGEMENT

Building permission means establishing rapport to a point where team members feel comfortable with more direct, even challenging, conversations. In coaching, rapport is essential for guiding clients through personal insights; similarly, leaders must create an atmosphere where team members feel safe enough to engage with difficult topics. Building permission is a skill that enables leaders to move from superficial interactions to more meaningful discussions that build trust and psychological resilience.

Example: When you sense a team member is uncomfortable with feedback, start by sharing a positive observation or an empathic comment. As rapport strengthens, introduce constructive feedback gradually, inviting them to share their own thoughts on the matter.

For instance, *"I really appreciate your commitment to the project. I think there's an opportunity to improve efficiency here—what's your view on how we might approach this?"* This gives them space to engage openly and without defensiveness.

STAGE 3: Behaviour

While observational and conversational skills set the foundation, behavioural skills allow leaders to embody safety priming and establish it as part of the team's culture. Behavioural cues, from controlled breathing to relaxed body language, send powerful signals of calm, openness, and readiness to engage. Through consistent use of these behaviours, leaders not only reinforce safety but also invite their team to mirror these states, promoting a collective sense of security and trust. Here, we delve into the essential behavioural skills leaders can develop to create and sustain a culture of safety.

. . .

Breath Control

Regulating one's breath may seem simple, but its effects on self-control and group dynamics are profound. In moments of high tension, slowing down and lowering your breath to your abdomen signals calm and presence, setting a foundation for others to mirror. When a leader models steady, controlled breathing, they signal that there is no need for alarm, which can profoundly influence the group's overall state.

Exercise: Practice "box breathing" before meetings or challenging conversations. Inhale for four counts, hold for four, exhale for four, and hold for four again. This exercise can help you enter a calm state, which, in turn, stabilises the emotional energy you bring into the room. Over time, you'll notice that your centred breathing has a subtle yet noticeable calming effect on your team, allowing co-regulation to take place.

Playful Engagement

Human connection thrives on direct, face-to-face interaction. Making eye contact, offering a sincere smile, and maintaining a relaxed posture are subtle yet powerful cues that activate the social engagement system. These small acts establish a baseline of trust and connection, reassuring team members that they are seen, valued, and safe. This is especially critical in times of change or stress when people may feel disconnected or anxious.

Pro Tip: *During team check-ins or feedback sessions, make a point of maintaining eye contact with each participant. Show genuine engagement with each person's input, signalling that their presence matters. This consistent face-to-face engagement will reinforce a culture where every individual feels acknowledged and valued.*

. . .

OPEN PHYSICAL CUES

Your posture communicates a great deal about your mindset, and as a leader, adopting a relaxed, open posture can encourage your team to do the same. Avoid crossing your arms or hunching your shoulders—stances that can come across as defensive or closed off.

Instead, aim for a relaxed, upright stance with uncrossed arms and open palms. This openness signals approachability and encourages others to mirror a similar stance, reducing tension and fostering a sense of security.

Pro Tip*: The next time you enter a discussion, pay attention to your posture. Relax your shoulders, uncross your arms, and adopt a balanced stance. Notice how this subtle change impacts the mood of the conversation, helping others feel comfortable and open to contributing their thoughts.*

VOCAL CO-REGULATION

The nervous system's response to auditory cues signalling safety is quite fascinating. The tone, pitch, and rhythm of your voice are integral to setting an emotionally safe environment. Dr. Stephen Porges points to famous American singer Johnny Mathis as an example of prosody.

Younger readers may find 'John Legend' a more relatable reference, with his smooth, warm, and intimate vocals in songs like *"All of Me"*. Either way, in the context of Porges's work on auditory safety and the calming effects of prosodic voices, he puts it this way:

"Our Nervous System is waiting for Johnny Mathis"

This remark underscores how the modulation of vocalisations in certain sounds (voice, music, etc) can convey safety to our nervous system. In doing so, it promotes relaxation and social engagement: good things for safety priming for groups.

A calm, rhythmic voice can have a powerful co-regulating effect on a group, gently guiding the emotional state. When discussing sensitive topics or leading a tense meeting, adopting a softer, melodic, more 'Johnny Mathis', tone helps others stay centred and engaged. This is especially helpful during high-stakes conversations where anxiety might run high.

Exercise: During your next high-stress discussion, consciously slow down your speech and soften your tone. Observe how this adjustment affects the room's energy and helps bring others into a more receptive, calm state.

Over time, using vocal prosody consistently in tense settings can reinforce an overall culture of safety and trust.

Turn Niggles *into Giggles*

Co-Regulating Humour can be a highly effective safety-priming tool. Gentle coxy humour helps to lighten the mood, reducing anxiety and encouraging people to let go of rigid thought patterns. More robust, well delivered 'chiding' humour, as exemplified by Frank Farrelly and Richard Bandler, takes more verbal and abductive acuity, but, when mastered, can be the gold standard of priming and probing.

Whatever style adopted, when leaders can turn minor annoyances or "niggles" into playful moments or "giggles", it fosters resilience and an ability to view challenges from a fresh perspective.

This doesn't mean making light of serious issues but rather helping the team keep things in proportion, transforming unnecessary tension into something constructive.

Example: If a team member voices a minor frustration, such as "We're always stuck in back-to-back meetings," respond with a touch of humour, like, "Maybe we should install bunk beds in the conference room!"

This playful reframing encourages the team to laugh and take the frustration less seriously, breaking down any tension and opening the door to solutions.

Pro Tip: Always gauge the team's response to humour. Playful commentary that is met with smiles and laughter signals a healthy rapport. Take subdued responses as a cue that they need more safety. As such, maintain a state of approachability and jolliness and continue to reframe playfully. In doing so, you are sending lots of safety cues and autonomic invitations to deepen connection.

DAILY SAFETY PRIMING

Safety priming is most effective when it becomes a daily practice rather than a one-time intervention. Embedding these skills into your regular routines reinforces safety as a constant. This might include starting each meeting with a brief grounding exercise, using humour regularly to diffuse tension, or reminding yourself to check your posture and breathing.

By making these behaviours routine, you reinforce an environment where safety is the norm, not the exception.

Exercise: Create a personal checklist of safety-priming actions that you can refer to before each team interaction. Include reminders such as "take a deep breath," "engage with eye contact and smile" and "use an approachable tone." This checklist will help you internalise these practices until they become second nature, gradually embedding safety priming into your leadership approach.

. . .

While safety priming begins at the individual level, its true power lies in its ability to transform entire teams and organisations. A leader can model these techniques, but if psychological safety is to become truly embedded, it must be woven into the organisation's culture.

Scaling safety priming ensures that safety is not dependent on individual leaders but is a shared responsibility reinforced at every level. The next section explores how to embed safety priming into the larger system, ensuring that it is not just a leadership practice but a core element of organisational culture.

Stage 4: Scaling Safety

While safety priming begins with individual interactions, its true power lies in its capacity to transform entire teams and organisations. By embedding safety priming practices into daily routines, training, and leadership development, safety that supports adaptability, resilience, and open collaboration on a larger scale, seeping into the deeper aspects of the organisation's culture.

In this final section, we explore ways to scale safety priming across teams and organisations, transforming it from an individual skill into a foundational cultural element.

Co-Regulation is Giving

As individuals begin to mirror the leader's calm and present demeanour, co-regulation emerges as a powerful force within the group. Co-regulation allows everyone to take collective responsibility for the team's emotional state, supporting one another through mutual reassurance and calmness.

When leaders intentionally model and encourage co-regulation, they create a team environment where emotional stability and openness become cultural norms.

Example: When introducing a high-pressure project or discussing challenging changes, maintain a calm, measured tone and your team members will mirror your calm. In moments of spiked emotion, remind everyone to take a moment to breathe before reacting, that way you are inserting *co-regulation* into their conscious thoughts.

Over time, this shared focus on calmness and receptivity will become a natural response to stress, helping the team navigate complexities with resilience.

Feedback Loops

Scaling safety priming requires regular feedback to gauge its impact and identify areas for improvement. Inviting team members to share their experiences with safety priming techniques can offer valuable insights, helping leaders refine their approach and adjust their strategies as needed.

Feedback loops also foster a sense of collective ownership over the team's emotional climate, enabling team members to feel actively engaged in maintaining a safe and supportive environment.

Exercise: Consider implementing regular team surveys or feedback sessions where team members can anonymously share their thoughts on the team's emotional climate. Ask *PACE Protocol* style questions like,

- *"Do you have the permission to share your ideas, even if contentious, in meetings?"*
- *"When things go wrong, does your group have your back? Does your boss?"*

- "Are you able to be fully transparent in your group without feeling vulnerable?"
- "Think of the future, is your group learning to get better, faster and smarter?"

This feedback can reveal insights into the effectiveness of safety priming efforts, guiding leaders in refining their practices.

Personal Resilience Training

Embedding autoregulation techniques into leadership development programs ensures that new and existing leaders possess the skills to foster safety. Training sessions can cover core skills like *The Worry Solver, Connect with Yourself,* and *Increasing Instinct Acuity* equip leaders with practical tools to control their own stress. Additionally, these programs reinforce the expectation that safety is an organisational priority, cascading the impact of autoregulation from leaders to the co-regulation of their respective teams.

Practical Step*: Design workshops that teach autoregulation skills, such as using breathing techniques to control stress and raises their awareness of their own unique VAK+B patterns. Encourage leaders to practice these techniques through role-playing scenarios and real-world simulations. This not only strengthens their confidence in their ability to autoregulate but also embeds these practices within the organisation's leadership framework.*

Group Resilience Training

Embedding safety priming techniques into leadership development programs ensures that new and existing leaders possess the skills to foster psychological safety across their teams. Training sessions can cover core skills like observational acuity, vocal prosody, and non-verbal communication, equipping leaders with practical tools to build trust and reduce defensiveness. Additionally, these programs reinforce the expectation that safety is an organisational priority, cascading the impact of safety priming from leaders to their respective teams.

Practical Step: *Incorporate safety priming training into leadership onboarding and ongoing development programs. Instead of treating it as an individual competency, integrate it into team-wide practices such as structured debriefs, coaching sessions, and collaborative reflection exercises.*

Train leaders in group-level co-regulation techniques, ensuring they can reinforce safety even in high-pressure environments. Conduct live simulations where teams practice responding to real-time safety ruptures together, reinforcing a collective approach to psychological safety.

Valuing Safety

To fully scale safety priming, psychological safety should be recognised as an organisational value, embedded into core principles and reflected in everyday practices. When safety is explicitly valued, it permeates all levels, shaping how teams approach problem-solving, decision-making, and interpersonal interactions. Reinforcing safety as a cultural value encourages everyone—from frontline employees to executives—to prioritise emotional well-being, making it a unifying aspect of the organisational identity.

Pro Tip: *Shift happens, so to speak. Therefore, secure experienced coaches on retainer with your organisation, in order to ensure that you have a fast response should things go wrong. The speed and efficacy of this approach are truly impressive, as demonstrated in* Chapter 8: Rupture Repair Coaching

. . .

External Stakeholders

Safety priming principles can be equally powerful when engaging with external stakeholders, including clients, partners, and the public[2]. By practicing transparency, empathy, and calm presence in high-stakes interactions, leaders can build trust and foster stronger relationships beyond the immediate team.

The same safety cues that promote emotional safety internally can strengthen credibility and collaboration externally, making negotiations, client presentations, and partnerships more productive.

Example: *Consider addressing a board of investors during a challenging financial period. By maintaining a steady, transparent tone and openly acknowledging the difficulties, you create a calm, trustworthy atmosphere.*

Stakeholders are more likely to remain receptive and cooperative when they feel they are engaging with a leader who is honest, composed, and considerate of their concerns.

Exercise: Before engaging with external stakeholders, review and employ the *'How Not to Get Shot'* technique in Chapter 10. Take a moment to check your emotional state using breath control or a brief body scan. Focus on presenting yourself with openness and empathy, listening actively, and responding thoughtfully.

This practice reinforces safety not just within your team but in every relationship your organisation fosters, strengthening your reputation as a trustworthy and emotionally intelligent leader.

Scaling safety priming across teams and organisations transforms it from an individual skill into a cultural pillar. By embedding safety priming in daily practices, leadership training, feedback mechanisms, and organisational values, leaders create an environment where psychological safety is not just a priority—it is an expectation.

When fully integrated, safety priming is no longer a leadership tool—it is the foundation of how people think, interact, and innovate together. In these cultures, trust is not something that must be continually rebuilt; it is the default state. Teams in these environments do not just function—they flourish.

SECTION FOUR SUMMARY

We have a nervous system that reacts to both danger and safety. Social connection triggers a calming response that enhances our ability to feel secure and connected[1]

Dr. Stephen Porges

The *Group Resilience Skills* section examines the dynamics of collective intelligence within teams and organisations, exploring how leaders can harness the instinctive behaviours of groups to build resilience, trust, and innovation. Grounded in neuroscience, behavioural psychology, and organisational theory, this section reveals how human groups function as interconnected systems, balancing creativity and collaboration with the risks of dysfunction and fragmentation.

Across three chapters—*The Hive Mind, Safety-Embedded Structures* and *Safety Priming Skills*—readers learn how to shape group behaviours that foster cohesion and adaptability.

The Hive Mind is a phenomenon of collective intelligence that emerges when individuals work toward shared goals. Drawing from nature, this chapter illustrates how systems like beehives or bird flocks achieve remarkable coordination without centralised control[2]. In human organisations, the Hive Mind thrives on shared purpose, interdependence, and dynamic communication. However, it is also vulnerable to pitfalls like groupthink, emotional contagion, and resistance to change. The chapter emphasises the leader's role in regulating the Hive Mind, ensuring it serves adaptability rather than self-protection.

Psychological Safety is the foundation of high-performing, resilient teams. This chapter explores how neuroception—our subconscious ability to detect safety or threat—**shapes team dynamics[3]. When psychological safety is high, individuals feel empowered to take risks and contribute openly. When it is absent, they default to defensive behaviours like withdrawal, conflict, or disengagement.

Leaders must cultivate both the Inner Game (self-regulation) and Outer Game (team regulation) to create environments where trust, respect, and open communication are the norm[4]. Structured techniques such as *After-Action Reviews* and strengths-based approaches ensure psychological safety is reinforced over time[5].

Safety Priming builds on structured safety by embedding real-time safety cues into daily interactions. While structured safety ensures long-term stability, safety priming ensures trust is actively reinforced in critical moments. Leaders learn to observe subtle emotional and physical cues, regulate safety using conversational tools like vocal prosody and humour, and model calming behaviours that influence group neuroception.

This chapter also explores how safety priming can scale across organisations, transforming psychological safety from an individual skill into a cultural cornerstone.

Techniques Introduced in This Section

To apply these concepts, leaders need a blend of structured processes and real-time interventions. The techniques below provide practical strategies to create, sustain, and repair psychological safety:

To build and sustain neuro-resilience, we introduced some approaches:

1. **After-Action Reviews** – Reflect on outcomes to foster learning and growth.
2. **Crumple & Toss:** Anonymises team member inputs to surface hidden tensions.
3. **PACE Strengths**: Strength-based storytelling for learning and cohesion-building.
4. **PACE Surfacing:** Safe engagement for tacit knowledge and emergent narratives.
5. **Gold Seam Mining:** for uncovering, refining and institutionalising strengths.
6. **Safety-Priming** – batched and sequenced verbal and non-verbal techniques the purpose of accelerated co-regulation.
7. **Breathing Patterns:** Gauge emotional states and regulate team energy.
8. **Co-Regulation** – Making one's regulated state available for others.
9. **Vocal Prosody** – Uses tone and rhythm to create calm and trust.
10. **Verbal Empathy** – Articulating the observable conditions of others.

In today's unpredictable, high-stakes environments, leaders cannot rely solely on strategy or expertise. Their ability to regulate group safety—both structurally and in the moment—determines whether their teams remain engaged, adaptive, and resilient under pressure. Those who master these skills build teams that thrive in complexity rather than succumb to it.

Toolbox Summary

After-Action Review (AAR)

Purpose: To reframe failure as a learning opportunity and foster a culture of continuous improvement.

Steps:

1. What really happened?

   - Build a shared understanding of events by integrating diverse perspectives.

2. What insights did we gain?

   - Reflect on what worked, what didn't, and why, without assigning blame.

3. How can we improve next time?

   - Turn insights into actionable strategies for future improvement.

Training Summary:

Leaders should model vulnerability by sharing their own failures and lessons learned. Conduct AARs after key projects or milestones, ensuring the focus remains on learning rather than blame. Use the three core questions to guide structured yet flexible discussions.

Crumple & Toss

Purpose: To create a safe, anonymous space for team members to share concerns and ideas.

Steps:

1. **Preparation**:

- Distribute half-sheets of paper and ask participants to write responses to:
    - "What concerns or issues are preventing progress?"
    - "What needs to happen for the group to move forward?"

2. **Crumple & Toss**:

- Participants crumple their papers and toss them into a central area or bucket.

3. **Reading Aloud**:

- Each participant picks a random paper and reads it aloud without commenting.

4. **Pattern Recognition**:

- Identify recurring themes or patterns in the responses.

5. **Solution-Focused Discussion**:

- Collaborate on actionable solutions to address the surfaced concerns.

Training Summary:

Use this technique in larger groups where open sharing may feel intimidating. Emphasise anonymity and non-judgmental listening to encourage honesty and build trust[6].

PACE Strengths

Purpose: To build trust and engagement by focusing on team strengths rather than weaknesses.

Steps:

- **Safety Pre-frame & Ensure Commitment**:
  - Set a positive tone by checking in with participants and ensuring they feel comfortable sharing.

- **Lead with Strengths, Pre-frame Weaknesses**:
  - Highlight team strengths and frame past challenges as learning experiences.

- **Let Them Tell Their Story**:
  - Encourage free-flowing storytelling about team journeys, successes, and turning points.

- **Learning & Understanding**:
  - Reflect on insights and identify opportunities for systemic improvement.

Training Summary:

Use this approach to boost morale and cohesion. Focus on what's working well, and frame weaknesses as opportunities for growth. Ensure the conversation feels natural and energising[7].

PACE Surfacing

Purpose: To uncover hidden team intelligence and cultural dynamics through storytelling.

Steps:

1. **Grounding & Framing Contributions**:
    - Create a safe space for storytelling by using humour and non-verbal cues to signal trust.

2. **Removing Barriers to Authenticity**:
    - Normalise subjectivity and ensure participants feel free to share without fear of judgment.

3. **Letting Stories Emerge Naturally**:
    - Allow conversations to meander, focusing on resonance rather than consensus.

4. **Turning Patterns into Insights**:
    - Identify recurring themes and use them to inform actionable strategies.

Training Summary:

Use this technique to uncover tacit knowledge and cultural insights. Avoid forcing conclusions; instead, let stories reveal weak signals and hidden patterns[8].

Gold Seam Mining

Purpose: To systematically uncover, refine, and institutionalise team strengths.

Steps:

1. **Prospecting**:
    - Identify team strengths by asking questions like:
        - "What do we consistently do well, even under pressure?"
        - "What strengths give us a competitive edge?"

2. **Excavation**:
    - Analyse why these strengths exist and how they function.
    - Encourage storytelling to uncover patterns and formulas for success.

3. **Refining**:
    - Codify strengths into principles and embed them into daily practices.
    - Shift the culture to view mistakes as stepping stones to mastery.

4. **Distribution**:
    - Spread strengths across the organisation through mentorship, cross-functional sharing, and training programs.

Training Summary:

Use this structured approach to transform local successes into scalable, repeatable practices. Focus on amplifying strengths rather than fixing deficits.

Observation Skills

1. **Breathing Patterns** – Observing breath patterns to gauge emotional states and using deep breathing exercises to regulate team energy.

Goal: To regulate emotional states by observing and adjusting breathing patterns.

1. **Observe** – Watch for shallow, high-chest breathing (stress) vs. deep, abdominal breathing (relaxation).
2. **Calibrate** – Identify baseline breathing patterns for each team member.
3. **Adjust Your Own Breathing** – Before key interactions, take slow, deep breaths into your abdomen.
4. **Model & Mirror** – Consciously slow your own breath to encourage the team to unconsciously match your rhythm.
5. **Cue Deep Breathing in the Team** – Subtly prompt them: "Let's take a moment to ground ourselves before we dive in."
6. **Co-Regulation** – Using one's emotional stability to influence and regulate the collective emotional state of the team.

Group Dynamics – Reading team rapport and cohesion through reactions to light-hearted interactions or challenging topics[9].

Goal: To use tone and rhythm to create a psychologically safe atmosphere.

1. **Check Your Voice** – Record yourself speaking under stress vs. relaxed; listen to your natural rhythm.

2. **Slow Down Your Speech** – Avoid rushed delivery; take pauses between key points.
3. **Lower Your Pitch Slightly** – A lower, steady tone signals authority and reassurance.
4. **Soften Your Cadence** – Use a rhythmic, melodic flow rather than a flat, monotone delivery.
5. **Practice in Key Moments** – Before tense discussions, take a breath, slow down, and soften your vocal tone.

Conversational Skills

1. **Vocal Prosody** – Using modulation in pitch, tone, and rhythm to create a calming and reassuring environment[10].

Goal: To use tone and rhythm to create a psychologically safe atmosphere.

1. **Check Your Voice** – Record yourself speaking under stress vs. relaxed; listen to your natural rhythm.
2. **Slow Down Your Speech** – Avoid rushed delivery; take pauses between key points.
3. **Lower Your Pitch Slightly** – A lower, steady tone signals authority and reassurance.
4. **Soften Your Cadence** – Use a rhythmic, melodic flow rather than a flat, monotone delivery.
5. **Charismatic Pattern** – A blend of up-and-down tones within the command-tone-down patterns
   - Picture a soft wobbly line starting high on the left hand side, moving down to the right hand side.
6. **Practice in Key Moments** – Before tense discussions, take a breath, slow down, and soften your vocal tone.

7. **Verbal Empathy** – Matching the intensity of team members' emotions in language to deepen engagement and create psychological safety.

Goal: To reflect emotions back accurately and make people feel understood[11].

1. **Listen Closely** – Pay attention to **exact words** and **emotional intensity**.
2. **Identify Their Emotional Language** – Are they

using strong metaphors? ("I feel like I'm drowning" vs. "I'm struggling").
3. **Match Their Wording** – Echo their metaphor back ("Drowning... just trying to keep your head above water?").
4. **Watch for Recognition** – If they nod or relax, you've signalled true understanding.
5. **Move to Problem-Solving** – Once rapport is built, guide them toward constructive next steps.

SECTION FIVE
MICRO-SKILLS FOR LEADERS

The strength of the pack is the wolf,
and the strength of the wolf is the pack
Rudyard Kipling

Leadership is often considered as the art of persuasion—a well-timed speech, a clever argument, a compelling narrative. Yet beneath the surface of eloquent words and polished rhetoric lies a more potent force: the unspoken. Non-verbal communication—gestures, posture, facial expressions, and tone—shapes how we are perceived long before we speak[1]. It is the elusive language that either reinforces or undermines every word we utter.

Picture a leader walking into a room. Shoulders squared, gaze steady, movements deliberate. Without saying a word, they command attention and set the tone for what follows. Now think of that same leader entering with slouched shoulders, eyes darting anxiously, and a restless shuffle. The room senses it instantly: uncertainty. Doubt spreads before any words are spoken. This is the quiet truth of leadership—our bodies speak louder and faster than our voices ever can.

This instinctive response to non-verbal cues is not a recent phenomenon. It is ancient, embedded deep in our evolutionary wiring[2]. Long before language shaped human societies, survival depended on reading physical signals—tense muscles, a sharp glance, a subtle shift in posture. These cues conveyed threat or safety, dominance or submission. Our ancestors survived by swiftly interpreting these signs and reacting accordingly. Today, those same instincts remain, guiding how we perceive authority, trustworthiness, and confidence. In a boardroom or a meeting hall, when a leader falters in their voice or avoids eye contact, it stirs the same unease that once warned of hidden predators. The threats have changed, but the instincts have not.

At the core of non-verbal leadership is *congruence*—the alignment of what we say and how we say it. When a leader speaks of certainty but their posture sags or their voice wavers, the disconnect is palpable. People trust what they feel more than what they hear. In contrast, congruence—where voice, posture, and expression reinforce the message—amplifies authority. A leader presenting a bold vision with steady breath, deliberate gestures, and calm confidence silently says:

> *"I believe this, and so should you"*

Yet non-verbal communication is a double-edged sword. It is our most powerful tool and our greatest vulnerability. Words can be rehearsed, but the body reveals the truth. A clenched jaw betrays frustration. A fleeting glance exposes doubt. Mastering leadership, therefore, begins with mastering the self[3]. Before we can influence others, we must first become aware of what we unconsciously project[4].

This section explores that journey—from understanding the foundations of non-verbal influence to refining and mastering its subtle techniques. Chapter Thirteen, *The Elusive Obvious*, uncovers the hidden power of non-verbal cues in leadership. Chapter Fourteen, *Non-Verbal Acuity*, offers practical strategies to sharpen these signals and align them with intent. Chapter Fifteen, *The Subtle Skills*, delves deeper into advanced techniques—how to harness pauses, synchronise breath with speech, and manage presence under pressure. Together, these chapters offer an enlightening guide to the wordless art of leadership.

In a world awash with words, it is easy to overlook what is left unsaid. But true leadership is not about abandoning speech—it is about enriching it. The leader who masters non-verbal communication gains more than a skill; they gain presence. They move beyond words into the deeper realm of human connection. They become a leader not only heard but felt.

Let us now step beyond language and into the silent power that shapes influence, builds trust, and defines leadership.

THIRTEEN
THE ELUSIVE OBVIOUS

Eyes are vocal, and they do speak
Anna Katharine Green

HOW MUCH IS SAID without uttering a word? A firm handshake, a subtle nod, the way someone enters a room—these silent actions reverberate far more than we often realise. Indeed, the words we speak are merely the tip of the iceberg. Beneath the surface, there is a far richer communication channel at play: the world of *non-verbal communication*. This elusive reality is what often determines the success or failure of our leadership interactions, as much as the words we say.

This is not to suggest that words lack importance, but rather to highlight that much of our instinctual reaction to leaders comes not from what they say, but from the myriad of signals they give off unconsciously. As leaders, we need to understand the power of the unspoken and harness it deliberately to lead effectively.

. . .

Evolutionary Roots

Why do we react so powerfully to non-verbal cues? The answer lies deep in our evolutionary past. Long before the invention of language, our ancestors relied on body language and facial expressions to navigate social dynamics, signal intent, and detect threats.

As an example, 'bid' is a small snippet of behaviour designed to reaffirm connection and, by extension, safety. Picture a quick glance by someone with which you instantly react with a smile or a nod. Mammals give one another bids because it is a part of our social engagement apparatus. Reptiles do not do bids.

Picture early humans gathering around a fire, wary of predators lurking in the shadows. A raised eyebrow, a tense posture—these were often the first clues to approaching danger or the intent of a rival. The ability to quickly interpret these signals was essential for survival.

Fast forward to the progressive office or boardroom, and those ancient instincts remain. Think of someone who is more powerful than you are, or someone you regard as an ally. You are on the other side of the busy room from them. You make casual eye contact and nod but do to receive a reciprocal gesture. Your gut will act as though something is wrong.

Mammals evolved with a safety sense that required sufficient cues of safety to be triggered: an apparent absence of danger was not enough. Afterall, there were an assortment of apex predators and poisonous creepy-crawlies, not to mention other humans, hiding waiting to strike. *Nothingness is somethingness* to our neuroception's threat detection.

OK, the threats are no longer sabertoothed tigers but the social risks—losing trust, missing opportunities, appearing weak—are still very real. Our brains are hardwired to read non-verbal cues faster than words. Non-reciprocation is a non-verbal cue as much as how confidently a person carry themselves.

To be a leader who commands respect and trust, we must acknowledge these instinctual mechanisms and learn to control the non-verbal messages we send. *It's not just what you say that matters—it's what you do and don't do.*

Case Story: **Bruce's Instinctual Leadership**

Consider the case of Bruce, a logistics operations lead, as he enters a critical meeting with his team. The stakes are high; the project is behind schedule, and Bruce needs to regain control. As he steps into the room, before he has the chance to speak, a wealth of non-verbal communication is already occurring.

Bruce's confident stride, the square set of his shoulders, and his open, relaxed posture send immediate signals of authority. His instinctual leadership begins the moment he steps through the door. Without saying a word, he projects competence and control. His team, sensing this, subconsciously adjusts their own posture, mirroring his energy and preparing for a productive discussion.

That's what *actually* happened but consider the counterfactual: Bruce enters the room with slouched shoulders, his gaze darting nervously around the table. He fidgets with his notes and avoids eye contact. The message is clear, even if it is unintended: Bruce is uncertain. And his team, picking up on these non-verbal cues, starts to feel uneasy. Trust in his leadership begins to erode, and before the meeting even begins, the dynamics are set against him.

The contrast in these two scenarios highlights how much leadership is conveyed non-verbally. *It's not what you say, it's how you say it—and more importantly, how you carry yourself when you say it.*

. . .

Projecting **Non-Verbal Cues**

The significance of non-verbal communication in leadership cannot be overstated. Our brains are tuned to pick up on subtle cues—facial expressions, posture, gestures—that influence how we perceive others. In fact, research consistently shows that up to *93% of the communication of emotions and attitudes are non-verbal*. If this statistic sounds staggering, it is because we tend to underestimate how much of our day-to-day interactions are driven by signals, we barely notice.

Let's break down some of the key components of non-verbal communication:

- *Body Language*: A leader's posture, gestures, and movement can signal confidence, openness, or defensiveness. Standing tall with open gestures conveys confidence and approachability, whereas crossed arms or slouched posture signals uncertainty or closed-off attitudes.
- *Facial Expressions*: The human face is capable of over 10,000 expressions, and even subtle changes can drastically alter how someone is perceived. A smile can disarm tension, while a furrowed brow can create discomfort. In shutdown and freeze states, the human face becomes flat and impassive, which might elude all but the most observant. As a leader, controlling your facial expressions is crucial in managing how others experience your presence.
- *Eye Contact*: Direct eye contact is one of the most powerful tools in a leader's arsenal. It signals attentiveness, trust, and connection. Avoiding eye contact can convey disinterest or insecurity, which can undermine authority and rapport.
- *Tone of Voice*: The way something is said often matters more than the content. A calm, measured tone instils

confidence, while a shaky or high-pitched voice can convey anxiety, even if the words being spoken are logical.

These cues are processed in an instant by those around us. And unlike spoken words, non-verbal cues are often unconscious and difficult to fake. Therefore, as a leader, controlling these signals—making them congruent with your words—is essential for effective communication.

TIPS FOR LEADERS

Now that we understand the critical role of non-verbal congruence, the next question is how can leaders improve their non-verbal skills? Here are some practical tips:

- *Awareness:* Start by becoming more aware of your non-verbal cues. Consider recording yourself in meetings or presentations and then review the footage to see how you come across. Are your gestures open? Is your posture confident? Awareness is the first step to improvement.
- *Posture:* Focus on standing tall with your shoulders back and chest open. Good posture signals confidence and authority. Avoid slumping or crossing your arms, as these can be interpreted as defensive or unsure.
- *Eye Contact:* Make a conscious effort to maintain eye contact, especially when delivering important messages. Direct eye contact builds trust and makes your audience feel seen and heard.
- *Tone and Volume:* Practice modulating your voice. Speak slowly and clearly, with a steady tone. Varying your volume to emphasise key points can also keep your audience engaged and convey confidence.

- *Controlled Breathing:* Your breathing pattern affects your voice and overall energy. Deep, steady breathing calms the body and mind, helping you project confidence and control.

By consciously controlling these aspects of non-verbal communication, you can greatly enhance your effectiveness as a leader. Remember, *people may forget what you said, but they will remember how you made them feel,* and much of that feeling comes from your non-verbal communication.

THE ELUSIVE REALITY of non-verbal communication plays a pivotal role in how you are perceived and, ultimately, how successful you are. It is not enough to speak well; you must also present yourself in a way that aligns with your words. By mastering the art of non-verbal communication, you can project confidence, build trust, and lead with greater authority. In the next chapter, we will explore how to refine and perfect these skills through specific techniques, allowing you to master the subtle but powerful world of non-verbal leadership.

FOURTEEN
NON-VERBAL ACUITY

A gesture cannot be regarded as the expression of a sentiment, which is meant to remain internal; it must be understood as a kind of declaration which tries to express itself publicly
Marcel Mauss

NON-VERBAL COMMUNICATION? As we explored in the previous chapter, it plays both a central and critical role in leadership. Now, it's time to move from theory into practice. Developing of non-verbal skills requires not only awareness but also the deliberate and thoughtful application of these tools in real-world situations. Just as a conductor wields subtle gestures to evoke harmony from an orchestra, a leader must use their body, voice, and presence to orchestrate an environment of trust, authority, and collaboration.

CASE STORY: A Non-Verbal Fumble

Let's examine two scenes that illustrate the power of a leader's body language. Picture Angus, the Managing Director of a supply chain business, announcing a major company culture change initiatives to one of his large distribution team called, *'Values & Behaviours'*.

The shop floor workforce is known for their irreverence to authority, which is one of the reasons for the new policy to begin with. Angus has prepared a detailed presentation, explaining the rationale and benefits of the change, a summary copy of which is placed on each chair prior to the meeting.

As he begins to speak, his non-verbal cues were telling:

- His shoulders are slightly hunched, suggesting tension or uncertainty.
- His gripping the podium tightly, his knuckles white with strain.
- His eyes dart around the room rather than making steady eye contact.
- His voice, though he is trying to sound confident, has a slight quaver.

Despite the carefully crafted words of his presentation, Angus's non-verbal cues are broadcasting uncertainty and anxiety. The workforce, picking up on these unconscious signals, begin to grumble and gesticulate about the proposed changes. They realise that they are about to have their wings clipped. As Angus continued to speak, the workforce started to point to their handouts and discuss things amongst themselves.

This makes Angus feel disrespected and embarrassed. Once he begins to blush, he stops talking and glares at the workforce. In shrill high-pitched voice, Angus demands respectful silence whilst he is speaking. Of course, this makes him appear flaky and, true to reputation, the audience is watching the spectacle in quiet grinning satisfaction.

Angus picks up the pace and, with the armpits of his blue business shirt wet with sweat, he gets through to the end of the presentation. When asked if there were any question, there were none. He thanks them for their time and permits them to return to work. Once the room is emptied, all but a few summaries were left behind on the chairs or had flopped into the floor.

So, that is what *actually* happened. However, consider an alternative reality, where Angus walks in with an upright, relaxed posture. He makes warm eye contact with team members as he welcomes everyone. He walks around shaking hands with people and acknowledging people he knows. His gestures are open and inclusive. His voice is steady, rich and resonant. He makes a few humorous remarks at his own expense that has everyone laughing together. Even before he delves into the details of the presentation, Angus's non-verbal communication has already sent a powerful message of confidence and reassurance.

In both versions, the content of Angus message is identical. But the non-verbal packaging dramatically alters how his words are received and interpreted by his team's instinctual brains. So, let's start to break down the elements of non-verbal cues and communication.

Points of Focus *in Communication*

Much like how sailors use the terms "port" and "starboard" to orient themselves in any direction, leaders can use distinct *points of focus* in communication to direct attention with precision. Understanding where to direct your focus—and that of your audience—can make or break the outcome of an interaction.

Here are four key points of focus that every leader should understand:

- **One-point**: This is when the leader focuses inward, looking down at themselves or their internal experience. Think of it as the introspective mode, where you are reflecting or gathering your thoughts. Leaders often use this when they pause to consider their next words carefully.
- **Two-point**: The leader makes *direct eye contact* with the person they're addressing. This is where rapport is built, where trust is established. Two-point focus is especially effective in one-on-one conversations or small meetings where personal connection is essential.
- **Three-point**: Both the leader and the listener direct their attention to an external *third point*, such as a document or a shared visual aid. This is particularly useful for discussing complex or sensitive topics, as it allows for a collaborative, less confrontational approach. It shifts the focus from being personal to being task oriented.
- **Four-point**: This is when the leader directs their focus to something outside the immediate conversation— perhaps *into the distance* or at an abstract point beyond the present moment. It's often used when discussing larger ideas, the future, or something conceptual. Leaders use four-point focus when they want to take the audience beyond the immediate and make them consider broader possibilities.

Example in Action:

Bruce is leading a discussion on a new project, *'Balancing Outbound Volumes'*, which is aimed at equalising the outbound volumes over several distribution centres. During the discussion, Bruce focuses on a three-point—a PowerPoint presentation to which he is gesturing to clarify the logistics.

But when the conversation shifts to the project's broader impact on the company's future, he adopts a four-point focus, gesturing outward as if to encompass larger ideas, pulling the team into a vision of what the future could hold. This shift subtly signals to the audience that they are moving from detail-oriented work to visionary thinking.

Peripheral Awareness

Peripheral awareness is another critical skill. Leaders must gauge their audience's reactions, even when not making direct eye contact. Sometimes cultural norms or specific situations discourage direct eye contact, but a leader can still be attuned to the room using peripheral vision. *Peripheral awareness* allows you to sense the energy, mood, and reactions of others without staring directly at them, which can be useful in tense negotiations or when speaking to a larger crowd.

Non-Verbal Pattern Clusters

On a spectrum of non-verbal pattern clusters, at one end there are approachable clusters and, on the other, there are credible clusters. The approachable cluster is typified with a movement, such as a bobbing head, swaying body, an angled posture and gesticulation; facial expressions, such as smiling and raised eyebrows; and a modulating voice pattern and upward inflexions. These behaviours connote safety and send an autonomic invitation to connect. A friendly flight attendant is the poster child for this cluster.

The credible cluster is typified with stillness, minimal facial expression, zero gesticulation, an upright posture, with a flat voice tone that turns down at the end of sentences. A great example of this would be an airline pilot, the poster child of which is Captain Sullenberger, who was played by Tom Hanks in the movie 'Sully'. His emotionless narrative as he pilots a plane full of passengers into the Hudson River is remarkable. It connotes safety due to perceived intelligence and competence.

As a thought experiment, imagine the flight attendant with the credible cluster, with complete stillness, zero facial expression and flat voice welcoming you aboard. Or a highly energised up-and-downy voice coming over the 'tannoy' excitingly telling you about the potential for bad weather and turbulence. I'm sure that you will find them comically incongruent with their new situations.

Of course, these clusters are extreme categories, however, they do give us clues on how we can modify our own non-verbals to be congruent for our teams given the different circumstances in which we find ourselves. In circumstances that benefit from a more cool, cognitive or sober approach, dialling up our inner 'Sully' would be highly advantageous. Reviewing and evaluating an important proposition, talking to the facts of an investigation or addressing people during an emergency are all times where we benefit the listener with increased credibility.

At the same time, in circumstances where a higher degree of energy, enthusiasm, empathy or human connection, dialling up our friendly flight attendant would better suit the moment. Meeting someone at a networking event, lightening the start of an interview or ending a meeting on an upbeat note are all example of where we benefit the listeners with increased approachability.

Eye-Hand Coordination

Effective leaders not only direct focus with their eyes but also with their hands. *Eye-hand coordination* helps guide the audience's attention to where the leader wants it to go. For example, if a leader gestures towards a specific point, synchronising their gaze with the movement of their hand, it creates a more powerful and cohesive message.

But there's a subtle art to this. There are two primary methods of gesturing that can shape how a leader is perceived:

1. *Bouncing the hand towards a point*: the movement makes the leader seem more approachable, encouraging a sense of openness.
2. *Holding the hand steady and vertical*: This communicates authority, signalling that the leader's message is serious and definitive.

The difference between these two gestures can change the atmosphere in a room. A bouncing hand invites dialogue; a steady hand commands attention.

Breath & Perception

The voice is an instrument, and breath is the bow that brushes over the vocal folds. Together, they shape how your message is perceived. A voice that is steady and aligned with controlled breathing carries authority; a voice paired with shallow, erratic breathing often projects insecurity or stress.

Breathing patterns directly influence vocal tone. When you breathe deeply, your voice resonates with warmth and steadiness. Shallow breathing, by contrast, produces a higher, more strained pitch, which can inadvertently signal nervousness or irritation.

Non-verbally, each pairing of tone and breathing creates a different perception to the observer:

- *Low Breathing + Approachable*: Signals warmth and reliability.

- *Low Breathing + Credible*: Conveys intelligence, authority, and composure.
- *High Breathing + Approachable*: Comes across as flaky or insincere.
- *High Breathing + Credible*: Risks being interpreted as hostile or impatient.

In the unlikely event that you want to be perceived as hostile, impatient, insincere or flaky, before addressing your team, take a moment to autoregulate yourself. Once you are breathing low, you are in the right state to project a positive emotional echo. If you aim to inspire trust, combine low, steady breathing with a measured, approachable undulations, throwing in a smile and flowy gestures. If you need to project clear authority, use the same low breathing, show less facial expression, be more still, and have flatter undulations with command-down intonation.

Your non-verbals are a vehicle for your message, but your breath pattern can support or undermine your communication. By practicing the interplay of these elements, you can align your intent with your impact, ensuring your communication resonates deeply with your audience.

NON-VERBAL SKILLS REQUIRE practice and awareness. Leaders who understand how to direct focus, modulate their voice, and engage with the room through subtle cues become far more effective in inspiring trust and authority. As with any skill, the more you practice, the more natural it becomes, allowing you to communicate effortlessly without needing to overthink the mechanics. In the next chapter, we will explore how to harness the power of the pause and breathing techniques to deepen your non-verbal influence.

FIFTEEN
THE SUBTLE SKILLSET

*Art is the imposing of a pattern on experience,
and our aesthetic enjoyment is recognition of the pattern*
Alfred North Whitehead

LEADERSHIP GOES BEYOND WORDS. It is created from gestures, silences, and the breath between sentences. See a leader entering a room where tension hangs like a storm cloud. Without raising their voice or uttering more than a word, they exude calm authority. Their movements are deliberate, their pauses resonate with meaning, and their breath—steady and measured—sets the rhythm of engagement.

Non-verbal communication is the silent language of influence. It wields more power than is often credited. From the depth of our breathing to the spaces between our words, non-verbal cues shape how others perceive us. These subtle signals determine whether we are trusted, respected, or dismissed.

In this chapter, we explore how to master the unspoken elements of communication. You'll learn to control the emotional atmosphere through breathing, punctuate your words with purposeful pauses, and align your voice with your intent. These are not mere techniques; they are tools to craft a leadership presence that inspires trust, amplifies authority, and fosters genuine connection.

By the end, you will see how silence, breath, and voice are not empty spaces or fleeting sounds—they are the scaffolding upon which skilled leaders build their influence.

Case Story: **Karen's Negotiation Success**

Let's take a closer look at Karen, a senior executive entrusted with negotiating a major contract for her firm. The stakes are high, and her counterpart—a seasoned negotiator—is known for dominating discussions with fast-paced, assertive speech. Karen feels the pressure mounting but recalls her preparation: she knows that controlling the flow of conversation without appearing confrontational will be key.

As the negotiation begins, Karen feels her pulse quicken. She instinctively wants to respond immediately to counter her opponent's aggressive tone. Instead, she pauses. She takes a slow, deliberate breath, grounding herself. The silence stretches, compelling her counterpart to lean back slightly, caught off guard by the unexpected stillness. Karen uses this pause to process the argument presented and carefully shape her response.

Karen takes a rapid *dual-mind reflection* and, using her internal dialogue, says:

"Stay composed. Own this silence. Let them fill it".

She consciously relaxes her shoulders, steadying her breath. The negotiation is no longer a verbal tug-of-war but a dance of controlled energy. Her deep, measured breathing sends subtle signals of confidence and control. She notices her counterpart beginning to slow down, mirroring her calm pace.

As the discussion intensifies, Karen's internal dialogue keeps her balanced:

"Breathe. Listen. Respond with clarity".

She poses thoughtful, open-ended questions and waits patiently for answers. The once dominant negotiator grows more reflective, unsettled by Karen's composure. The tension in the room slowly dissolves, replaced by a steady rhythm of dialogue.

By the meeting's end, Karen has secured favourable terms for her firm. Her success wasn't rooted in aggressive tactics but in the quiet strength of deliberate pauses and controlled breathing. Her poised presence turned a potentially combative negotiation into a collaborative exchange. Karen left the room not only with a signed contract but with her reputation solidified as a negotiator who commands respect without raising her voice.

LEADERSHIP BREATHING

Just as pauses can control the tempo of a conversation, breathing can control the emotional energy in the room. Deep, steady breathing helps leaders manage their own stress, while simultaneously influencing the emotional state of those around them.

When *probing for permission*, one very effective visual cue is 'BLIP' (Breathing Low Indicates Permission). We can use this insight to infer whether someone has given us permission. At the same time, when a leader breathes deeply, it sends an autonomic invitation to 'approach and connect'. It's the 'welcome' mat on your front step. Conversely, shallow, high breathing signals an autonomic warning 'I am danger. Stay away'. It's the 'beware of the dog' sign on your fence. Others can pick up on, often unconsciously, and will connect or disconnect, accordingly.

Let's explore two ways leaders can use breathing to their advantage:

1. *Managing Personal Stress:* When under pressure, the instinct is often to breathe rapidly and shallowly, which can increase stress. By consciously breathing deeply and slowly, leaders can activate the body's parasympathetic nervous system, which promotes relaxation and reduces the effects of stress hormones like cortisol.
2. *Influencing Others:* People tend to mirror the body language and breathing patterns of those around them. When a leader breathes calmly and deeply, other's mirror neuron induces others to do the same. This can be particularly useful in tense meetings or during difficult conversations. If the leader remains calm, it helps create a more relaxed atmosphere for everyone involved.

Example: Think of a leader entering a tense meeting where emotions are running high. By focusing on their breathing—taking slow, deep breaths—they not only keep their own nerves in check but also influence the breathing patterns of their team. As the leader speaks, the team members, noticing the calm, begin to mirror this slower, more relaxed pace. The atmosphere shifts from one of tension to one of constructive dialogue.

SILENCE PROJECTS INTELLIGENCE

Pausing during speech isn't just about giving yourself time to think—it also enhances how others perceive your intelligence. In Western cultures, pauses are often interpreted as a sign of thoughtfulness and depth. When you pause, it signals to your audience that you are considering your words carefully, which in turn makes your speech feel more deliberate and meaningful.

In fact, studies have shown that people who pause before responding are often rated as more intelligent, trustworthy, and composed. This is because a pause conveys confidence—you're not rushing to fill the silence with unnecessary words. Instead, you're allowing yourself space to breathe, reflect, and respond with clarity.

But what exactly makes a pause so powerful? It comes down to a few key elements:

1. *Visual*: During a pause, remain still with your mouth closed. Movement during a pause can signal nervousness or uncertainty. Breathing through your mouth reduces your perceived intelligence. So, hold your posture confidently, breathe through your nose and make direct eye contact.
2. *Auditory*: Silence is golden during a pause. Don't rush to fill the space with filler words like "um" or "ah." Let the silence speak for itself.
3. *Kinaesthetic*: Stay grounded. Keep your weight evenly balanced on both feet and avoid shifting or fidgeting. Your body language should reflect that you are in control of the moment.

When done effectively, a pause can raise your perceived intelligence quotient and reinforce your authority. It gives the impression that every word you utter has been carefully considered, which in turn elevates the impact of your message.

GETTING Attention Professionally

See yourself walking into a crowded room, the air buzzing with conversation. Laughter ripples through pockets of chatter, and the hum of voices fills every corner. It's time for you to give a speech, a briefing or make an announcement. As a leader, you must first earn the attention of the group before guiding them anywhere. And this begins with how you address them.

Your opening sets the tone, letting everyone know you have something important to share. So, start strong - with pulse of volume that is sufficient to punch through the loud rumbling hum of conversation and noise.

The bigger group or the louder the noise, the louder the vocal pulse of volume required. The smaller the group, the quieter the noise, the softer the pulse of volume needed. In either case, you're aiming for brevity, clarity and authority; because the important thing is not what you say but the way that you say it. Indeed, it could be as simple as, "Good morning!"

Once you have their attention, stop. Let the silence linger for two or three beats. This isn't hesitation—it's strategy. A deliberate *pause* is like the steady draw of breath before a leap, charged with energy and anticipation. While you pause, scan the room. Look at your audience calmly and purposefully. This moment of quiet creates intrigue and signals that what comes next is worth hearing. You've caught their full attention, now allow them to approach and connect with you.

When you begin to speak, *lower your voice*, as though you're sharing a secret that everyone in the room needs to hear. In smaller spaces, speak just below a conversational volume; in larger ones, ensure your voice still carries softly enough to make people lean in to listen. This shift from *strong to silence to soft* draws the audience closer with intent. It makes your message feel intimate and profound.

Competent vocal dynamics transforms the way you connect with others. A strong voice grabs attention; a pause builds anticipation; and a whisper draws people closer, creating a powerful rhythm that prevents monotony. Michael Grinder's *"ABOVE (Pause) Whisper"* technique is a beautifully crafted sequence. It taps into human instinct, where changes in tone signal importance and evoke emotion.

Tense Conversations

In 2006, I stood before seven hundred and fifty employees to deliver the words they feared most: they were being made redundant. Rumours had rippled through the workforce for weeks, softening the blow only in theory. Yet, when spoken aloud, the confirmation struck hard. To my left, a large screen displayed a summary of the plan. Blue background, deep yellow lettering—an intentional choice for clarity in the mottled light of the hall. Every phrase I spoke had been crafted with care, every pause deliberately placed to give the weight of the words room to settle.

I told them the site would close after a five-week inventory rundown. I explained that the decision was final, irreversible. For most, that very day would be their last. The remaining few would stay to wind things down. My voice was slow, measured. I spoke with a prosodic calm designed not to soothe in a patronising way, but to give them space to think, to breathe, to understand.

As I spoke, I watched it happen—that quiet moment when comprehension turns cold and heavy. Bodies stilled. Faces slackened. Eyes fixed not on me but on the slides behind me, as though hoping the text might contradict what their ears had heard. It was easy, almost painfully so, to think of the mental arithmetic each person was performing. Mortgage payments. School fees. Pensions. Futures rearranged in an instant.

This was no gentle crowd. The workforce had a history of industrial action, and violence wasn't beyond possibility. We had security in place, discreet but ready. Yet, not once was it needed. No shouts, no threats. Only silence. A few low murmurs after I finished, the sound of people cautiously stepping back into a world that had just changed. Within twenty minutes, each person had their letter, detailing entitlements and final payments. One by one, they left. Quietly. Thoughtfully.

Outside, two news vans idled, cameras poised to catch whatever anger or despair might spill out onto the pavement. Later that night, I watched the broadcast, the reporter calling it 'sickening'. Perhaps it was, though not for the reasons they intended.

That day, I learned something critical about leadership under pressure. In volatile moments, a leader's presence can either steady the ground beneath people's feet or shake it loose entirely. We knew the psychological responses we might provoke—anger, fear, paralysis—and we planned meticulously to guide people through it. This wasn't about manipulation but about responsibility. It was our duty to carry them through that moment with dignity.

PACE YOURSELF...

Leadership is not just about the words we choose but how we carry ourselves when delivering them. Preparing oneself before facing a group—especially when delivering difficult news—is a profound act of respect and courtesy to those we lead. Through thorough autoregulation, we stabilise our internal state. In doing so, we honour the emotional weight our audience must bear, ensuring that our own unregulated emotions do not spill over and burden them further. This is where the PACE Protocol supports not just our resilience but our ethical leadership.

To stand before a group and guide them through challenging news requires more than information—it requires presence, steadiness, and empathy. Leaders must first extend the principles of the PACE Protocol inward, grounding themselves so they can responsibly guide others through moments of volatility.

... to Lead

Too often, leaders rush into difficult situations half-prepared, weighed down by doubt or distraction. This unfocused, scattered mental state is unacceptable. Instead, a deliberate internal check-in reframes the moment:

"Have I given myself full permission speak with compassion, precision and credibility?"

This self-questioning is not indulgence—it is responsibility. If you cannot answer in the affirmative, you need to do the 'Inner Game' work. At the point of delivery is no place for the 'impostor syndrome' or public speaking anxieties. Your duty is to be autonomically regulated to be able to step fully into the role of *guide*, ready to carry both the message and its emotional consequences. If you are struggling to get there by yourself, accept it and seek coaching and support.

This is important because, in moments of high stress, our instinct is to fight, flight or freeze. Yet leadership demands grounded, credible and effective response. Before and during the engagement, ask yourself:

> "Is my next action driven by instinct, intuition or thoughtful choice?"

This simple question interrupts the automatic patterns that can derail effective communication. This pause is not hesitation, nor will it be perceived as such. Rather, it will be perceived as self-control. It is the conscious decision to respond with Primate purpose rather than Reptile reflex.

And, whilst leaders must learn to control themselves, leadership is not about control. It is about connection. However, stress severs connection and locks us in survival mode. As people mirror their leaders, we must ensure our bodies are transmitting *autonomic invitations* to 'approach and connect'. Ask:

> "Am I feeling good with full access my social engagement behaviours?"

This ensures that the leader as safety primed themselves. By doing so, they are emotionally available to the group, capable of meeting them where they are and leading them forward.

Resilience is not an improvised accident. Rather, it is prepared for through practice and contemplating future with a problem-solver's mindset.

"What scenarios can I mentally prepare for to stay composed and present?"

This question needs to be answered thoroughly. However, most leaders and influencers fail to give it it's due diligence. They believe that, once they've written their speech or presentation, or pulled together their support material for their difficult discussion, that they're done. They are not. Mentally rehearsing successful outcomes means integrating new learnings and understandings in a useful way.

In the PACE Protocol, we refer to this as *embedding new strategies*. These strategies can be new *inner game* patterns of thinking and feeling. They can be *outer game* observational, conversational and behavioural patterns. They can be verbal and non-verbal patterns. Its purpose is to get the speaker's particular brain and body ready to deliver a particular message to a particular group, in a way that best maintains the accuracy of the information and the safety of all parties. This is so important that I shall reprise 'Preparing to Win' at the end of the chapter

... for Bad News

So, before engaging in a challenging conversation, it's essential to centre oneself within the framework of the *PACE Protocol*. After ensuring that you have given yourself full permission to have a successful (if challenging) encounter, check in with your instinct/cognition status with a *Dual-Mind Reflection*.

Instinct (Thinking Fast)	Cognition (Thinking Slow)
• Rapid pattern recognition • Driven by experience • Quick, intuitive decisions • Effective in familiar contexts • Emotionally charged reactions	• Analytical reasoning • Deliberate and logical • Time-consuming decisions • Mitigates emotional biases • Effective in novel situations

Here a quick and effective technique that Michael Grinder calls: *Break & Breathe Twice*:

- *Break*: Snap out of the negative state into which you are going. Change your physiology is a highly effective way of doing this: shift your position by standing up, or sitting back, or look in another direction, etc.; then
- *Breathe*: Take two deep, intentional breaths. Regain your mental clarity, your cognition and inner calm.

I have found this to be very practical technique with which to assert *agency over instinct* before, during and after difficult encounters. I like it, first, because it's simple: you're breathing anyway, so breathing a little differently on purpose is an easy way to exercise personal agency over one's instinctual *autonomic nervous system*. Second, in meetings, it is a quick, covert and low concentration technique.

Either way, the technique allows me to easily phase-transition into *connect and socialise* by applying one or more technique from Part 1. 'The Inner Game'. For me that's spinning a good feeling – calm, jovial, fascinated. Then I engage my peripheral vision, which keeps me alert to what's happening around me, regardless of on what I am focused.

That's what I do. Try it for yourself. If it doesn't work for you, ditch it. If it works OK, tweak it, so it works better. The point isn't doing my particular technique but finding your own 'go-to' autoregulation techniques. Whatever your recipe ends up being, my *state management* strategy prepares me to approach a challenging conversation clear headed and with my full social engagement functions available to me.

BASELINE CALIBRATING

As the conversation initiates, you are almost always going to begin in 'two-point' communication. As you do so, ensure you take full advantage by observing and understanding the other person's state and responses. This is done through *sensory acuity*, paying close attention to the sensory details of the other person's verbal and non-verbal cues. *Then calibrate to their state at that moment.*

If this is your first encounter, this becomes your baseline for the conversation, and you can watch for variation as the discussion progresses. This allows you to track as the other person becomes more or less socialised, mobilised or immobilised. If you already have a baseline from prior engagements, contrast (seek for differences) with how they are behaving against their baseline. Are you beginning the conversation from a point where they are more or less socialised, mobilised or immobilised than their baseline?

As always, this includes noting visual, auditory, and kinaesthetic (VAK) signals, as well as breathing patterns. By concentrating on what is genuinely happening for the other person, you remain attuned to the other's *Instinct-Cognitive* status... then comes the moment you've been (not) looking forward to... share the bad news!

. . .

How Not to Get Shot

Delivering difficult news is one of the most challenging tasks a leader faces. Missteps can erode trust, damage relationships, and escalate tension. Michael Grinder's communication technique offers a powerful solution by guiding leaders through emotionally charged conversations with greater composure and professionalism. This approach empowers both messenger and recipient, fostering understanding and collaboration even in tough moments.

Grinder's method comprises three core strategies designed to prevent defensive reactions and encourage constructive dialogue: shifting to third-person phrasing, using visual communication, and introducing a third point of focus. Together, these techniques can transform how difficult conversations unfold.

Go Third-Person: In high-stakes conversations, the words we choose can either defuse tension or intensify conflict. Using third-person phrasing, particularly through the passive voice, naturally creates a calmer, more neutral tone compared to the immediacy of first- and second-person language. This shift directs attention to the situation rather than individuals, reducing personal blame and emotional charge.

For example, saying "Respect was not maintained" focuses on the issue, whereas "I feel disrespected" or "You didn't follow the procedure" personalises the problem, often triggering defensive reactions. In tense situations, this subtle linguistic shift fosters problem-solving rather than blame.

However, leaders must balance the passive voice with active, solution-oriented statements to maintain clarity and accountability. For example, "Let's find a way to ensure procedures are followed next time" promotes collaboration without assigning blame.

Go Visual: Humans are wired to process visual information more effectively than text alone. Presenting challenging information visually—through letters, slides, or diagrams—empowers the recipient to absorb the message at their own pace. *You* control how the content is framed: plain or technical language, formal or informal tone, structured layouts, and visual aids like graphs or images.

Visual aids act as emotional anchors, engaging the analytical Primate Brain and tempering the Reptilian Brain's fight-or-flight response. In Polyvagal Theory terms, visuals support the vagal brake, sustaining social engagement behaviours. This approach promotes clarity and retention, especially for complex or emotionally sensitive information.

Consider how a financial report, presented as a clear graph rather than dense text, softens the impact of poor performance data. When recipients can revisit the information independently, they regain agency, reducing stress and emotional reactivity.

If the recipient becomes overwhelmed, cognitive function can drop by up to 35%. Allowing them to re-engage with visual material mitigates this effect, offering space for understanding and thoughtful response.

Go Three-Point: Direct eye contact during difficult conversations can intensify emotional states, whether positive or negative. Imagine two lovers sharing a gaze across candlelight versus two rivals locked in a stare-down. This is two-point communication—an intense, direct energy exchange.

Introducing a third focal point, such as a document or visual aid, diffuses this intensity. By redirecting attention to the information rather than the messenger, the emotional load is reduced. This stabilises the interaction, preserving cognitive clarity and emotional balance.

Orally delivering bad news forces the recipient to depend solely on the messenger, increasing stress and reducing personal agency. Repeated clarifications can lead to the messenger becoming associated with negative emotions. Providing a shared reference point (like a handout or chart) allows both parties to engage with the content without amplifying interpersonal tension.

Ultimately, by proactively priming one's own safety first and applying Grinder's *'How Not to Get Shot'*, leaders (and other messengers) remain connected, approachable and credible. In doing so, create the conditions for sound cognitive problem-solving and group collaboration, all which will lead to a more resilient future.

In turn, their team (or other recipients, like bosses, clients and peers) feel more connected, engaged and in control. Becoming competent in these strategies will not only defuse tension but also strengthen relationships and build trust. Start integrating these PACE aligned strategies into your daily practice and resilient team outcomes

... for Future Wins

Neuro-resilient rehearsal isn't about dreamy wishful thinking. It's about conditioning your mind and body to perform with clarity and confidence under pressure. By vividly pre-living a desired outcome, leaders can strengthen their emotional readiness and align their actions with their goals.

Consider how elite athletes prepare for high-stakes moments. Before ever stepping onto the field or into the ring, they have already 'lived' the victory in their minds. They visualise every detail—the sound of the crowd, the feel of the environment, the precise movements they'll execute. This mental preparation primes their nervous system and sharpens their focus, guiding their real-world actions toward that desired outcome. Champion boxer and cultural icon, Muhammed Ali, called this technique, 'future history'.

You can apply this same strategy to leadership. Before entering a challenging conversation or delivering difficult news, take time to mentally walk through the experience. Visualise yourself standing confidently, speaking with composure and empathy. See what you will see—the room, their faces, your slide show, your notes in your hand. Hear what you will hear—the chatter before you begin, your voice as you deliver the message, their voices asking questions and making comments. Feel what you will feel—the emotions, the sensations, your energy levels.

Then switch from two-point to four-point and witness yourself. See how you look and how you move; hear your vocal pattern, hear your words. Did you need to get their attention with an "ABOVE (pause) Whisper", was the room already deathly silent or did a cordial initial conversation morph into the main discussion?

If it is a volatile situation:

- Are you using third-party language, depersonalising your initial statements and answers to any question.
    - What questions are likely to be asked?
    - What topics must be discussed in the passive voice
- Did you deliver the message visually?
    - Are you using handouts or individual computer devices?
    - Is there a slide show?
- Are you engaged in a three-point conversation
    - Standing in front of a group, referring to slide show off to the side?
    - Sitting at a table, at 90 degrees to the listener, using your pen to step them through the information?

This process is more than visualisation—it's strategic mental conditioning. By rehearsing success, your mind becomes attuned to recognising opportunities and responding to challenges effectively. Your actions naturally align with your preparation, making you more adaptable and resilient.

Try this practice the next time you face a difficult task:

1. *Set the Scene*: Find a quiet space and close your eyes. Imagine the setting in detail—where you'll be, who will be present, and the atmosphere in the room.
2. *Engage Your Senses*: What do you see, hear, and feel in this moment? Listen to your voice calm and steady, your posture strong yet approachable.
3. *Visualise Success*: Picture yourself navigating the situation smoothly. See guiding others toward the best possible outcome; hear yourself responding thoughtfully; and feel your body moving smoothly and feel how good you feel.
4. *Anchor the Feeling*: Squeeze your thumb and index finger—because what is fired together is wired together—let your body become a resource you can draw upon.

The PACE Protocol's a very thorough *future pacing*, designed to *embed new strategies* by detailed mental rehearsal, so that your desired responses easily and naturally in that future moment. It is another example of *agency over instinct*, as you programme yourself to feel and act differently in the future. In doing so, you are mentally preparing thoroughly to be the best version of yourself. You are chasing perfection vainly, rather you are making sure that a lot of little things will be done well.

LEADERSHIP IS OFTEN MISTAKEN for the loudest voice in the room or the sharpest command issued. Yet, as this chapter has shown, true leadership lies in mastering the subtleties—the silent pauses, the steady breath, the poised stance. These understated elements are not ancillary to leadership; they are foundational. They shape perceptions, guide emotions, and foster trust, often without a single word being spoken.

Karen's negotiation success exemplifies how a composed breath and strategic pause can shift the dynamics of power. The deliberate control of silence, the conscious modulation of voice, and the intentional use of body language are not theatrical performances but authentic expressions of authority and empathy. They are tools that signal to others, "You are safe. We can get through this together."

In moments of high tension, it is the leader's regulated presence that can anchor a group, transforming volatility into stability. The PACE Protocol, the "Break & Breathe Twice" technique, and the strategic use of visual and third-point communication are more than techniques—they are disciplines of emotional intelligence and social mastery. They enable leaders to respond with thoughtfulness rather than react with instinct, ensuring that even the most challenging messages are delivered with dignity and clarity.

These subtle skills not only help navigate difficult situations but also elevate moments of success. They make great moments greater and bad moments better, allowing leaders to amplify celebration and soften hardship. The ability to adapt and apply these techniques across varying circumstances strengthens a leader's capacity to inspire and unify their teams.

This subtle skillset, when honed, does more than prevent miscommunication or manage conflict. It builds resilient teams, fosters emotional safety, and creates environments where people feel connected and understood. The ability to project calm, invite trust, and command attention without force is a leader's greatest strength.

As you move forward, remember that your leadership presence is crafted not only by what you say but by how you breathe, pause, and engage. Each silent moment and every measured breath become a building block in the architecture of trust and influence. By practising these subtle skills, you are not just leading—you are guiding with intention, inspiring with authenticity, and cultivating resilience within your teams.

Master these nuances, and you will find that influence is not seized but naturally extended to those who lead with presence and poise.

SECTION FIVE SUMMARY

The most important thing in communication is hearing what isn't said
Peter Drucker

Leadership is often thought of as verbal persuasion—the power of eloquent words and compelling arguments. However, beneath every great leader's voice lies a subtler, more profound layer of influence: non-verbal communication. Section Five, *Non-Verbal Leadership*, illuminates this silent yet powerful domain, showing how gestures, tone, posture, and even breathing shape perceptions, fosters emotional and psychological safety, and deepen trust.

Non-verbal leadership is not a supplementary skill—it is the foundation upon which all effective communication is built. Our evolutionary heritage has hardwired us to react instinctively to non-verbal cues—faster than we process words[1]. Long before language, body language and vocal tone signalled danger, communicated intent, and fostered cooperation. Today, those same primal sensitivities still govern how we trust and follow others, even in boardrooms and meeting spaces. Leaders who fail to recognise this instinctual layer risk miscommunication and mistrust, while those who master it inspire confidence and unity.

At the heart of non-verbal leadership lies *congruence*—the alignment between what is said and how it is expressed[2]. When a leader's words and non-verbal cues are in harmony, their message resonates with authenticity and authority. Conversely, misalignment—like nervous fidgeting paired with confident words—creates discomfort and doubt, eroding trust. Effective leadership begins with self-awareness: recognising and refining these unconscious cues is essential to influencing others with credibility.

This section takes readers on a journey from understanding non-verbal basics to mastering nuanced leadership presence.

- **Chapter 13, *The Elusive Obvious*,** introduces the power of non-verbal cues, tracing their evolutionary roots and explaining how they silently shape interactions before words are spoken. It highlights how non-verbal communication is processed instinctively, influencing trust and perception.
- **Chapter 14, *Non-Verbal Acuity*,** deepens this understanding by offering practical tools to refine non-verbal communication. Frameworks such as the PACE Protocol and techniques like the "Break and Breathe" method teach leaders how subtle adjustments in posture, eye contact, and tone can transform their presence and guide team dynamics.
- **Chapter 15, *The Subtle Skillset*,** explores advanced strategies—like the power of the pause, breath control, and third-point communication—that allow leaders to maintain authority and empathy even in high-pressure scenarios. Case stories, such as Karen's negotiation success and Angus's failed presentation, illustrate how non-verbal

SECTION FIVE SUMMARY

mastery can either strengthen or undermine leadership outcomes.

Non-verbal leadership is not just about making a good impression—it is about creating an environment of trust, safety, and resilience. By mastering the silent language of leadership, you can amplify your impact, foster deeper connections, and guide your team with both authority and empathy. These subtle skills are the cornerstone of building high-performing teams that can thrive in complexity and adapt to change.

Techniques Introduced in Section Five

1. **Non-Verbal Congruence**[3]: Aligning verbal and non-verbal cues for highest impact.
2. **Posture Awareness**[4]: Using open, upright posture to convey confidence.
3. **Eye Contact**[5]: Building trust and attentiveness through direct gaze.
4. **Tone Modulation**[6]: Controlling vocal tone to convey authority or approachability.
5. **The Power of the Pause**[7]: Using silence to create thoughtfulness and authority.
6. **Breath & Perception**[8]: Understanding how high/low breathing affects how you are perceived
7. **BLIP**[9]: Using deep breathing to project calm and co-regulate group emotions.
8. **Peripheral Awareness**[10]: Sensing audience reactions without direct observation.
9. **Points of Focus**[11]: Shifting between inward focus, direct engagement, task-oriented focus, and conceptual vision.
10. **Non-Verbal Pattern Clusters**[12]: Switching and blending *approachable* and *credible* patterns based on context.

11. **Eye-Hand Coordination**[13]: Guiding attention with synchronised gestures and gaze.
12. **How Not to Get Shot**[14]: Arranging non-verbals to minimise emotional discussions.
13. **Above (Pause) Whisper**[15]: A sequence for gaining and maintaining attention.

SECTION SIX
NARRATIVE & UNITY

> *I suggest that the story of the last few years strongly indicates that human action is nonlinear, that time and place matter a great deal*[1]
> **Ralph Stacey**

Leadership in times of transition tests the very limits of influence. As explored in Section Five, *Non-Verbal Leadership*, leaders must master the silent language of gestures, tone, and presence to shape group dynamics and create safety. Yet, non-verbal communication alone cannot guide people through the complexities of change. To move teams from paralysis to progress, leaders must give voice to the unspoken. They must craft stories that bridge the gap between instinctive trust and purposeful action, turning ambiguity into clarity and fear into hope.

Section Six, *PACE Storytelling*, introduces the art and science of using narrative as a leadership tool in complexity. It builds on the non-verbal foundation of Section Five by adding words into the mix —not just any words, but those deliberately chosen to transform how people think, feel, and act.

Stories for Sense & Meaning

Stories hold a unique power in leadership because they operate on two levels. First, they help us make sense of objective reality, providing coherence in a world that is often chaotic, ambiguous, and uncertain. This is where the work of Ralph Stacey, Dave Snowden, and Meg Wheatley becomes invaluable. In complex systems, where cause and effect are unclear, stories reveal patterns, uncover tacit knowledge, and foster shared understanding. As Snowden's Cynefin framework teaches, storytelling becomes a vital sense-making tool in environments where traditional logic falters[2].

Second, stories shape subjective experience. They do not merely describe reality; they transform how people perceive it. Drawing on insights from Stephen Porges' *Polyvagal Theory*[3] and Daniel Kahneman's work on cognitive biases, storytelling taps into the instincts and emotions that govern human behaviour. A well-told story can reframe adversity as opportunity, align people's emotional states with a shared vision, and inspire action even in the face of uncertainty.

Reframing & Transforming

Change is the crucible of leadership. Transitions—whether they involve uniting disunited teams, navigating crises, or inspiring bold ventures—amplify disconnection, mistrust, and fear. In such moments, logic and directives alone are insufficient. Leaders must connect with the human experience of those they lead, weaving narratives that validate emotions, foster safety, and align diverse perspectives.

Ralph Stacey reminds us that human action is nonlinear and deeply influenced by context. Leaders cannot impose order on complexity, but they can guide people through it by crafting stories that resonate. These narratives act as bridges, linking individual roles to a collective mission and transforming isolated efforts into cohesive action.

Consider the fractured dynamics of a team divided by silos, mistrust, or resistance to change. A leader employing narrative framing does not merely communicate operational goals—they tell a story that illuminates the "why" behind the mission. The story transforms individual contributions into indispensable pieces of a greater whole, fostering trust, empathy, and shared purpose.

A Framework for Influence

PACE Storytelling provides leaders with a structured approach to crafting and delivering these transformative narratives. Rooted in insights from complexity theory, neuroscience, and Richard Bandler's human change technologies[4], the framework bridges the gap between sense-making and meaning-making. It equips leaders to navigate two critical tasks:

1. **Sense-Making**: Revealing the hidden dynamics of complexity, helping teams understand their context and navigate ambiguity.
2. **Meaning-Making**: Shaping how people interpret their circumstances, enabling them to reframe challenges, align with shared values, and act with purpose.

By addressing both the objective and subjective dimensions of human experience, PACE storytelling transforms leadership into an art of influence and alignment. It is designed to resonate across the three levels of the human mind:

- **Instinctual (Reptilian Brain)**: Engaging survival instincts through high-stakes risks and vivid imagery[5].
- **Emotional (Mammalian Brain)**: Fostering connection, trust, and empathy through shared experiences.
- **Rational (Primate Brain)**: Providing logic, vision, and intellectual stimulation to guide decision-making.

Story Structures for Transitions

Stories become indispensable during transitions, which are often fraught with fragmentation and paralysis. Whether leading a team fractured by silos, navigating a crisis that threatens morale, or inspiring a stagnant group to embrace bold change, leaders must tell stories that address their teams' instinctual, emotional, and rational needs.

For example, in moments of disunity, stories can bring people together by reframing divisions as opportunities for collaboration. During times of despair, stories can inspire hope by positioning adversity as the beginning of a shared journey toward renewal. And when teams are too comfortable to change, stories can spark the imagination, showing them a future worth striving for.

The stakes for leaders in these moments are high. Without effective narratives, they risk being perceived as irrelevant, obstructive, or even threatening. But when leaders succeed, the rewards are profound: they create environments where individuals feel safe, valued, and empowered to act.

A Preview of What Lies Ahead

The chapters in this section equip leaders to craft narratives that meet the demands of three iconic leadership transitions:

Chapter 16: Of Sense & Meaning focuses on the dual power of storytelling as both a sense-making and meaning-making tool. Leaders learn to unify teams and foster resilience through narratives that engage instinct, emotion, and intellect. By framing reality, building shared understanding, and inspiring collective purpose, this chapter demonstrates how storytelling provides clarity amidst complexity. It introduces the evolved PACE framework and examines practical applications of sense-making through Dave Snowden's insights and meaning-making through Richard Bandler's transformative approaches.

Chapter 17: "Band of Brothers" explores the unifying power of storytelling during challenging transitions. Using the *Unity BRIDGE* framework, leaders discover how to dismantle silos, align diverse groups around shared values, and establish psychological safety. The chapter highlights how storytelling can transform fractured teams into cohesive, resilient units, with real-world examples that illustrate its fractal application across organisational scales.

Chapter 18: "Les Misérables" delves into how leaders can guide teams through moments of despair to renewal and growth. Drawing lessons from historical figures like Nelson Mandela, Mahatma Gandhi, and Abraham Lincoln, the chapter highlights the power of narrative to rebuild trust, align values, and inspire resilience. It introduces the *FOCUS UP* framework, offering leaders tools to transform crises into opportunities for collective progress, uniting teams with compassion, clarity, and purpose.

These chapters provide leaders with actionable tools like Unity BRIDGE and FOCUS UP to influence group dynamics, rebuild trust, and inspire transformation. By mastering the art of storytelling, leaders can create neuro-resilient organisations that thrive in complexity, uniting their teams under shared values and a common vision.

The Leadership Challenge

Unlike world leaders with teams of strategists and speechwriters, most organisational leaders must rely on their instincts, experience, and resolve to guide teams through uncertainty. They are the mid-level managers, CEOs of small nonprofits, and owners of struggling family businesses who bear the weight of these responsibilities alone. This section is written for them, offering practical, actionable frameworks to help them craft stories that inspire, unite, and move their teams forward.

Leadership begins with what is unsaid, but it is the words leaders choose—woven into compelling narratives—that turn silence into strength and complexity into opportunity. As we delve into *PACE Storytelling*, consider the stories you want to tell. What will you say to shape the future of your teams, organisations, and communities?

SIXTEEN
OF SENSE & MEANING

The most powerful person in the world is the storyteller.
The storyteller sets the vision, values,
and agenda of an entire generation that is to come.
Steve Jobs

STORYTELLING IS A PRIMARY SKILL — it is not something to be added once the 'real' leadership work is done. History and neuroscience confirms this. The leaders who shaped history were those who shaped the stories that defined it.

The Steve Jobs quote encapsulates the timeless influence of storytelling. In a world filled with complexity and uncertainty, leaders who can craft and share compelling narratives possess a unique power: the ability to connect, align, and inspire.

Consider a ship navigating turbulent seas. Without a unifying story to guide its crew—a narrative compass to bring purpose and direction—they risk drifting aimlessly, consumed by confusion and distrust.

Conversely, a shared story transforms a fragmented group into a cohesive team, resilient and focused on reaching their destination. This is the transformative power of storytelling.

For leaders, storytelling is more than an art—it is a necessity. It bridges the gaps between chaos and clarity, sense-making, meaning-making, teaching, and individual growth and collective purpose. It is not just a tool for communication but a means of fostering meaning and unity.

This chapter explores why stories matter, how they enable sense-making and meaning-making, and how leaders can use frameworks like PACE to inspire and sustain their teams. Leadership, at its core, is *storytelling*.

Why Stories Matter

Since the first humans, stories have been our most enduring tool for survival, understanding and sharing knowledge. From ancient cave paintings to futuristic digital media, stories have shaped our understanding of the world, our place within it, and our relationships with others. Stories are far more than entertainment; they are blueprints for survival, teaching us lessons, values, and shared purpose.

Consider a small group of early humans huddled around a fire. One recounts a successful hunt—where to find prey, which dangers to avoid, and the strategies that led to triumph. In that moment, the storyteller is not just sharing an event but transferring knowledge, building connection, and fostering confidence. Thousands of years later, though the contexts have changed, the essence of storytelling remains the same: it binds people together, passes down wisdom, and mobilises collective action.

Stories engage the human mind in ways facts and data alone cannot. Stories have an extraordinary ability to touch the deepest recesses of our minds, engaging not just our cognition but also our emotions and instincts. Stories play right across the Reptilian, Mammalian and Primate Brains, captivating us in ways that transcend facts and data.

The Reptilian Brain responds to stories which contain high stakes risks. A tale of survival, with its vivid descriptions of peril and triumph, grips this part of the brain. Think of a story where a character narrowly escapes a predator or endures an unrelenting storm. Our Reptilian Brain reacts as though the events were happening to us, "right here, right now". It sharpens our focus, heightens our awareness, and sets our bodies on edge, ready for action.

The Mammalian Brain operates as the centre of our emotional life. This brain thrives on connection and compassion, finding resonance in stories of love, loss, friendship, and community. When a story portrays a parent sacrificing for their child or friends overcoming adversity together, this brain floods us with emotions. These narratives release oxytocin, deepening our sense of trust and attachment. A well-told story does more than entertain; it builds bridges between the teller and the listener, creating a shared emotional reality.

The Primate Brain is humanity's evolutionary crowning achievement, the realm of abstract thought, logic, and imagination. The Primate Brain loves puzzles, thrives on moral dilemmas, and savours complex ideas. It delights in stories that challenge conventional wisdom or offer intellectual surprises. Consider a plot twist that recontextualises the entire narrative or a philosophical parable that forces us to question long-held beliefs. Such stories invite reflection, spurring us to connect the dots, consider alternatives, and perhaps even change our worldview.

A well-told story weaves together instincts, emotions, and intellect, creating a seamless thread that speaks to the gut, heart and head alike. A masterful narrative works by weaving together survival stakes, emotional resonance, and intellectual depth into a rapture of engagement.

Think of the classic hero's journey: the protagonist faces life-threatening danger (Reptilian Brain), wrestles with emotional challenges and relationships (Mammalian Brain), and ultimately achieves a transformative insight or victory that carries profound meaning (Primate Brain). It is no wonder that such stories endure across cultures and generations—they speak to the entirety of our humanity.

This interplay of brains also explains why stories are evolutionarily effective. For the Reptilian Brain, they act as simulations, preparing us for real-world risks and opportunities. For the Mammalian Brain, they provide a shared emotional language that strengthens social cohesion. And for the Primate Brain, they encode complex knowledge in a form that is both memorable and compelling. In this way, stories are not just thrilling; they are tools of survival, connection, adaption and resilience. For leaders, these characteristics of storytelling hold a transformative power.

A leader who understands how stories engage instincts is not at the mercy of group emotions but can guide them. By shaping narratives that resonate with all three levels of cognition, leaders move teams from reactivity to resilience.

Consider Nelson Mandela, who united a fractured nation not through statistics or policy details but by framing a narrative of hope, justice, and shared destiny. His story inspired belief and action, demonstrating that stories do not just communicate—they galvanise.

During times of uncertainty, stories become even more essential. They provide clarity and direction, helping teams navigate ambiguity and align around a shared vision. Without a guiding story, anxiety spreads, and disunity takes hold. But with one, leaders can foster resilience, purpose, and progress.

Stories matter because they connect us to each other, shape how we see the world, and inspire us to move forward together. To lead, the leader must tell stories that matter to the people they lead.

The Sense-Maker

Dave Snowden helps people and organisations grapple with the volatility, ambiguity and uncertainty that define complexity. He has developed an array of ways to glimpse into complexity to get some inkling into what is really going on. Snowden is a *sense-maker*.

Sense-making is the process of creating coherence from chaos, a vital skill in leadership. In today's fast-changing environments, leaders often face ambiguity and complexity that challenge even the most robust plans. Here, storytelling emerges as a powerful tool—not just for explaining complexity, but for navigating and transforming it into shared understanding.

At its core, sense-making connects disparate observations into a unified narrative, aligning individuals toward a common purpose. Dave Snowden, a leading thinker in complexity science, highlights storytelling's role in this process. In his *Cynefin Framework*, Snowden argues that in complex systems, cause and effect are not always clear. Leaders must instead use tools like *Anecdote Circles* (augmented in Chapter 11 into PACE Surfacing), which gather micro-narratives—short, lived experiences—to reveal patterns within the system.

Consider a manufacturing company transitioning to semi-automation. Tensions between shop floor workers and management escalate, and productivity plummets. Instead of imposing a top-down solution, leaders facilitate small-group discussions to capture employee narratives. Workers share concerns about job security, pride in craftsmanship, and frustrations over exclusion from decision-making. These narratives, collected through *Anecdote Circles*, reveal underlying emotional dynamics: resistance is not rooted in opposition to automation but in a lack of trust and a low sense of agency.

Using these insights, leaders craft a new narrative. This story acknowledges workers' fears, celebrates their expertise, and frames semi-automation as a collaborative effort to improve outcomes for everyone. The narrative transforms resistance into engagement, fostering trust and alignment.

Snowden's approach also incorporates *Safe-to-Fail Experiments*, small-scale interventions designed to explore solutions without fear of major repercussions. For example, the company might involve workers in co-designing workflows for semi-automation. By framing these experiments as part of a shared story—one where employees are active contributors rather than passive recipients—leaders create a sense of ownership and shared purpose.

It integrates logic and emotion, engaging both the Primate mind that seeks patterns and the emotional core that craves meaning. A purely rational explanation may satisfy the intellect but leave people disengaged. A compelling story, on the other hand, weaves facts and feelings into a relatable narrative that inspires action.

Sense-making through storytelling is particularly critical in complex systems where solutions are not linear. Leaders who embrace this approach can illuminate hidden dynamics, align diverse perspectives, and guide their teams through uncertainty. As Snowden's work demonstrates, stories are not static—they are living tools that adapt and evolve with the challenges they address.

In the hands of a skilled leader, storytelling is the compass that turns ambiguity into shared understanding, enabling teams to navigate complexity with clarity and confidence.

THE MEANING-MAKER

Richard Bandler is a teacher. His teaching is more than just the transmission of information, although there is that aspect. Rather, his teaching is the art of transforming meaning and, in doing so, change the way people think, feel and behave afterwards. Bandler is a *meaning-maker*.

Stories, with their unique ability to inspire and engage, are the ultimate teaching tool. They connect with people on a deeper level, bypassing resistance and fostering new perspectives. Leaders who master storytelling as a teaching method can guide their teams to embrace change and grow beyond their limitations.

Richard Bandler, co-creator of Neuro-Linguistic Programming (NLP), recognised the transformative power of storytelling. Amongst the array of storytelling and linguistic tools that he has created, Bandler uses techniques like *reframing, nested loops,* and *heteromorphic metaphors* to help people see challenges differently and unlock new possibilities. For Bandler, stories are active agents of change, capable of bypassing conscious resistance and speaking directly to the unconscious mind.

Consider a leader addressing a team paralysed by fear of failure. Instead of delivering a lecture on resilience, the leader shares a personal story: how they faced rejection early in their career but reframed those setbacks as stepping stones. The story subtly plants a new perspective—failure is not an endpoint but part of a larger journey. Without explicit instruction, the team begins to see challenges as opportunities for growth.

Bandler's *nested loops* technique illustrates how storytelling can embed profound lessons. Picture a story within a story, each layer adding depth and nuance. For example, Bandler might recount a client overcoming anxiety by learning to reframe their fears, interwoven with a metaphor about a river carving its path through obstacles. Bandler engages all three levels of the triune brain to get the desired response from the listener.

As soon as he detects the response, without concluding the story, he switches the story in search of his next desired response. He closes the loops, by concluding the stories, in the reverse order from which they were originally told. It is a beautiful piece of highly effective meaning-making where the listener has internalised its message within each triune level, often without realising it.

Reframing is especially powerful in leadership and a critical leadership ability to reframe the narratives surfaced during the sense-making phase. A team that views obstacles as insurmountable will struggle to act. But when those same obstacles are framed as challenges to overcome, the team gains momentum and determination. For instance, a struggling organisation might be galvanised by a story of past crises where collective effort led to success. The leader's narrative does not deny current difficulties but places them within a broader arc of resilience and renewal.

Storytelling also fosters connection. When a leader shares a story, it humanises them, allowing the audience to see themselves in its characters and scenarios. This shared identification builds trust and empathy, essential foundations for any transformation to take root.

Meaning-making through storytelling is not a soft skill; it is the most effective way a leader can successfully engage with and influence the complex adaptive system of the Hive Mind. To paraphrase Bandler:

"By influencing the way that the Hive Mind thinks and feels, you influence the way it behaves"

By crafting narratives that reframe perspectives and inspire new ways of thinking, leaders empower their teams to move beyond limitations. They are not merely imparting knowledge, they transform its meaning, creating a bridge to transform the group—one story at a time.

In leadership, meaning-making is about more than delivering solutions. It is about creating the conditions for growth, fostering group resilience, and inspiring belief in the groups own agency to alter their current circumstances—all through the timeless power of storytelling.

From Sense to Meaning

Superficially, sense-making and meaning-making might seem like separate processes. Sense-making focuses on interpreting ambiguity and uncovering tacit knowledge, while meaning-making reframes this knowledge into explicit insights that can inspire action. Yet, these two processes are deeply intertwined, forming an iterative cycle where each amplifies the other. Storytelling is the bridge that connects them: storytelling is both the input into and the output out of these combined processes. They enable leaders to move seamlessly between sense-discovery and the transformation of meaning.

Consider a river system as a metaphor. Sense-making is the network of tributaries collecting streams of tacit knowledge—anecdotes, emotions, and experiences—from the landscape. Meaning-making channels this raw material into a focused current, shaping it into triune brain understanding that provides direction. Without sense-making, meaning-making lacks depth and breadth. Without meaning-making, sense-making risks remaining diffuse and unfocused.

Without both, just like the proverbial butterfly whose flapping wings cause a tornado on the other side of the planet, organisations and societies can be subject to destructive positive feedback loops. Think of the 'Arab Spring' which spread like a wildfire destabilising and toppling regimes across North Africa and the Middle East; or the spontaneous riots and attacks on illegal migrants across England because of three children being stabbed to death.

Consider a tech start-up grappling with market disruption. Through sense-making techniques, the leadership gathers micro-narratives from employees, uncovering fears of obsolescence, pride in innovation, and frustrations with unclear priorities. These insights reveal a fragmented organisation, but they also point toward hidden strengths. The leader then uses storytelling to reframe these narratives, weaving them into a story of resilience and adaptability that hits all parts of the triune brain. The new narrative aligns the team's understanding and inspires a shared commitment to innovate.

This iterative process underscores storytelling's dual role: it illuminates hidden dynamics while reframing them into actionable insights. Leaders skilled in storytelling can guide their teams through ambiguity by uncovering the group's unconscious patterns and aligning them with a collective vision.

By bridging sense-making and teaching, storytelling transforms complexity into clarity, fostering both understanding and action. In an era where adaptability is paramount, mastering this dynamic is essential for leaders seeking to inspire, align, and sustain their teams.

The PACE Storytelling Model

The *PACE framework* has already demonstrated its versatility in this book. Its applications evolving through multiple repurposing to meet the demands of different leadership challenges.

First introduced in Chapter Eight, the PACE Protocol was designed as a tool to help coaches and practitioners track their progress during *safety rupture repair sessions*. Of course, the client was oblivious to the phases through which they were being transitioned. However, the protocol served as a *straightforward 'outer game' map and compass*, allowing practitioners to keep oriented and on track as they move sequentially through the rupture repair process.

PACE functions like a *flight navigation system*, guiding leaders and coaches through a structured sequence where each phase builds on the last.

1. *Set the foundation* – Establish initial safety conditions, ensuring readiness to engage by probing for permission.
2. *Navigate the journey* – Address the key objectives of the current phase, ensuring progress and alignment.
3. *Clear for transition* – Once the criteria for the current phase are met, transition naturally into the next stage.
4. *Land and integrate* – When the final phase is complete, exit the structured process, allowing the new insights and strategies to take root.

This sequential approach provided clarity and structure, helping coaches teach their clients about their own 'inner game', training them how to repair their own safety ruptures. That is, by the end of the session, the client walks away with a set of new understanding and ways of thinking, with which to sustain a their socially connected state: in simple terms, they learn how to 'feel safe from the skin in'.

Later, in Chapter Nine, PACE was adapted for 'inner game' support for *leader autoregulation and event prep*, empowering leaders to stabilise their internal states before 'outer game' engagements.

In Chapter 11, Dave Snowden's *Anecdote Circles* idea was augmented, in the first instance, into *PACE Strengths*, which had the narrow focus of strength-led conversations, to surface tacit knowledge and latent narratives towards the improving at the local level.

In the second, *PACE Surfacing*, had no topic of focus. It sought to uncover raw emergent narratives, from plural and diverse sources. Each occasion a narrative is recorded, it is treated as a data point. These data are analysed, grouped into types, clusters and patterns, from which inferences can be drawn, and distributed throughout the organisation.

While all these earlier versions were guided through an imperceptible phased process, they were worked because their application was in constrained environments, such as small group conversations, with specific goal criteria: achieve 1) safety and permission, 2) 'inner game' control, 3) 'outer game' sociability and 5) new learnings and understanding. In addition, the leader, coach or facilitator was present throughout and would respond to the vicissitudes of these conversations, guiding participants through to a conclusion.

In short, it was a 'closed system', a straightforward process, operating for a short duration, on a consciously chosen end goal.

However, the leadership function of 'narrative framing' is not about surfacing emergent narratives. It is about reframing those narrative data-points towards a useful way of thinking about what is happening and, by proliferating that new frame, influence the beliefs and behaviours of the Hive Mind.

Of course, this is easier said than done. The Hive Mind is not a closed system, it is an open one. It is not straightforward, it is complex. It is not of short duration, it is an ongoing long-term entity. It does not have a specific consciously chosen goal, it has multiple conscious and unconscious, overt and covert, interests and agendas. Some of these are mutually compatible, some incompatible; and some are cooperative and competitive.

In environments of *volatility, uncertainty and ambiguity*, leaders face multiple points of instability. These points of instability are due, in part, because of the complex and adapting dynamics of their system (Hive Mind) within which they are operating. They are also due to how this system responds to the larger external complex and adapting system, in which their Hive Mind is a participant.

Exhausted leaders find themselves constantly tackling sporadic, plural and diverse problems. Their traditional linear management methodologies fail to get control over the nonlinear dynamics, both within and from without, the system in which they lead. The Hive Mind does not respond to top-down logic alone. It requires a story compelling enough to override its internal contradictions. To navigate these challenges, the PACE framework was modified to address the iterative, concurrent, and responsive needs of *complex adaptive systems*.

The PACE Storytelling Framework

At its core, *PACE Storytelling* helps leaders navigate complexity by addressing both the socio-psychological and behavioural dimensions of group dynamics. It provides four key points of ongoing focus that guide the crafting and delivery of stories:

1. *Prime & Probe:* Leadership storytelling begins with establishing group safety. By creating an environment where people feel heard and valued, leaders gain implicit permission to influence. This step ensures that the audience is receptive and engaged, setting the stage for deeper connections.
2. *Agency over Instinct:* Narratives must empower groups to rise above instinctual reactions, such as fear or defensiveness, in order to enable collective, thoughtful responses. 'Leadership credibility' as expressed in their verbal and non-verbal cues, as well as their cognitive reasoning and action, is an important variable.

Framing challenges as opportunities is only believable if it is delivered by leaders who are perceived to be grounded, credible and intelligent. Such leaders are able to guide their teams to act with intentionality rather than impulsivity.

3. *Connect and Socialise:* Effective narrative framing fosters unity and alignment by creating shared meaning and group cohesion. Narratives should resonate with collective values and goals, transforming a diverse group into a unified team

with a common purpose; or a distressed group towards somewhere better.
4. *Embed Strategies & Meanings:* The ultimate goal is to influence thoughts, feelings, and behaviours of the Hive Mind in a way that builds flexibility and resilience. By embedding new meanings into the group's narrative, leaders can foster adaptability, innovation, and sustained progress in the face of complexity.

Phase Shift

In its *narrative framing* form, the prior 'phases', each with its own goal/ exit criteria, become *Unity-Stabilising Inputs* (USIs). Once initiated, like the Hive Mind, the USIs are ongoing and have no exit criteria. Rather, they have operating criteria, which are monitored and sustained through leadership interventions.

USIs are not phases to complete but *rhythms to maintain*—like spinning plates, each element requires continuous attention during and after their roll out:

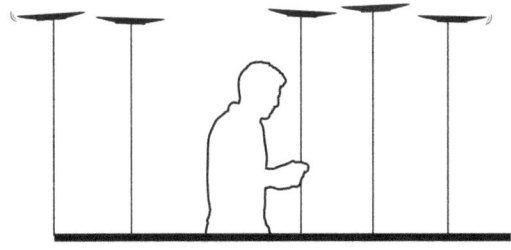

1. *Start the first stabiliser* – Establish psychological safety as the first key input and ensure it remains steady as permission is secured.
2. *Expand stability* – Introduce additional stabilisers while maintaining those already in motion.
3. *Sustain the balance* – Adapt to shifting conditions, reinforcing alignment as needed.
4. *Intervene as required* – Leadership is a constant act of recalibration; respond proactively to instability before it cascades.

This adaptation turns the PACE Protocol into a flexible framework that supports group resilience. Much like a juggler in a 'spinning plates' routine, leaders must ensure that each USI—once initiated—remains stable and responsive to the group's shifting needs. This monitoring often combines *hard metrics* (e.g., KPIs) with *soft metrics* (e.g., trust surveys or anecdotal insights), ensuring that narratives remain grounded in the group's lived experiences.

Importantly, these performance indicators will be *indicative*, not definitive: they are proxies for what is really happening. As such, these indicators themselves should be subject to revision. Whilst such metrics are often omitted, they should form part of an AAR in the aftermath of a 'surprise'. Because misplaced trust and confidence in nondefinitive KPIs can erode quickly and strip leadership of its perceived credibility.

As Mark Twain put it:

> "It ain't what you don't know that gets you into trouble. It's what you know for sure that just ain't so".

Or, as my colleague, Michael Grinder, says:

> 'Surprise is the enemy of competence'.

The importance of sensitive and reliable performance indicators is important, for example:

- How do you know exactly whether you have broad-based permission for a strategic initiative?
    - If you are operating under that assumption falsely, the success of your initiatives will be compromised.
    - In the event of failure, you may be convinced that it was the project's execution that was at fault.
    - But it might well have been the Hive Mind's willingness to adopt the initiative that was the issue.

Storytelling for Resilience

Through this evolution, the *PACE Storytelling framework* transforms leadership narratives into adaptive, *living frameworks*. Drawing on *Polyvagal Theory* and *Neuro-Linguistic Programming* (NLP), PACE addresses group safety, autonomy, cohesion, and resilience as ongoing processes. Among its many strengths, it equips leaders to:

1. Take disunited and estranged groups and unite them.
2. Guide teams from challenging circumstances to better outcomes.

The result is more than effective communication; it is the creation of a *neuro-resilient group dynamic*, where individuals and teams alike thrive in the face of complexity. By evolving from a protocol into the iterative flexibility of USI frameworks, PACE ensures that leadership storytelling becomes the foundation for *growth, adaptability, and long-term success*.

Leaders who influence effectively do not simply tell a story once and expect it to hold. They tend to it, reinforce it, evolve it. Unity-Stabilising Inputs (USIs) allow leaders to maintain the delicate balance between reinforcing a shared reality and adapting to new challenges.

USI Frameworks

PACE Storytelling is a very useful generic framework is a quick and easy go to and can suit small to medium organisations well. It's easy to understand, teach and review. In addition, over the years, I have developed other USI frameworks, many of which do not fall within the PACE structure. However, I would like to introduce you to two which were derived from PACE, each refined to better suit two specific leadership contexts.

- *'Unity BRIDGE'* focuses on uniting disparate groups, such as merging teams or diverse stakeholders, by emphasising shared values and goals.
- *'FOCUS UP'* guides leaders in moving teams from adversity to progress by framing challenges as stepping stones toward a brighter future.

These frameworks maintain PACE's iterative nature, ensuring that narratives evolve alongside the group's needs.

The next two chapters are dedicated to exploring these two frameworks in depth. By examining Unity BRIDGE and FOCUS UP, leaders will gain practical tools to stabilise group cohesion, foster trust, and guide their teams through the complexities of current challenges.

Key Takeaways

The PACE framework transforms storytelling from an abstract concept into a structured, actionable leadership tool. By addressing safety, agency, connection, and resilience, it equips leaders with a narrative compass that fosters trust and alignment. Whether uniting fractured teams or navigating crises, PACE extends beyond communication to create resilient group dynamics.

Two derivative frameworks, Unity BRIDGE and FOCUS UP, were developed to enable leaders to craft living narratives that evolve with their teams. In complex systems where uncertainty prevails, PACE-style frameworks empower leaders to transform ambiguity into progress, inspiring sustainable growth and shared purpose.

STORYTELLING IS NOT an ornament of leadership; it is its essence. A well-told story does more than transmit information—it reorganises perception, reshapes belief, and reorients action. It transforms disorder into clarity, doubt into resolve, and disunity into shared direction. It is, in every meaningful sense, the bridge between complexity and understanding.

Steve Jobs once claimed that the storyteller is the most powerful person in the world, setting the vision, values, and agenda for the future. He was not speaking metaphorically. Every major shift in history—every great movement, every profound transformation—has been preceded by a story that reframed reality. The Enlightenment did not begin with a set of policies but with a shift in narrative about reason, liberty, and human potential. The Civil Rights Movement gained momentum not through statistics but through stories that made injustice visceral, undeniable, and urgent. Leadership, at its core, is the craft of narrative shaping.

Yet, storytelling in leadership is not mere rhetoric—it is a structural necessity. A leader without a story is a ship without a compass, drifting at the mercy of external forces. Teams without unifying narratives fragment under pressure. Organisations without compelling stories fail to cohere, leaving individuals navigating uncertainty alone. A well-structured story is not just a means of making sense of the present but an invitation to participate in a shared future.

This chapter has explored the two intertwined dimensions of narrative: sense-making and meaning-making. Sense-making, as Dave Snowden argues, is how we detect patterns within complexity, gathering micro-narratives and surfacing implicit tensions before they become fault lines. Meaning-making, as Richard Bandler demonstrates, is the art of reframing those patterns, embedding new significance into familiar experiences, and unlocking fresh pathways for action. The most skilled leaders oscillate between these two processes, using stories to reveal, reframe, and realign.

The PACE framework, introduced in earlier chapters, provides a structured approach to this process. First, a leader must 'prime and probe', creating the psychological safety necessary for narratives to take hold. Without this, even the most compelling story will be met with resistance. Second, they must empower agency over instinct, ensuring that storytelling does not merely evoke emotion but mobilises action. Third, they must connect and socialise, crafting narratives that bind individuals into a collective, making the story a lived experience rather than an abstract ideal. Finally, they must embed strategies and meanings, ensuring that narratives are not fleeting moments of inspiration but enduring, adaptive frameworks for resilience.

A static story dies. A living story evolves. The next chapters will explore how frameworks like Unity BRIDGE and FOCUS UP extend these principles, providing structured tools for leaders to forge shared identities and mobilise teams through adversity. These are not theoretical exercises; they are essential practices for leading in a world where uncertainty is not an exception but the rule.

So, the question is not whether you will tell stories. You already do. The question is whether you will tell them consciously, with precision and purpose, shaping the minds, emotions, and instincts of those you lead. In a world brimming with competing narratives, only those who master the craft of storytelling will have the power to set the direction for what comes next.

What story will you tell? And who will follow you because of it?

SEVENTEEN
"BAND OF BROTHERS"

> *Narrative is critical to our landscapes, relationships, interactions, and actions; <u>it defines us</u>*[1]
> **Dave Snowden**

"BAND OF BROTHERS" was more than a book; it was a testament to what happens when individuals, bound not by blood but by purpose, forge a unity stronger than circumstance. Easy Company's story is not unique to war; it is the same thread that runs through every organisation that must transform itself from fragmented individuals into a cohesive whole. The title of this chapter is not just a nod to history—it is a lesson in what it takes to build something greater than the sum of its part.

Have you ever walked into a new workplace where half the faces are unfamiliar, where old alliances linger, and where the future feels uncertain. How does a leader turn that loose collection of individual and cliques and uncertainty into unity? Snowden's insight reminds us that narrative is not just how we communicate—it's how we cohere. It is the thread binding individuals into a collective, the bridge between unfamiliarity and shared purpose.

Bringing people together is not enough. Co-location does not create collaboration. A leader's true challenge is not in moving bodies into the same space, but in weaving a shared identity. Take, for instance, the opening of a new distribution centre (DC), a transition that reveals the full complexity of unity in motion.

Indeed, this transition story is about a large-scale *consolidation* involving the closure of four previous sites, a significant reorganisation of roles, and a mixture of both voluntary and involuntary redundancies. It's a period marked by profound change and, naturally, a mix of apprehension and optimism among team members.

The workforce now encompasses individuals from various levels—shop floor workers, supervisors, administrative staff, and management—each bringing different experiences and expectations. And as they come together, the need to forge a unified identity is crucial. Without this unity, the new DC would struggle to establish the foundation it needs to thrive.

Much like the Hive Mind discussed in Chapter 10, an organisation's strength lies not only in its individual components but in the ability of these components to operate harmoniously as one. However, unity doesn't simply materialise from co-location or organisational mandates. Instead, it's cultivated, nurtured, and strengthened through deliberate efforts to break down barriers, rally around shared values, and establish a common purpose. This is where the *Unity BRIDGE* framework comes into play.

True unity isn't about removing differences—it's about synchronising them. A great orchestra does not demand that every instrument play the same note; it demands that each musician contributes to the whole. The Unity BRIDGE framework operates on the same principle: it transforms individual differences into collective strength, aligning diverse perspectives into a single, dynamic force.

Each *'Unity Stabilising Input'* (USI) of the framework supports the overall goal of creating a single, resilient entity out of many subgroups or factions. Through this framework, the new DC team will transition from disparate groups to a unified force, bringing out the best in each member and fostering a truly collaborative environment. While narrative shapes the collective identity of a workforce, the patterns of interaction within that workforce also play a critical role in maintaining unity.

Fractal Structure

> *I see fractals in the turbulence of human life*
> *each action may seem independent,*
> *but they are part of a larger self-organizing system*
> **Benoit Mandelbrot**

In Chapter 10, we explored collective intelligence as an emergent phenomenon, often seen in complex adaptive systems. Mandelbrot's observation reminds us that what appear to be isolated actions—decisions, conversations, or team efforts—are in fact interconnected, shaping and being shaped by the larger dynamics of the system. This principle holds true in organisations, where even small acts or statements can ripple across teams, influencing morale, communication, and performance.

In a distribution centre, for example, a single decision about scheduling can cascade through the system, amplifying trust or sparking friction depending on how it is perceived. This interconnectedness is characteristic of what I prefer to call "living systems," which we see in nature—storm formations, locust swarms, or starling murmurations.

These systems exhibit repeating patterns at different scales, providing stability while remaining adaptable.

Leadership is not about grand pronouncements; it is about repeated patterns of connection. The strength of an organisation, much like a fractal, is found in the symmetry between small moments and large outcomes. A single act of trust—one recalibration, one alignment—creates ripples that reorganise the entire system. These Unity Stabilising Inputs (USIs) provide leaders with tools to influence the system both broadly and in specific situations, from strategic initiatives to team meetings.

These *negative feedback loop*s are like a built-in self-correction system. Think of it as your car's cruise control. When the car goes too fast, the system automatically slows it down; when it's too slow, it speeds it up. This keeps the car at a steady speed.

In organisations, negative feedback loops work the same way. They help maintain balance by automatically adjusting to keep things on track. For example, if trust between teams starts to drop, a good leader might notice the signs—like miscommunication or tension—and take action to rebuild trust before it causes bigger problems.

It's called "negative" not because it's bad, but because it reduces or counters something that's going off-course—like slowing a car that's speeding or stopping a team conflict before it escalates. These loops help organisations adapt and stay stable in changing environments.

Like the repeating patterns of a fern leaves at large and small scales, Unity BRIDGE ensures consistency and coherence across all communication levels, creating alignment even in dynamic and unpredictable environments. Leaders are not simply following sequential steps; they are managing multiple elements simultaneously, addressing emerging challenges to maintain equilibrium.

For example, if communication breaks down between shop floor workers and supervisors, it may destabilise other areas like trust or collaboration. Leaders must act swiftly to restore alignment, much like a juggler doing a spinning plates routine will stabilise a plate that is beginning to wobble. This iterative, non-linear approach enables leaders to keep the system cohesive while adapting to real-time conditions.

By understanding the fractal nature of organisations, leaders can better anticipate ripple effects and intervene effectively. Unity BRIDGE not only helps establish initial alignment but ensures that this alignment persists through the inevitable turbulence of a living system.

Snowden's narrative insights and Mandelbrot's fractal patterns equip leaders with practical tools to achieve unity in complex organisations. Together, they form the backbone of the Unity BRIDGE framework.

Unity BRIDGE Framework

USI 1: **B**reak Down Barriers

The first endeavour towards creating unity within any organisation, especially one as large and complex as a consolidated distribution centre (DC), is to address and dismantle the barriers that naturally arise between different groups and roles. Picture a landscape divided by fences and gates, each segment occupied by teams that have developed their own ways of doing things, honed by years of familiarity. These 'territories' serve a purpose—they define roles and responsibilities. But they also breed suspicion, limit collaboration, and create a fragmented organisational culture.

In our DC example, the individuals from the four closed sites bring with them different work practices, habits, and often an ingrained sense of loyalty to their former teams. Each group has its unique history, shared experiences, and perhaps even internal jargon or shorthand that feels foreign to others.

Now, imagine these groups coming together under one roof. It's like asking players from different sports to form a single team. While they may all be 'athletes', their training, language, and approaches differ. To succeed as a team, they must learn each other's strengths, respect each other's perspectives, and adopt a shared way of working.

CROSS-FUNCTIONAL INTERACTION

The practical approach to breaking down these barriers begins with creating opportunities for meaningful interaction. This isn't just about placing people from different teams at the same table; it's about designing situations that require real collaboration. Cross-departmental projects and collaborative training sessions are essential first steps.

For instance, as the DC team adapts to new semi-automated processes, a training programme that includes shop floor workers, supervisors, admin staff, and management can facilitate shared learning. Not only does this approach break down practical knowledge silos, but it also builds mutual understanding as each group gains insights into the other's contributions and challenges.

Additionally, open forums and structured dialogues can create safe spaces where team members can voice their thoughts without fear of judgment. Leaders must encourage transparency and demonstrate that they are receptive to input. When team members across roles see that their insights are not only heard but also respected, trust begins to grow organically. In this way, the psychological fences start to come down, making it harder for an 'us vs. them' mentality to persist.

Key Insight: *Breaking down barriers is about more than erasing physical or logistical divides; it's about dismantling the psychological walls that often isolate groups within organisations. With that in mind, humans form cliques all the time. With respect to the 'plate-*

spinning' point, leaders need to be alert to old cliques can come back as well as new cliques spontaneously emerging.

For the new DC team, this means moving beyond individual roles and creating a shared culture where everyone's perspectives are valued. Unity begins to flourish when team members recognise each other's contributions as essential.

USI 2: **R**ally Around Shared Values

Once the physical and psychological barriers begin to dissolve, the next step is to rally the team around shared values. Shared values act as the unifying core of an organisation, providing a collective foundation that goes beyond job titles or functional roles.

Consider shared values as the roots of a large tree; while the branches may spread in different directions, each branch draws nourishment from the same source. In organisations, values like respect, resilience, and quality serve this function, uniting diverse individuals under a common purpose.

In the case of the DC, rallying around shared values is especially important. The team includes people who have had very different experiences, not only in terms of job roles but also in terms of workplace culture.

For example, shop floor workers may have priorities that differ significantly from those of administrative staff, just as supervisors may have different viewpoints compared to senior management. However, by focusing on shared values, we can transcend these differences.

Building a New Culture

For the DC, core values such as *Respect, Resilience,* and *Quality* provided a guiding framework. Respect ensures that every member—regardless of role—feels valued and acknowledged for their contributions. Resilience emphasises the importance of supporting each other through the transition, recognising that each person is adapting to new systems, environments, and expectations.

Commitment to quality unites the team around a shared goal of excellence in everything they do, from logistical efficiency on the shop floor to meticulous data management in admin roles. Leaders can actively reinforce these values through regular "values-alignment" sessions, where team members from different roles discuss how these values translate into their specific tasks.

For example, during a session focused on quality, a shop floor worker might share how their attention to detail in packing ensures accuracy, while an admin staff member could explain how timely data entry supports the entire chain of distribution. Such sessions enable the team to see how each role, in its unique way, upholds the organisation's values, fostering mutual appreciation.

Key Insight: *Shared values are more than aspirational statements; they are the glue that binds diverse teams together. Values, therefore, have to be manifested in all aspects of organisation life. With our plate-spinning analogy in mind, leaders need to be vigilant for any degrading of values in action. If respect, resilience and quality are no longer the lived values, some other values will be. Regardless of whether they are espoused in official documents, the lived values are those in operation.*

By rallying around these values, the new DC team can create a collective identity that bridges differences, reduces fragmentation, and enhances cooperation.

USI 3: Inspire with Vision

As barriers are coming down and shared values in generalising through the organisation, inspiring the team with a convincing and compelling vision is the next 'plate to spin'. Extending the metaphor, if shared values are the roots of the tree, vision is the sunlight, drawing everyone upwards and guiding their collective endeavour and growth. A clear and resonating vision is essential, especially during times of transition, as it provides direction and instils a sense of purpose in each member.

Inspiring with vision, however, requires more than setting a direction; it demands communication that is both vivid and meaningful. Leaders must create the connective tissue between the abstract and the practical, making the vision feel personal and immediate.

Allan, the General Manager of the new DC, encapsulated his vision in his opening speech to the team. His message, titled *"Many Boats to One Ship,"* set the tone for unity, resilience, and shared purpose. This is how he described his process of using the *Unity BRIDGE* framework:

"I was struggling to write my 'big speech' to a bunch of people, many who were pissed off by the closure of their old place of work, some that were new and starry-eyed, and many that would rather have been made redundant. This included many of my management team. So, I decided to use the UB framework like a jelly-mould, pouring into it the flavour of jelly that would support the unification process".

We will review and analyse Allan's speech in detail once we've covered all the USIs.

USI 4: **D**efine Actions

With barriers broken down, shared values established, and vision communicated, the next USI in *Unity BRIDGE* is to translate that vision into reality by defining specific actions. Defining actions in *Unity BRIDGE* operates at both broad and detailed levels, transforming vision into reality whether through large-scale initiatives or individual team tasks. This flexibility ensures that each team member has a clear sense of purpose and direction, aligning daily efforts with overarching goals.

For instance, defining actions for the new DC could include creating a roadmap for the training programme, setting milestones for semi-automated system integration, and establishing channels for regular progress feedback. Each action provides clarity, making the transition process more manageable and ensuring that every team member knows their role in the shared journey.

Key Insight: *Defining actions transforms vision into reality. By outlining specific steps, leaders provide clarity, reducing ambiguity and ensuring that every team member understands their role in the collective journey.*

USI 5: **G**et Commitment

Now that actions have been defined, the next USI is to ensure commitment. In *Unity BRIDGE*, commitment-building is a fractal process, where leaders build dedication not only to broad initiatives but also in specific settings like meetings, training sessions, and individual check-ins. This approach transforms commitment from a passive agreement into an active engagement with the team's shared goals.

Building commitment in the new DC can involve a variety of methods, from informal discussions where team members voice their hesitations to formal agreements on shared goals. This creates an environment where everyone is actively participating, strengthening unity through each interaction and ensuring accountability.

Key Insight: *Commitment turns unity into a cohesive force. By fostering genuine buy-in, leaders transform passive agreement into* *active engagement, ensuring that the team's energy is consistently aligned with its goals.*

USI 6: **E**xcite to Act Now

The final USI in *Unity BRIDGE* is perhaps the most immediate: Excite to Act Now. Enthusiasm and motivation are core elements of *Unity BRIDGE* that energise teams at every scale, from setting milestones on major projects to fostering enthusiasm in daily tasks. By applying these principles in all interactions, leaders ensure that the team's energy translates into progress, sustaining unity and direction.

For example, setting short-term goals—such as achieving a specific milestone in the semi-automation process—can create immediate momentum and highlight the team's progress. Recognising early successes in team meetings or individual conversations helps maintain enthusiasm, reinforcing unity with each achievement.

Key Insight: *Excitement and urgency turn unity into momentum. By creating a sense of immediate purpose, leaders ensure that the team's energy translates into tangible progress, propelling them forward on their shared path.*

Unity **BRIDGE** in Action

Here is Allan's speech[2], a direct example of how a unification vision can be communicated with empathy, inclusiveness, and clarity:

Speech Excerpt: "Many Boats to One Ship"

Good morning, everyone.

Today marks the opening of this new distribution centre—a milestone for the company and a big step for all of us here. It's the first day in our new workplace, one that brings with it lots of changes.

For many of us, these changes have stirred up mixed emotions. I want to address those feelings openly because I know this journey hasn't been easy, and I believe that by acknowledging the challenges together, we can steer our way through them together.

First, let's acknowledge the obvious—some of us are here from different centres that were closed to make this one possible. We have colleagues who are no longer with us due to redundancies, some who didn't want to leave and others who did.

This situation has created uncertainty, and I understand that many of you may still be adjusting. You're not alone in feeling that way. Each of us has had to adapt, and it's normal to feel some strain and disorientation.

But I ask that we look at this as an opportunity. Today, we're coming out of many boats to one ship. This ship—the new DC—isn't just going to be a place of work; it's going to be a community where every person here, regardless of their role, brings something valuable.

Our shared values—resilience, respect, and quality—are what unite us, regardless of title or tenure.

My vision is simple and ambitious: to become not just a well-oiled machine but a supportive, innovative, and resilient team that becomes the standard for efficiency and collaboration in our business.

Think about a future where we're not just adapting to new systems but we're first in class in operating them, where each of us feels free to contribute ideas, offer solutions, and grow alongside this centre.

To start, we have a few initial steps to ease the transition: comprehensive training sessions, regular check-ins, and open channels for feedback. I urge each of you to engage fully, take part in these activities, and bring your strengths to the table. You have my commitment, and the commitment of every manager and supervisor here, to support you and to ensure that your voice is heard.

Together, we're building a workplace that we can all be proud of, one where our combined efforts will not only create a better environment for us but set an example in our industry. Let's make today the start of a new journey, a shared journey, where we move forward not as loose collection of boats but as one united ship.

Thank you.

To UNDERLINE, Allan wasn't a professional speechwriter: he was an operations leader. His words and sentiment were simple, clear and to the point. Yet, by using the Unity BRIDGE framework, he gave himself the psychological permission to:

1. Surrender to the framework's overall USI structure, including their sequence
    1. Focus on the things he wanted to say personally, within each of the USIs, to this particular assortment of managers, supervisors and shopfloor workers, in that particular business unit, at that particular moment in time.

Allan's talk not only exemplifies the mission of *engaging for unity*, it highlights the framework's fractal characteristics: not only can the USIs be used to structure the communications strategy, developed a dashboard of KPIs, it was used the compose the speech. As this pattern was allowed to be replicated at these different scales, a cohesive and adaptable narrative structure emerged.

Later in the transition, there were a few key milestone moments. Some milestones had gone well, some not so well. At these moments, Allan and his leadership team leaned on *Unity BRIDGE* framework for these high-impact moments.

As Allan put it:

"Retaining cohesion amongst stakeholders when the news is good is a lot easier than when the results are poor. We used the UB structure regardless. The focus was always on working together better, being true to the principles and priorities, and moving in the right direction as a unit.

If the results were great, we talked about unity, commitment and pride in our work. If the results were poor, we did the same. We presented our outcomes this way to the business, to ourselves and to the shopfloor."

How ALLAN's Speech Influences the Hive Mind

Allan's speech effectively engages all three levels of the Triune Brain (reptilian survival instincts, mammalian bonding emotions and primate cognition), which influence how groups respond behaviourally. By crafting his message in a way that resonates with these levels, Allan not only communicated his vision but also inspired action and built trust across the organisation.

1. Break Down Barriers

- *Instinct*: Allan acknowledges the uncertainty and strain caused by redundancies and site closures, addressing the team's basic survival fears. This transparency helps reduce the instinctual defensiveness and fight-or-flight responses that often accompany significant change.
- *Emotion*: By validating mixed emotions and shared struggles, Allan builds an empathetic connection, fostering emotional safety and reducing feelings of isolation or resentment.
- *Cognition*: Allan uses clear, logical language to explain the reasons behind the changes, offering a coherent narrative that helps the team intellectually process the situation and see a path forward.

2. Rally Around Shared Values

- *Instinct*: Shared values like resilience, respect, and quality act as grounding principles, providing a sense of stability in a time of upheaval. These values align with the brain's need for safety and predictability.
- *Emotion*: Allan reinforces emotional bonds by highlighting how these values unite the team, creating a shared identity that fosters belonging and trust.
- *Cognition*: The articulation of shared values also appeals to higher-order thinking, helping team members connect their roles and tasks to broader organisational goals and cultural ideals.

3. Inspire with Vision

- *Instinct*: The metaphor of "many boats to one ship" speaks to the primal need for security and unity, reassuring the

team that they are stronger together in navigating the uncertain "seas" ahead.
- *Emotion*: The imagery of working together on a shared journey evokes a sense of camaraderie and collective purpose, appealing to the emotional drive for connection and support.
- *Cognition*: Allan's ambitious vision—becoming a "well-oiled machine" and an industry leader—challenges the team intellectually, inspiring them to think beyond immediate challenges and strive for excellence.

4. Define Actions

- *Instinct*: Outlining tangible steps like training sessions and feedback channels provides the team with a sense of control and direction, reducing uncertainty and instinctual resistance to change.
- *Emotion*: These actionable steps demonstrate Allan's commitment to supporting the team, fostering trust and reinforcing the emotional bond between leader and team.
- *Cognition*: The clear roadmap satisfies the need for logic and structure, helping the team intellectually understand how their efforts contribute to achieving the vision.

5. Get Commitment

- *Instinct*: By inviting engagement and participation, Allan reduces the instinctual fear of being left behind or overlooked, encouraging active involvement rather than passive compliance.
- *Emotion*: The call for commitment is framed as a mutual pledge, strengthening emotional ties and creating a sense of shared responsibility and accountability.

- *Cognition*: Allan's emphasis on collaboration and contribution appeals to the team's rational side, encouraging them to think critically about how they can add value to the organisation's goals.

6. Excite to Act Now

- *Instinct*: Allan's rallying tone generates energy and urgency, tapping into the team's instinctual drive to take immediate action and "move forward."
- *Emotion*: Celebrating the start of a shared journey reinforces emotional investment, making the team feel valued and motivated to contribute.
- *Cognition*: The focus on building a workplace to be proud of challenges the team to think long-term, aligning their immediate actions with a broader vision of success and innovation.

Why the Speech Resonates Across the Triune Brain

1. *Balanced Engagement*: Allan ensures his message appeals to instincts, emotions, and intellect, creating a multi-dimensional narrative that resonates deeply with his diverse audience.
2. *Emotional Safety*: By addressing fears and validating emotions, he disarms the instinctual resistance to change while fostering trust and connection.
3. *Visionary Clarity*: Allan provides both the "why" (shared values and vision) and the "how" (tangible actions and commitment), satisfying the team's intellectual need for clarity and coherence.
4. *Motivational Energy*: His concluding call to action inspires immediate engagement, aligning the team's instincts, emotions, and logic toward a shared purpose.

. . .

Because Unity BRIDGE is derived from PACE Storytelling structure, Allan's speech embodies it. His speech begins with a clear acknowledgment of the emotional challenges of redundancies and closures, which fosters safety, builds trust and evokes psychological permission. He encouraged agency over the group survival instincts by reframing the transition as an opportunity for growth, empowering the team to move beyond instinctual defensiveness toward purposeful engagement.

By rallying the team around shared values like resilience, respect, and quality, and using the unifying metaphor of "many boats to one ship," he created emotional connection and strengthens group cohesion. Finally, Allan embeds a new narrative of collaboration and progress through a clear vision and actionable steps, replacing uncertainty with unity, momentum, and shared purpose.

Key Takeaway

Allan's speech is a masterclass in narrative leadership, effectively targeting the Triune Brain to foster unity, resilience, and forward momentum. By engaging instincts, emotions, and intellect, he creates a multi-layered message that aligns his team's collective efforts with a shared vision, ensuring the new distribution centre starts its journey on a solid foundation.

As we conclude *Band of Brothers*, it's worth reflecting on the bigger picture. Each USI in this framework builds safety, aligns team members, and creates a unified force that is resilient to disruption. This is not a method for resolving disputes, albeit its fractal nature means that the core themes within the narrative frame as well as the USIs can be employed effectively in the conflict resolution process. Rather it is a means of creating an environment where individuals feel safe, valued, and motivated to contribute to a shared mission. In doing so, it makes the groups collective 'vagal brake' more antifragile and less likely to fail.

Not every leadership moment starts with unity. Some begin in discord, inertia, or even despair. How do you lead when the road ahead is unclear? When the past holds more gravity than the future? How do you turn frustration into momentum, resistance into renewal?

This is not just about managing a team—it's about leading through turbulence, when certainty is a luxury and doubt is the default. The next chapter, "Les Misérables", will explore the art of leading through adversity—when where we are is not where we want to be. Because knowing what we do not want is not the same as knowing where we must go. And in those moments, the right story isn't just a tool—it's the turning point.

EIGHTEEN
"LES MISÉRABLES"

> *The field of narrative in organizations is a new discipline that draws on many traditional sources but is neither confined nor represented by those traditions*[1]
> **Dave Snowden**

"LES MISÉRABLES" is a novel written by Victor Hugo in 1862, which later inspired numerous adaptations, including films, stage productions, and one of the world's most famous musicals. Its enduring legacy across different media reflects its universal themes of redemption, tenacity and justice. It was chosen as the title for this chapter because it symbolises the transformative power of leadership and narratives to turn despair and adversity into unity, resilience, and progress.

Many leaders earn their reputation by transforming dire circumstances into opportunities for renewal and growth. Through talent, vision, and resolve, they guide their people from despair to stability, laying the foundation for new beginnings. Their legacies endure because they inspire generations with narratives of resilience and hope.

Some dismiss storytelling as mere rhetoric, believing that leadership rests on strategy and execution. But history shows that movements are not sustained by policies alone. People do not rally around spreadsheets—they rally around stories that give meaning to their struggle. A leader who fails to provide a compelling narrative does not merely lack inspiration; they forfeit control over the collective imagination of their people.

Figures like Nelson Mandela, Mahatma Gandhi, and Abraham Lincoln illustrate the power of leadership to unite fractured societies. Mandela, speaking during his 1964 trial, transformed personal struggle into a collective vision for justice:

> *"I have walked that long road to freedom. I have tried not to falter; I have made missteps along the way. But I have discovered the secret that after climbing a great hill, one only finds that there are many more hills to climb. With freedom comes responsibilities, and I dare not linger, for my long walk is not ended.[2]"*

Gandhi, during India's independence struggle, stirred a divided nation with urgency and resolve:

> *"Here is a mantra I give you: 'Do or Die.' We shall either free India or die in the attempt; we shall not live to see the perpetuation of our slavery.[3]"*

At Gettysburg, Lincoln transformed a devastating Civil War into a call for unity and democracy, beginning:

> "Four score and seven years ago, our fathers brought forth on this continent a new nation, conceived in Liberty, and dedicated to the proposition that all men are created equal.[4]"

These leaders wielded words to inspire resilience and collective action, reminding us that even in the direst moments, a compelling narrative paired with vision can ignite transformation.

Today's leaders face an increasingly complex, fast-changing world, they need flexible frameworks to provide structure for creating unity and guiding teams through uncertainty. In dark and difficult moments, narratives are not merely speeches; they align and energise people, addressing instinctual, emotional, and rational needs. Without a unifying alternative, human nature gravitates toward division—tribalism, territorialism, and groupthink—creating silos, ideological fractures, or sectarian tensions.

By employing storytelling frameworks, leaders can rebuild trust, align values, and transform fragmented teams into resilient groups capable of thriving through adversity. Impactful leadership is not just about solving problems but about telling stories that inspire collective progress and resilience.

THE 4CS OF **Effective Leadership**

Throughout history there have been moments of immense challenge. From fractured societies to oppressive regimes and national crises, these moments called for leaders with the qualities necessary to inspire unity, resilience, and progress. They required leadership was not just about what had to be done but how it all was communicated.

Inspiring leaders share four fundamental qualities. First, they demonstrate _compassion_, recognising and addressing the emotions of those they lead to build trust and connection. Second, they establish _credibility_, earning trust through authenticity and integrity so that their words carry weight. Third, they apply _cognition_, framing challenges with clarity and insight to help others navigate complexity. Finally, they lead through _campaign_, rallying collective energy toward a shared mission, transforming vision into action. These qualities shape narratives that do not merely describe the world as it is but envision it as it could be.

Take Nelson Mandela. His speech during his trial in 1964 was a masterclass in *compassion*, as he validated the pain of oppression while offering hope for the future. His unwavering *credibility* stemmed from his personal sacrifices, which aligned his words with his deeds. By articulating the fight for justice with clarity (*cognition*), he transformed despair into resolve. And through his call to action, he united a nation under a campaign for freedom.

Similarly, Mahatma Gandhi's leadership during India's independence movement was rooted in *compassion* for the suffering of millions, paired with an unshakeable commitment to nonviolence (*credibility*). His speeches clarified the stakes of their struggle (*cognition*) and rallied the people to a campaign of sacrifice and determination: "Do or Die."

Abraham Lincoln's *Gettysburg Address* encapsulated these same qualities. With humility and grace, he connected with a grieving nation (*compassion*), rooted his words in democratic ideals (*credibility*), and framed the Civil War as a fight for equality and unity (*cognition*). His resolve to see the nation reborn as a government "of the people, by the people, for the people" became the campaign that carried the United States forward.

From Timeless Principles to Practical Framework

While Mandela, Gandhi, and Lincoln shaped the course of nations, today's leaders must navigate equally complex human dynamics in workplaces, communities, and organisations. The challenge is no longer just about shaping national movements but about aligning diverse teams, resolving internal tensions, and guiding people through uncertainty. The question is not whether we will face crises, but how we will lead our teams through them. This is where structured narrative tools like *FOCUS UP* become essential.

FOCUS UP distils the 4Cs into a dynamic framework for narrative framing[5]. It is a practical tool that helps leaders guide their people through uncertainty, fostering unity and resilience while inspiring the collective action needed to move from adversity to opportunity. By structuring communication around these principles, leaders can turn paralysis into momentum, ensuring that their teams not only survive challenges but emerge stronger.

Whether addressing a missed target, navigating a hostile stakeholder meeting, or leading a team through market upheaval, *FOCUS UP* equips leaders to reframe adversity, inspire belief, and rally efforts toward a shared vision. It transforms the timeless lessons of historic leadership into actionable steps, enabling today's leaders to inspire their teams to journey toward—and build—something better.

Framework Overview

The adaptive framework offers leaders a clear roadmap for navigating uncertainty with clarity, empathy, and purpose. It is designed to address the instinctual, emotional, and rational needs of teams, transforming confusion into confidence and inertia into action. The framework comprises seven interconnected components, each targeting a specific facet of leadership communication:

1. **F***rame the Context*: Establish a shared understanding of the situation, eliminating ambiguity and aligning perspectives.
2. **O***bserve Shared Experiences*: Validate emotions and foster empathy, ensuring team members feel seen, heard, and connected.
3. **C***oncretise the Challenge*: Define the specific problem, channelling energy toward manageable and actionable goals.
4. **U***plift with Vision*: Present a hopeful and realistic future, inspiring the team to view the challenge as a pathway to growth.
5. **S***et the Steps*: Outline clear, tangible actions that bridge the gap between the current state and the desired outcome.
6. **U***nite Their Hearts*: Anchor actions in shared values, forging a deeper emotional commitment to the mission.
7. **P***ress for Action*: Turn alignment and energy into purposeful momentum, ensuring decisive forward movement.

These components form a flexible narrative arc, addressing both immediate challenges and long-term aspirations. Unlike rigid, linear models such as Kotter's Eight-Step Process, *FOCUS UP* is fluid and iterative. Leaders can activate its elements simultaneously or shift focus as conditions evolve, maintaining balance and momentum across the team.

To fully appreciate the potential of FOCUS UP, it's important to understand its fractal nature—a characteristic that enables it to adapt dynamically to challenges at any scale.

Group Safety Rupture Repair

At its heart, FOCUS UP isn't just a structural tool—it's a way to repair safety ruptures at the group level. Leaders who effectively employ the framework guide their teams on a journey from negative emotions like fear, helplessness, and despair, toward positive states like trust, empowerment, and hope.

This emotional transformation is not accidental; it is deeply rooted in the PACE Storytelling framework from which FOCUS UP is derived. PACE's structured process—*Prime & Probe, Agency over Instinct, Connect and Socialise, Embed New Meanings*—guides the shift in emotional states, ensuring the group moves intentionally through vulnerability, empowerment, connection, and renewal. By adapting these principles, FOCUS UP transforms fragmented or fearful teams into cohesive and motivated units. Each step actively addresses the instincts, emotions, and cognition of the group, ensuring the transformation from safety rupture to resilience is not only possible but predictable.

Using PACE as a foundation, the emotional arc within FOCUS UP can be made explicit:

1. *Prime & Probe*: At the outset, leaders establish psychological safety by validating fears and anxieties. By acknowledging the shared challenges that people face (e.g., through Frame the Context and Observe Shared Experiences), leaders defuse defensiveness and create openness to dialogue.
    - Emotional Transition: From defensiveness to openness.

2. *Agency Over Instinct*: By framing challenges as surmountable and providing actionable steps forward (Concretise the Challenge and Set the Steps), leaders empower teams to shift from passive helplessness to active engagement. Reframing adversity as an opportunity for growth taps into the team's instinctual drive for survival, channelling it into purposeful action.
   - Emotional Transition: From helplessness to empowerment.
3. *Connect and Socialise:* Teams often begin in fragmented or isolated states, exacerbating uncertainty. By fostering emotional resonance through shared values and experiences (Observe Shared Experiences and Unite Their Hearts), leaders cultivate a sense of connection and belonging, reducing anxiety and creating trust.
   - Emotional Transition: From isolation to connection.
4. *Embed New Meanings*: Finally, leaders solidify the emotional transformation by offering a vision of hope and progress (Uplift with Vision) and translating it into tangible action (Press for Action). By doing so, they redefine current struggles as stepping stones toward a brighter, collective future, replacing despair with optimism and determination.
   - Emotional Transition: From despair to hope.

FOCUS UP is not just about organising ideas or clarifying actions; it's about repairing disconnected states, fostering connection, cohesion, and unity. The framework leverages the PACE Storytelling structure to address and guide instinctual, emotional, and cognitive responses, ensuring teams feel safe, connected, and inspired.

Each USI of is designed to move teams along this emotional arc; by monitoring these USIs diligently and taking corrective action, leaders maintain the group's unity. In doing so, leaders can transform negative instinctual states into positive emotional states, enabling the full cognitive capacity of the group to problem-solve and flourish together.

Narratives do not merely define the present; they shape the future. A great leader's story is never static—it evolves, responding to challenges, crises, and transformations. The leader who understands this does not merely react to circumstances but actively reshapes them through the power of narrative. This is not a one-time process but an ongoing practice of storytelling, adaptation, and influence.

THE FRACTAL NATURE

The FOCUS UP framework is not a rigid, linear process; instead, it mirrors the complexity and adaptability of living systems. Its fractal nature lies in its ability to be applied consistently across varying scales—whether in addressing a crisis affecting an entire organisation, resolving tensions within a team, or guiding a one-on-one conversation with a colleague. At every level, the same principles and Unity-Stabilising Inputs (USIs) remain relevant, yet they adapt dynamically to the context.

Fractals in Leadership Communication

1. **Core Consistency Across Scales**
2. Just as fractals exhibit self-similar patterns regardless of scale, the FOCUS UP framework provides a stable structure that works across micro and macro levels. For example:
    - At the *organisational level*, "Frame the Context" might involve addressing the entire workforce about a restructuring initiative.
    - At the *team level*, it could mean clarifying specific project roles and goals to ensure alignment.

- At the *individual level*, it might involve acknowledging a colleague's unique struggles and aligning on shared objectives. Despite the difference in scope, the same process of aligning understanding and setting a foundation for action applies.

3. **Adaptability to Complexity**
4. Leadership challenges often resemble complex adaptive systems: they are dynamic, interconnected, and unpredictable. The fractal nature of FOCUS UP enables leaders to navigate this complexity by breaking large challenges into smaller, manageable pieces. Each USI can be applied iteratively and repeatedly, scaling up or down as necessary, while maintaining alignment with the broader vision.

Practical Examples of Fractals in Action

- **Crisis Management at Different Scales**
    - *Macro-Level*: A CEO addressing the company during a major market disruption uses FOCUS UP to Frame the Context of economic uncertainty, Concretise the Challenge of declining sales, and Uplift with Vision for pivoting to new markets.
    - *Micro-Level*: A team leader within that same organisation uses FOCUS UP to Frame the Context of adapting to new KPIs, Observe Shared Experiences of team fatigue, and Press for Action to prioritise short-term goals.
- **Iterative Implementation**
- Each USI can be revisited multiple times within a single initiative:
    - *Framing the Context* might evolve as new information emerges, requiring leaders to re-establish shared understanding at each stage.

- *Uniting Their Hearts* might need reinforcement to sustain morale over time, particularly during prolonged or complex projects.

Fractals and Feedback Loops

In complex systems, feedback loops help maintain balance. Similarly, the fractal nature of FOCUS UP incorporates continuous feedback:

- Leaders can revisit earlier USIs as new challenges or opportunities arise.
- For instance, after implementing steps to address an immediate problem, a leader may need to return to "Observe Shared Experiences" to reassess team morale and make adjustments.

Why Fractals Matter in Leadership

1. *Scalability*: The framework provides leaders with a single tool that can be scaled up or down without losing its core utility.
2. *Sustainability*: Its iterative application ensures adaptability over time, supporting sustained progress rather than one-time fixes.
3. *Resonance*: By maintaining consistency across different levels, the framework builds trust and alignment, as team members see coherent leadership in every interaction.

The Framework as a Living System

Much like a fractal design in nature—a fern leaf or a coastline—the FOCUS UP framework reflects the patterns of human communication and collaboration. It adapts dynamically to challenges and scales seamlessly, ensuring leaders can address the big picture while never losing sight of the details.

Key Insight

The fractal nature of FOCUS UP reinforces its effectiveness in addressing both the complexity and nuance of leadership. Leaders who internalise this concept can seamlessly apply the framework across diverse contexts, ensuring clarity, alignment, and progress at every level of their organisation or team.

Having explored the adaptability of the framework, let us now examine how these principles manifest in real-world scenarios, showcasing the power of narrative to align, inspire, and propel action.

Adaptability for Every Scenario

The strength of narrative framework lies in its adaptability. It's not limited to large-scale transformations or formal presentations. It can be seamlessly applied to diverse contexts, such as:

- *Engagement Framework* for internal and external stakeholder engagement
- *One-on-One Conversations*: Supporting a team member through personal or professional challenges.
- *Team Huddles*: Realigning priorities and boosting morale during periods of high stress.
- *Ad Hoc Problem-Solving*: Quickly framing context and solutions in moments of crisis.

Whether addressing a workforce after a major setback, engaging stakeholders during organisational change, or navigating high-pressure situations, the framework scales to meet the unique demands of each moment.

Beyond Crisis Management

At its core, *FOCUS UP* builds trust and momentum. By balancing transparency with inspiration, it equips leaders to address challenges constructively while maintaining sight of the bigger picture.

It turns adversity into opportunity, enabling teams to emerge not just intact but stronger, more united, and better prepared for future challenges.

This is not just a tool for managing crises—it's a method for cultivating resilience and forging progress. By guiding teams through ambiguity and adversity, **FOCUS UP** empowers leaders to create lasting change, uniting people around a shared vision and ensuring forward motion.

FOCUS UP Framework

As with Unity BRIDGE, the FOCUS UP framework is fractal in its nature. In this case, the framework provides seven *Unity Stabilising Inputs* (USIs), each addressing a key element of leadership communication. Together, these components guide teams from uncertainty to purposeful action, building trust, clarity, and momentum.

USI 1: **F**rame the Context

Framing the context is the first step in aligning your team. It's more than stating facts—it's about establishing a shared foundation for understanding the situation. Without this, assumptions diverge, leading to confusion and conflict.

Framing the context is like orienting a map. Before determining the destination, you must clarify where you are. Without this reference point, a team risks heading in the wrong direction.

Tone is as critical as content. Leaders who catastrophise can spark panic, while those who sugar-coat risk complacency. Effective framing strikes a balance: presenting the truth with composure, clarity, and confidence.

For instance, an operations leader addressing a severe backlog began:

> "We've faced challenges—resource shortages, client demands, and system failures—but your resilience has kept us going. Now, for the first time, the backlog is shrinking. We're gaining momentum, and I know we can clear this together."

This leader acknowledged the difficulty without exaggeration, celebrated progress, and set a positive tone. Transparency like this reinforces psychological safety and aligns the team.

Key Insight: Framing the context grounds the team in reality, fostering clarity and reducing ambiguity. With a shared understanding, teams are better equipped to focus on solutions.

USI 2: **O**bserve Shared Experiences

Acknowledging emotions is crucial for unity. Leaders who validate team members' feelings foster psychological safety and empathy, helping to build trust and camaraderie.

Emotions in a team are like unseen ocean currents—if ignored, they can pull the team off course. By recognising and sharing these experiences, leaders steer with empathy, creating a supportive environment.

For example, during the height of COVID-19, a factory owner told their team:

> "I know many of you are exhausted. The shortages and delays have tested us all. But know this: your dedication is what's keeping us afloat, and we'll get through this together."

This simple acknowledgment validated the team's effort and emotions, reinforcing trust and a sense of shared purpose.

Key Insight: Observing shared experiences builds an emotional bridge. Recognising and validating team struggles fosters resilience and strengthens group cohesion.

USI 3: **C**oncretise the Challenge

Turning vague concerns into actionable problems helps focus the team's energy. Concretising the challenge shifts the narrative from emotional overwhelm to productive clarity.

A factory manager facing a 168% surge in demand addressed her team:

> "Our orders have quadrupled, and we need to adapt quickly. First, we'll reset client expectations. Then, we'll ramp up overtime and improve workflows. Let's focus on stabilising operations while exploring long-term capacity solutions".

This clarity redirected the team from feeling overwhelmed to addressing tangible tasks, transforming anxiety into agency.

Key Insight: Concretising the challenge channels energy into action. A clear, objective focus minimises blame and defensiveness, fostering an environment for problem-solving.

USI 4: **U**plift with Vision

A compelling vision shifts focus from immediate challenges to future possibilities, inspiring hope and energising the team.

A leader's vision acts like a lighthouse in a storm—it doesn't calm the waves but provides a guiding light. Effective visions are inclusive, balancing clarity with room for team contributions.

After defining a capacity challenge, a factory manager said:

> "Imagine a workplace with optimised workflows,

> state-of-the-art tools, and flexible schedules. That's our future, and your creativity and resilience will get us there".

This vision connected short-term struggles to a greater purpose, motivating the team with a shared goal.

Key Insight: Vision connects present struggles to a brighter future. By offering realistic hope and inclusivity, leaders inspire collective action.

USI 5: **S**et the Steps

To turn vision into reality, leaders must outline clear, actionable steps. Without this, even the most inspiring vision risks feeling unattainable.

Beth, the factory manager, told her team:

> "Here's our plan: First, we'll reset client expectations. Next, we'll identify workflow bottlenecks for quick wins. Finally, we'll scope long-term capacity expansions, with input from all of you".

Breaking tasks into manageable steps creates clarity and accountability, giving the team confidence in their ability to progress[6].

Key Insight: Setting the steps translates vision into action. By defining clear tasks and ensuring accountability, leaders provide a roadmap that bridges present struggles and future success.

USI 6: **U**nite Their Hearts

While logic informs decisions, it is emotion that drives commitment. Leaders who unite their team's hearts create a shared identity, transforming individual efforts into collective purpose.

A healthcare leader told their team:

> "No matter the changes, our commitment to dignity and compassion remains. Together, we're not just meeting challenges; we're shaping a future aligned with our values"

Anchoring actions in shared values strengthens emotional bonds and commitment, fostering unity and resilience.

Key Insight: Uniting hearts appeals to shared values, inspiring genuine emotional commitment. Authenticity and consistency from leaders build trust and reinforce group identity.

USL 7: **P**ress for Action

The final step turns alignment into momentum. Pressing for action provides the spark to translate preparation into progress.

A manufacturing leader concluded their address:

> "We've done the groundwork. By week's end, I want each team to submit recommendations for streamlining workflows. Let's take the first step today".

Urgency and achievable goals create momentum, while celebrating early wins sustains motivation.

Key Insight: Pressing for action converts unity into progress. Leaders who set clear starting points and create urgency ensure immediate, purposeful motion.

Practical Applications

The *FOCUS UP* framework is dynamic and scalable, applicable in various scenarios:

- *One-on-One:* Reconnecting disengaged team members by observing shared struggles and setting clear goals.
- *Team Huddles:* Aligning a team during stress with clear context and concrete steps.
- *Large-Scale Presentations:* Inspiring alignment across diverse groups with vision and decisive action.

FOCUS UP equips leaders to transform uncertainty into clarity and challenges into opportunities, ensuring progress even in the most adverse conditions.

Douglas's Team Address

"Good morning, everyone.

Earlier this week, something happened that we can't ignore. Many of you witnessed Jerry's incident. He froze—physically, mentally, emotionally. He couldn't move, speak, or act.

Stress got to him. It built up silently over time until his body shut down. Jerry isn't injured, but what he went through should remind us all of how much pressure we carry in this job —and how dangerous it can be if we don't address it.

This isn't just Jerry's story; it's a story about all of us[7]. Who here hasn't felt that weight? The pressure to hit targets, keep everything running smoothly, and not let anyone down? It impacts all of us differently, but when one of us breaks, it's a sign that something deeper needs to change.

Let me ask you to imagine a different kind of workplace. One where we don't wait until someone reaches their breaking point. One where it's safe to speak up, to say, 'I'm not okay,' before it's too late. A place where leaders, myself included, notice when someone's struggling and step in with real support. Can you picture that?

We can build that place, but it's going to take all of us. Starting today, we'll be making some changes. First, we're introducing regular check-ins so we can talk honestly about what's working and what isn't. Next, we'll be rolling out training for leaders to spot the early signs of stress and act before things escalate. And most importantly, we'll put well-being on par with productivity. That means creating a culture where trust and safety come first.

This isn't just about reducing stress. It's about becoming the kind of team that lifts each other up, a team that thrives under pressure without breaking. Let's commit, together, to making this change. Let's make safety—not just physical but mental—a priority. When we do, we'll not only become stronger as individuals but unstoppable as a team."

How the Speech Affected his Group's Hive Mind

Douglas's speech artfully engages all three levels of the Triune Brain (reptilian survival instincts, mammalian bonding emotions, and primate cognition), creating a narrative that fosters trust, unity, and purposeful action. By addressing these layers, Douglas transforms a moment of vulnerability into a catalyst for resilience and collective progress[8].

1. **Frame the Context**
    - *Instinct*: Douglas begins by addressing the immediate survival concern—stress-induced breakdowns like Jerry's incident. This acknowledgment calms the primal fear of instability and danger by signalling that the leader recognises the issue and is taking control.
    - *Emotion*: By connecting Jerry's experience to a shared team reality, Douglas validates the collective emotional struggle, reducing feelings of isolation and fostering psychological safety.
    - *Cognition*: Framing the context as a reflection of deeper systemic issues shifts the focus from individual blame to a broader intellectual understanding of the problem, creating clarity and shared perspective.
2. **Observe Shared Experiences**
    - *Instinct*: Douglas explicitly acknowledges the pressure everyone feels, reducing instinctual defensiveness by showing that struggles are recognised and normalised.
    - *Emotion*: Validating the team's emotional burden builds empathy and connection, making team members feel seen, heard, and supported.
    - *Cognition*: By linking individual stress to a collective reality, Douglas helps the team intellectually understand how shared challenges affect them as a group, fostering alignment.

3. **Concretise the Challenge**
   - *Instinct*: Defining the challenge as a culture that prioritises productivity over well-being reassures the team that the problem is tangible and solvable, addressing primal fears of unpredictability.
   - *Emotion*: Douglas shifts the narrative from overwhelming stress to actionable change, giving the team emotional relief and a sense of agency.
   - *Cognition*: Clearly articulating the systemic issue allows the team to focus on logical, constructive solutions rather than being paralysed by uncertainty.
4. **Uplift with Vision**
   - *Instinct*: Douglas paints a vision of a workplace where safety and well-being are prioritised, appealing to the primal desire for security and stability.
   - *Emotion*: His aspirational vision of trust and support inspires hope and emotional investment, motivating the team to believe in a better future.
   - *Cognition*: The vision connects the team's current struggles to a long-term goal, encouraging them to think critically about how their efforts contribute to this transformation.
5. **Set the Steps**
   - *Instinct*: Concrete actions like check-ins, leader training, and a well-being culture provide a roadmap, reducing uncertainty and satisfying the need for control and direction.
   - *Emotion*: The actionable steps demonstrate leadership commitment, strengthening trust and emotional buy-in.
   - *Cognition*: Outlining clear steps transforms the vision into a logical, achievable plan, empowering the team with clarity and purpose.

6. **Unite Their Hearts**
   - *Instinct*: Anchoring the new culture in shared values like teamwork and mutual support are strong cues of safety, obviating primal responses.
   - *Emotion*: Douglas appeals to the team's emotional connection to their shared mission, reinforcing bonds and a sense of collective identity.
   - *Cognition*: Highlighting shared values aligns individual goals with the team's broader purpose, fostering intellectual and moral commitment.
7. **Press for Action**
   - *Instinct*: Douglas's direct call to action activates the team's survival-driven need for immediate progress, providing momentum and focus.
   - *Emotion*: His emphasis on collective commitment energises the team, creating a sense of urgency and shared responsibility.
   - *Cognition*: By clearly linking the call to action with specific steps, Douglas ensures logical alignment between the team's efforts and the desired outcome.

Why It Resonated Across the Triune Brain

1. *Instinctual Engagement*: Douglas addresses fears of stress and burnout by acknowledging vulnerabilities, outlining practical steps, and providing a vision of safety, thereby reducing fight-or-flight responses.
2. *Emotional Connection*: Through empathy and validation, he strengthens bonds within the team, creating a supportive environment that fosters trust and collaboration.
3. *Intellectual Clarity*: By framing the problem clearly, providing a roadmap, and connecting actions to values, Douglas satisfies the team's need for logical understanding and purpose.

Key Takeaway

Douglas's speech demonstrates the power of narrative to address the Triune Brain holistically, transforming a crisis into an opportunity for growth. By engaging instincts, emotions, and intellect, he builds trust, inspires action, and aligns the team around a shared vision of resilience and progress. His structured use of the FOCUS UP framework ensures the message resonates at every level, fostering a culture of safety, unity, and forward momentum.

Other Narrative Applications

The flexibility of the FOCUS UP framework extends beyond formal speeches, enabling leaders to address diverse scenarios, from brief conversations to team meetings and organisational presentations:

- *Brief Interactions*: For a disengaged team member, a leader might *Frame the Context* by acknowledging recent pressures, *Observe Shared Experiences* by validating their struggles, and *Set the Steps* for improvement with clear, supportive actions.
- *Meetings*: In tense discussions, leaders can *Frame the Context* to align the group, *Concretise the Challenge* to clarify focus, and *Unite Their Hearts* around shared goals, ensuring the meeting remains productive and aligned.
- *Presentations*: When launching new initiatives, leaders can *Uplift with Vision* to inspire belief and *Press for Action* to energise the audience into taking decisive steps forward.

The adaptability of FOCUS UP makes it indispensable for leaders working within complex, living systems. Whether addressing a crisis, facilitating discussions, or rallying a team, the framework's *Unity-Stabilising Inputs* (USIs) counteract the tendency toward disunity and positive feedback loops. It reinforces focus, resilience, and alignment, ensuring leadership communication drives meaningful and lasting change.

KEY INSIGHTS

> *"The universe is a continuous web. Touch it at any point and the whole web quivers.[9]"*
> **Stanley Kunitz**

In times of strife, leaders are measured not just by their plans or performance but by the narratives they craft—stories that guide, unite, and inspire people to make things better. As we've explored throughout this chapter, narratives are indispensable tools for sensemaking, especially in the face of uncertainty, ambiguity, and complexity.

Historic leaders like Nelson Mandela, Mahatma Gandhi, and Abraham Lincoln mastered the art of narrative to connect with their people's instincts, emotions, and cognition. Their speeches were not mere calls to action but transformative moments that reshaped meaning, instilled clarity, and created shared purpose.

In today's volatile and fast-changing world, leaders must similarly harness their own and their teams' instinctual drives. By mastering narrative tools like FOCUS UP, leaders can portray shared experiences, demonstrate compassion, and inspire collective action. This framework provides a way to move people from instability, discomfort, or fear toward hope, stability, and renewed purpose. Without such guidance, many would remain stuck in familiar, unproductive patterns.

FOCUS UP is more than a crisis management tool—it is a dynamic framework for leading people out of adversity. By aligning with the fluid and adaptive nature of leadership, it offers flexibility across a range of scenarios, from high-stakes speeches to team discussions and one-on-one conversations.

Its true value lies not in rigid linear steps but in its dynamic, *USI-driven approach*, underpinned by the *4Cs of Effective Leadership*: compassion, credibility, cognition, and campaign. These qualities ensure leaders remain responsive to the human complexities that influence team dynamics, enabling them to sustain unity and momentum even in turbulent environments.

As leaders navigate the ever-changing landscapes of their organisations, they must remember that their words shape their legacies. A well-crafted narrative is not merely a strategy; it is a beacon—a light that transforms confusion into clarity, disconnection into unity, and inertia into progress.

Leaders who know how to influence the Hive Mind do not merely solve problems. They tell stories that help others believe in solutions, commit to action, and persevere through uncertainty. The question is not whether you will lead with stories—you already do. The question is whether you will do so *consciously, with precision and purpose.* The narratives you craft today will define the reality you and your team will face tomorrow. So, what story will you craft? And who will you inspire because of it?

SECTION SIX SUMMARY

*Nature always finds a way;
we must simply allow it*
Leonardo da Vinci

Leadership in times of profound change demands far more than technical expertise or meticulous planning. It requires the ability to navigate the uncertain terrain of human emotions, instincts, and intellect—a realm where ambiguity thrives and traditional logic falters. Leaders are not merely decision-makers; they are weavers of meaning, capable of crafting stories that cut through the fog of complexity, build unity from fragmentation, and transform fear into hope.

PACE Storytelling, the focus of this section, is a leadership framework that equips individuals to create these transformative narratives. It builds on the foundation of non-verbal leadership explored earlier, adding language as a tool—not just any words, but those chosen with precision to resonate with both heart and mind.

To understand the power of storytelling in leadership, we must first recognise its dual function. As Dave Snowden articulates, stories serve as mechanisms for 'sense-making'—the process of discerning patterns amidst chaos—and for 'meaning-making'—reframing those patterns to inspire purposeful action. Together, these capabilities make storytelling indispensable for leaders navigating the tangled networks of human systems.

Consider a leader addressing a fractured team, their cohesion eroded by silos and suspicion. A direct command to collaborate may fail to resonate. But a narrative that reframes their predicament as an opportunity to achieve something greater together has the power to unite. This is not storytelling as a 'soft skill'; it is an essential leadership tool, particularly in environments where uncertainty reigns, and human dynamics take centre stage.

Neurological Anchors

Stories are ancient tools that connect our past experiences with present challenges and future possibilities[1]. Their resonance is rooted in the structure of the human brain, as Paul MacLean's triune brain model so elegantly demonstrates. At the most primal level, stories engage the Reptilian Brain, addressing our survival instincts. Tales of danger narrowly avoided, for instance, trigger visceral responses that prepare us for action, as if we were reliving the moment ourselves.

The Mammalian Brain, responsible for emotion and connection, is drawn to stories of love, loss, and triumph—narratives that build trust and foster shared identity. Finally, the Primate Brain engages with stories that challenge our assumptions and expand our understanding, offering intellectual stimulation and new insights.

Stephen Porges' Polyvagal Theory extends this understanding by showing how stories can shift the autonomic nervous system from defensive states (fight, flight, or freeze) to states of social engagement. A narrative that acknowledges collective anxieties while offering reassurance signals safety to the listener, unlocking the emotional and intellectual resources necessary for collaboration and creativity.

Take the archetypal hero's journey as an example. The protagonist faces life-threatening danger, emotional trials, and finally, transformative insight. This enduring narrative resonates because it engages the whole of our humanity: our instincts, our emotions, and our intellect. Leaders must take note—a story that appeals only to the intellect may inform but rarely inspires; a story targeting only emotions may lack clarity. The most impactful narratives weave all these elements together into a cohesive whole.

Reframing Adversity

Leadership is often tested most during transitions—when fear and disconnection amplify. Ralph Stacey's insight into the nonlinear nature of human behaviour reminds us that leaders cannot impose order on complex systems. Instead, they must guide people through them by crafting narratives that resonate with lived experience.

Consider a team divided by conflicting priorities and mistrust. A directive to 'work together' is likely to ring hollow. However, a story that highlights shared victories from the past can reframe the current challenges as opportunities to replicate those successes. This act of reframing, grounded in both collective memory and future potential, creates alignment and fosters trust.

Daniel Kahneman's work on framing provides a further dimension. By reshaping how challenges are presented—turning threats into opportunities, for instance—leaders can alter the way their teams perceive adversity, shifting them from paralysis to purpose.

Physiological Arc

The PACE Storytelling framework is not just a method; it is an emotional journey. Its arc transforms states of defensiveness, helplessness, and despair into openness, empowerment, and hope. The process begins with 'Priming & Probing', where leaders validate emotions and create psychological safety. This is the starting point for shifting from defensiveness to openness.

The next phase, 'Agency Over Instinct,' encourages individuals to transcend their reactive instincts, framing challenges as opportunities for choice and action. This transformation replaces helplessness with engagement. In 'Connect and Socialise,' leaders build emotional bonds through shared values and experiences, fostering unity. Finally, the narrative concludes with 'Embedding New Meanings,' reframing adversity as a catalyst for growth and replacing despair with optimism.

Complexity & Evolution

PACE is more than a linear framework; it is a living system, reflecting the principles of complex adaptive systems as articulated by Meg Wheatley, Ralph Stacey, and Dave Snowden. Its negative feedback loops—Unity-Stabilising Inputs (USIs)—allow leaders to address multiple dynamics concurrently, dampening adverse developments while maintaining coherence.

Dave Snowden's Cynefin framework highlights the importance of adaptable approaches. PACE embodies this adaptability. Whether aligning an entire organisation during a restructuring, guiding a team's project discussions, or addressing individual challenges, PACE provides a scalable structure for coherence and alignment.

Richard Bandler's influence is woven into the DNA of PACE, particularly his foundational concept of 'pace and lead.' This idea, reframed for leadership contexts, underscores the importance of aligning with a team's current emotional and cognitive state before guiding them toward new possibilities.

Some of Bandler's toolkit were discussed —reframing, nested loops, and metaphors—which he uses to elevated storytelling into a transformative art. *Reframing* allows leaders to shift perspectives, turning obstacles into opportunities. *Nested loops* engage the triune brain, embedding deep insights by weaving multiple stories that resolve in reverse order. *Metaphors* provide leaders with a bridge between abstract concepts and lived experience, making complex ideas tangible and relatable.

These techniques ensure that PACE is not just a framework for storytelling but a methodology for transforming instincts, emotions, and behaviours in real-world leadership scenarios.

The derivatives of PACE are both plural and diverse and I have developed many over the years. The two selected for a detailed unpacking were Unity BRIDGE and FOCUS UP, which demonstrated its scalability and versatility. Unity BRIDGE focuses on uniting diverse groups, emphasising shared values and collective purpose—essential during transitions like mergers.

FOCUS UP, on the other hand, addresses crises, guiding teams from despair to resilience through visionary leadership and actionable steps. Both frameworks retain PACE's iterative, fractal nature, ensuring adaptability to any challenge.

Leadership is Storytelling

It is the ability to frame and reframe narratives that align instincts, emotions, and intellect, transforming complexity into clarity and disconnection into unity. The PACE Storytelling framework equips leaders with tools to navigate the shifting sands of organisational life, inspiring trust, alignment, and action.

What stories will you tell to guide your teams? How will you craft narratives that resonate with the whole of their humanity? In the end, the stories we tell shape the futures we create—building environments where flourishing, resilience, and unity are possible.

And, when we look back at our careers as leaders, isn't that what we all want?

Summary of Tools & Techniques

This section presents a series of frameworks and strategies that leaders can use to create **unity, resilience, and alignment** through storytelling. The frameworks provide structured approaches to sense-making, meaning-making and mobilising action within complex adaptive systems.

- **PACE Storytelling** - helps leaders navigate complexity through narrative framing.
- **Unity BRIDGE** - helps leaders designed for uniting diverse groups and factions.
- **FOCUS UP** - helps leaders navigate out of adversity and crisis by inspiring action.

Story Structures Summary

PACE Storytelling Framework

Purpose: This framework (along with Unity BRIDGE and FOCUS UP) is straightforward to implement. It empowers leaders to navigate complexity through *narrative*, turning chaos into clarity by engaging hidden patterns.

More than a communication tool, it engages the full spectrum of human cognition—resonating viscerally with the Reptilian Brain, fostering trust through the Mammalian Brain, and aligning decisions with the analytical Primate Brain. This makes storytelling a structured approach to sense-making, meaning-making, and deep engagement.

1. Prime & Probe

- *Establish group safety* the test for new narrative receptiveness.
- **Action:** Use shared experiences, acknowledging struggles, fears, and concerns.
- **Example:** "Many of you feel uncertainty about the changes ahead. I hear you."

2. Agency Over Instinct

- Reframe the situation to diminish the need for fear and defensiveness.
- **Action:** Highlight collective control; share other times they overcame adversity.
- **Example:** "We've been here before, and each time we've adapted and got better."

3. Connect and Socialise

- Align individuals with a *collective identity* through shared values and vision.
- **Action:** Use metaphors and stories to unify perspectives.
- **Example:** "Many boats, one ship—we are all navigating these waters together."

4. Embed Strategies & Meanings

- Ensure the new meanings are reinforced with repeated storytelling.
- **Action:** Use *fractal patterns* for narrative alignment across different scales.
- **Example:** Regular team debriefs for shared narrative perspectives.

Story Arc of PACE

Purpose: Move teams through states to foster safety, cohesion, unity and action.

1. *Self-protection* → *permission*: Validate emotions and reduce resistance.
2. *Powerless* → *Empowerment*: Reframe challenges as opportunities.
3. *Isolation* → *Connection*: Build shared values, goals and experiences.
4. *Old Beliefs* → *New Meanings:* Provide insights to connect the '*As Is*' to the '*To Be*'.

Unity BRIDGE Framework

Purpose: This framework was specifically designed for uniting diverse groups, such as during mergers, reorganisations, or cultural integration efforts.

1. Break Down Barriers

- Address *psychological silos* and emotional divisions.
- **Action:** Encourage cross-department collaboration and shared problem-solving.
- **Example:** "Let's rotate teams in training to learn from diverse experiences".

2. Rally Around Shared Values

- Define a *common cultural foundation* to unify the group.
- **Action:** Identify 3-5 **core values** and integrate them into daily conversations and decisions.
- **Example:** "Respect, resilience, and quality will guide how we work together."

3. Inspire with Vision

- Articulate a *compelling future* that aligns with the shared values.
- **Action:** Use vivid imagery and storytelling to *paint the future*.
- **Example:** "Imagine a centre where we set the standard in the industry for efficiency and collaboration."

4. Define Actions

- Turn abstract vision into *concrete actions*.

- **Action:** Break down the path forward into clear, actionable steps.
- **Example:** "We will start by implementing weekly open forums for feedback."

5. Get Commitment

- Ensure *active participation* rather than passive agreement.
- **Action:** Foster ownership through clear role expectations and accountability measures.
- **Example:** "Each team will assign one ambassador to track our progress and share concerns."

6. Excite to Act Now

- Create *urgency and momentum* to initiate immediate action.
- **Action:** Set short-term milestones and *celebrate early wins*.
- **Example:** "In the first 30 days, let's complete our first project to set the tone for success.

SECTION SIX SUMMARY

FOCUS UP Framework

Purpose: This framework is designed for navigating adversity and crisis, transforming fear and paralysis into momentum and action.

1. Frame the Context

- Create a *shared understanding* of the situation.
- **Action:** Clearly and accurately state the current reality in ways that is verifiable.
- **Example:** "We're facing an increased workload and fatigue is showing."

2. Observe Shared Experiences

- Validate *team emotions* to build psychological safety.
- **Action:** Share a common struggle to make people feel heard and understood.
- **Example:** "I know many of you feel frustrated. This pressure affects all of us."

3. Concretise the Challenge

- Define the *problem in clear, actionable terms*.
- **Action:** Shift focus from overwhelm to problem-solving.
- **Example:** "Production is 20% behind target—let's focus on the three bottlenecks."

4. Uplift with Vision

- Paint a *motivating picture of the future*.
- **Action:** Frame adversity as an opportunity for collective growth.
- **Example:** "We can be the team that performs best and leads the industry".

5. Set the Steps

- *Break down* the vision into actionable steps.
- **Action:** Set clear milestones and assign responsibilities.
- **Example:** "By next Friday, we'll have tested a new workflow to increase efficiency".

6. Unite Their Hearts

- Anchor progress in *shared values.*
- **Action:** Reinforce the emotional commitment to a greater purpose.
- **Example:** "We're not just hitting targets; we're building a culture of excellence."

7. Press for Action

- Drive *momentum with an immediate call to action.*
- **Action:** Set short-term challenges that drive engagement.
- **Example:** "Today, I challenge each of you to identify one area for improvement."

CONCLUSION
OWNING YOUR OUTER GAME

Leadership today is a test of resilience in the face of complexity—not a test of technical competence. The old playbooks—rigid hierarchies, top-down directives, and one-size-fits-all strategies—are crumbling under the weight of an increasingly volatile, uncertain, and ambiguous world. Leaders who attempt to control every outcome, eliminate uncertainty, or impose stability through force soon find themselves in a paradox: the harder they try to stabilise, the more fragile their teams become.

This book has explored both the inner and outer dimensions of neuro-resilient leadership. At its heart lies a fundamental truth: mastering one's own instinctual responses—the *Inner Game*—is a prerequisite to leading collective intelligence—the *Outer Game*. The leader's first responsibility is not to the organisation or the strategy, but to the governance of their own nervous system. A leader who cannot regulate their internal state will, consciously or not, impose their dysregulation onto others. The difference between a leader who fosters psychological safety and one who erodes it is often measured in moments: a misplaced sigh, a glance of disapproval, an impatient dismissal of an idea. These micro-signals are not trivial; they are the signals that shape the group's sense of safety, engagement, and trust.

A leader does not sculpt results—they sculpt the conditions in which results emerge. The best leaders act as architects, designing an environment where intelligence, trust, and resilience become the natural state of the team.

Just as a skilled gardener does not *force* plants to grow but ensures they have the right soil, light, and water, the leader's craft is in shaping an environment where high performance becomes a natural consequence. And this is where the *Hive Mind* emerges—not as a mystical or abstract concept, but as the unseen force that dictates how teams function.

A well-led team is more than the sum of its individual members; it becomes an intelligent, self-regulating system. In the presence of safety, teams adapt fluidly, challenge ideas constructively, and move towards solutions with shared ownership. In its absence, even the most talented individuals retreat into defensive postures—rigidity, avoidance, and passive compliance. Talent, experience, and intelligence are wasted when people operate in self-protection mode. The determining factor between a team that thrives and one that suffocates is not raw ability but the level of psychological safety that exists between them.

Of course, some argue that psychological safety is a luxury, that too much comfort breeds complacency. But this is a fundamental misunderstanding. Safety is not the absence of challenge—it is the precondition for taking risks. The best teams are not those free from tension, but those where people trust that challenge will be met with curiosity rather than punishment. Neuroscience affirms this: the human nervous system is constantly scanning for social cues of trust or threat. Stephen Porges' *Polyvagal Theory* explains that when people feel psychologically unsafe, their physiology shifts into a defensive state, impairing cognitive flexibility, creativity, and problem-solving.

In contrast, safety unlocks engagement. A leader who understands this does not merely manage behaviour; they shape the very conditions under which performance becomes possible.

This is why neuro-resilient leadership is fundamentally a practice, not a position. The best leaders do not simply manage teams; they sculpt the environment in which high-functioning teams can emerge. They do this by developing three essential skills:

First, they *regulate themselves under pressure*. A leader's state is the baseline for the team's state. Just as a fire crew does not look to a manual in a crisis but to the calmest, most experienced firefighter in the room, teams attune to their leader's nervous system. A leader who exudes control, confidence, and trust will set a physiological tone that allows others to follow suit.

Second, they *understand and influence the Hive Mind*. Teams are not collections of individuals; they are interdependent, emergent systems. A leader who grasps this recognises that minor shifts in team culture—who gets to speak, how failure is handled, whether people feel truly heard—have profound effects on overall performance.

Third, they *embed psychological safety into the team's fabric*. This is not a matter of policies or mission statements. It is a lived experience that must be reinforced in the moment-to-moment interactions that define group culture. Safety is not built in grand gestures but in subtle, repeated confirmations that it is safe to contribute, to challenge, to innovate.

And so, we return to one final question:

Are you shaping the conditions where your team can operate at its highest level of intelligence, trust, and resilience? Or are you, however unintentionally, creating an environment where safety is uncertain, engagement is selective, and potential is left untapped?

Because in the end, leadership is not about the individual leader. It is about what they enable in others.

Power & Peril of Crowds

The most persistent illusion in leadership is the belief that teams are merely collections of individuals, each acting independently, making rational decisions based on self-interest. But human systems do not operate this way.

Teams are not like neatly arranged puzzle pieces, each contributing its part in isolation. They behave more like a murmuration of starlings—fluid, synchronised, shifting dynamically in response to unseen forces. Every action, hesitation, and unspoken cue ripples through the group, shaping the collective behaviour. This is the Hive Mind—an emergent intelligence that can be greater than the sum of its parts or, just as easily, a breeding ground for dysfunction.

A well-led Hive Mind is a force multiplier, capable of processing complexity in real-time, integrating multiple perspectives, and generating insights that no individual could reach alone. But when mismanaged, it collapses into rigidity, conformity, and self-protection. Leaders who fail to understand this dynamic often misdiagnose the symptoms. Low engagement? They assume a motivation problem. Resistance to change? A competence issue. Lack of innovation? A skills gap.

Yet, the issue is rarely with individuals. It lies within the system itself.

The Silent Architecture

Every group develops an invisible architecture—an unspoken social contract dictating whose voice carries weight, whose ideas gain traction, and whose contributions fade into silence. This architecture is not crafted through formal policies or hierarchical structures but emerges through an intricate exchange of neurobiological signals.

In any team, there are those who speak freely and those who hesitate. Some people are interrupted mid-sentence while others command uninterrupted attention. Certain ideas spark discussion, while others sink beneath the surface, unacknowledged. Some emotions are mirrored and amplified, while others are met with blank stares. Risks are selectively rewarded or subtly punished.

Over time, these micro-patterns accumulate, forming the unwritten rules that govern group behaviour. Whether they foster psychological safety or corrode it depends largely on the leader, who—knowingly or not—is the chief architect of this invisible structure.

Intelligence vs Dysfunction

A team operating under psychological safety functions as adaptive intelligence—a collective network capable of learning, integrating new ideas, and navigating uncertainty with agility.

But when safety is compromised, even subtly, this network does not simply slow down; it shifts from intelligence to defensiveness. The change is profound and immediate:

- Silence becomes the safest strategy. Instead of contributing insights, individuals hesitate, scanning for signs that speaking up is worth the risk.
- Compliance replaces commitment. People follow instructions, but without psychological investment. They execute, but they do not engage.
- Innovation disappears. Taking risks requires trust, and trust cannot exist in an environment where failure, ridicule, or exclusion loom as possibilities.

These are not abstract effects. Studies show that teams with low psychological safety experience heightened stress, slower problem-solving, and increased errors. Conversely, organisations that prioritise psychological safety report greater innovation, stronger cohesion, and resilience under pressure.

Yet, the critical point is this: *safety is not a logical conclusion—it is a biological state.*

Safety is Felt Before Understanding

Long before a person consciously decides to trust, engage, or contribute, their nervous system has already made the decision for them. This process (neuroception) operates below conscious awareness, continuously scanning the environment for signals of safety or threat.

- A hesitant glance from a leader can be interpreted as doubt.
- A tense posture can be processed as disapproval.
- An unexpected interruption can trigger a micro-threat response, shutting down creative thinking.

The leader's role, therefore, is not simply to declare a space safe, but to *demonstrate* it—through every interaction, every gesture, and every moment of presence.

The Hive Mind's Regulator

At any given moment, a team is leaning toward one of two states:

1. *Adaptive Intelligence*—where psychological safety enables engagement, curiosity, and collective problem-solving.
2. *Defensive Rigidity*—where uncertainty and fear lead to withdrawal, compliance, and self-protection.

The leader sets the tone. Their ability to regulate their own state—to remain calm, clear, and composed under pressure—determines whether the Hive Mind becomes an asset or a liability.

The question, then, is not whether you are leading a team.

It is whether you are leading a Hive Mind that is awake, engaged, and adaptive—or one that is stagnant, hesitant, and defensive.

Because in leadership, the difference is never neutral.

The Hidden Engine of High-Performance

The greatest misconception about psychological safety is that it is about being nice. It is not. It is not about eliminating conflict. It is not about ensuring people always feel comfortable. If anything, the opposite is true—psychologically safe teams argue more, not less. The difference? Their arguments are constructive rather than corrosive.

To understand psychological safety, envisage an orchestra. In an ideal performance, musicians challenge each other, adjust their timing, experiment with new phrasing, and lean into tension rather than avoiding it. If a conductor silences every error with a sharp look or a dismissive wave, the musicians learn one thing: play it safe. Stick to the notes. Take no risks. And while the music may remain technically accurate, it will lack something vital—life. The same is true in teams. The moment people fear that mistakes will be punished, creativity dies, and all that remains is compliance.

At its core, psychological safety is about *permission*—the permission to speak, to challenge, to contribute, to fail. It is what allows a team to think, adapt, and problem-solve at its highest level of intelligence. Without it, even the most talented individuals will operate at a fraction of their capacity, diverting energy into self-protection rather than innovation, playing to authority rather than pursuing solutions.

But psychological safety is not something that can be declared. It must be *demonstrated*. A leader who says, 'We have an open-door policy' but subtly flinches when challenged has already communicated the real rule. And the nervous system, exquisitely attuned to signals of approval and rejection, does not negotiate with words—it obeys experience.

The Dual Nature of Psychological Safety

Psychological safety is not built in grand pronouncements or policy documents; it is forged in two complementary ways—*structural safeguards* that ensure safety exists beyond the leader's personal disposition, and *moment-to-moment priming* that determines whether safety is genuinely felt.

If psychological safety were a bridge, its *structural integrity* would be upheld by well-designed rules, routines, and expectations. Without these, safety is fickle—dependent on personalities, shifting moods, and external conditions.

Consider a Formula 1 pit crew. Every team member must act with precision under extreme time pressure, but they also know that mistakes will happen. If the culture treats errors as personal failings rather than process flaws, the crew will tighten up, hesitate, and play defensively. If, instead, errors trigger an immediate process review— 'What do we adjust? What do we learn?'—then performance continuously improves.

High-performing teams operate in the same way. They establish clear norms and shared expectations—defining what engagement looks like, what risks are acceptable, and how failures are handled. They normalise structured reflection, using After-Action Reviews and debriefs to ensure that setbacks are treated as data, not as evidence of incompetence. They incorporate deliberate trust-building rituals, from check-ins to open forums, ensuring that vulnerability is met with reinforcement rather than silence. And they maintain transparency in decision-making, allowing people to see how their input shapes outcomes—because nothing erodes safety faster than the sense that engagement is merely performative.

But structures alone do not create safety. They create *predictability*. The human brain does not process 'safe' in the abstract—it determines safety in real-time interactions.

The Internal Reinforcement

Consider a leader who praises creativity but stiffens slightly when someone challenges their idea. A manager who invites feedback but habitually interrupts before an idea is fully formed. A team member who takes a risk, only to be met with an awkward silence rather than reinforcement. These micro-moments may seem trivial, but they accumulate. And in an environment where psychological safety is fragile, they signal: 'Think twice before speaking.'

A leader who *masters* safety priming ensures that *safety is felt, not just stated*. This happens through:

- *Non-Verbal Acuity*: Safety is detected before it is understood. A leader who maintains a relaxed posture, uses open gestures, and sustains steady vocal prosody communicates receptivity. Conversely, a leader who glances at their phone mid-conversation signals disengagement, undermining any verbal assurances of openness.
- *Conversational Framing*: People rarely take risks in a vacuum. They take risks when the environment *invites* them to do so. Compare: 'Any thoughts?' versus 'I'm particularly interested in challenges to this idea—where might I be wrong?' The latter signals that dissent is not merely tolerated; it is *expected*.
- *Pacing & Leading*: Safety is not about dismissing tension—it is about meeting people where they are and guiding them forward. A hesitant team will not respond to forced enthusiasm, but they will follow a leader who first mirrors their state and then gradually shifts them towards engagement.

- *Co-Regulating Humour:* Well-placed humour acts as a neurological reset, shifting teams from defensiveness to receptivity. But **precision matters**—a joke at someone's expense reinforces insecurity rather than trust.
- *Modelling Psychological Safety:* If a leader never admits uncertainty, their team will never feel safe to do so. If a leader never asks for help, their team will fear appearing incompetent. Safety is demonstrated, not demanded.

The Invisible Erosion

Leaders rarely *intend* to undermine safety—but they do so nonetheless, often in imperceptible ways. A team member voices a concern, and the leader unconsciously tenses their jaw. Someone suggests an unconventional approach, and the leader acknowledges it but swiftly moves on. No words were spoken, yet the lesson was learned: *risk is unwelcome here.*

Sometimes the erosion is more obvious. A leader claims to value openness but dominates discussions. They invite feedback but only act on suggestions that confirm their existing views. This inconsistency creates *uncertainty, and uncertainty is processed as a threat.*

Even well-intended corrections can become micro-punishments. A leader publicly corrects someone's comment rather than asking for clarification privately. A joke lands at a team member's expense, triggering laughter—except for the one who will think twice before speaking next time. None of these moments may seem dramatic, but the nervous system registers them all the same.

The Key to Collective Intelligence

Teams are not intelligent or unintelligent. They are either safe enough to engage fully or uncertain enough to withdraw.

A safe team will:

- Challenge outdated assumptions without hesitation.
- Think in solutions rather than self-protection.
- Generate creativity and insight that would not exist in a less safe environment.

An unsafe team will:

- Default to risk-avoidance and compliance.
- Suppress real concerns until they explode into conflict.
- Lose their ability to innovate under pressure.

Psychological safety is *not a soft concept*—it is the single greatest predictor of whether a team will function at adaptive intelligence or defensive paralysis.

And so the leader's responsibility is clear:

Are you creating a climate where people can engage at their highest level of intelligence? Or are you unknowingly fostering an environment where silence and self-protection are the safest options?

Because leadership is never neutral. It always shapes the group—towards resilience or rigidity, towards engagement or withdrawal, towards intelligence or survival mode.

Which will you choose?

Micro-Skills for Macro-Impacts

True leadership is not about grand gestures. It is not about rousing speeches, imposing authority, or the illusion of unwavering confidence. These may create moments of impact, but they do not sustain trust. Instead, true leadership rests on a far subtler foundation: the micro-skills that shape perception, behaviour, and engagement in real time.

A leader's influence does not come from declarations—it comes from signals. The most powerful shifts in psychological safety, engagement, and performance do not occur during formal leadership moments but in the quiet, imperceptible ones. The moments that accumulate into the team's lived experience.

This is why *The Elusive Obvious*—the subtle, easily overlooked signals—separates a high-trust, high-engagement team from one that operates in cautious self-protection.

The Currency of Leadership

A leader's words are never the full story. The team listens not just to what is said, but to how it is said, when it is said, and, most crucially, what remains unsaid.

A conversation is never just about content. A leader might nod imperceptibly, encouraging someone to continue—or glance at their phone mid-discussion, subtly signalling disinterest. They might pause for a breath after a team member speaks, inviting further thought—or jump in too quickly, shutting down exploration. These micro-signals operate beneath conscious awareness, but the brain processes them *before* logic, before reasoning, before words even register.

A leader might *say* that a team is safe to speak freely, but if their tone, posture, or facial expressions betray tension, the nervous system believes the signals, not the statement.

The best leaders refine this non-verbal acuity. They develop an invisible power—the ability to shape the emotional and psychological state of a room without uttering a single word.

What Sets Leaders Apart?

The leadership ideal is often thought of as charisma or authority. But the most effective leaders rely on precision in their micro-skills.

How a leader frames a question, a challenge, or a response determines whether it expands possibility or shuts it down. Consider two responses to the same situation:

- *"I don't think that will work—what else do you have?"*
- *"There's an interesting tension here—what assumptions are we making that might need adjusting?"*

One response narrows the map, making the speaker defensive. The other opens the map, inviting exploration. The difference is subtle, yet profound.

Most leaders underestimate the power of silence. The instinct is to fill gaps, keep conversations moving, respond quickly. But silence, when used deliberately, does something remarkable—it shifts ownership.

A leader who allows three seconds of silence after a team member speaks does not just create space. They signal *thoughtfulness*, they allow psychological safety to expand into the room, they invite reflection. The team, in turn, does not just wait for orders—they engage in thinking, discovery, and ownership.

Trust is rarely built in grand moments. It emerges from a thousand micro-moments of reinforcement.

A slight nod as someone shares an idea signals 'keep going'. A pause before responding shows that their words are worth considering. A genuine 'That's an interesting perspective—I hadn't thought of that' encourages contribution without needing to declare agreement.

These moments seem insignificant, yet they determine whether a team expands into engagement or contracts into self-protection.

Leading with an Emotional Anchor

A leader's emotional state is contagious. If they radiate calm, clarity, and confidence, the team absorbs it. If they carry tension, anxiety, or frustration, the team mirrors that instead.

The Emotional Echo

This is co-regulation: the unseen mechanism behind psychological safety. Some leaders enter a room and immediately settle an anxious team; others inadvertently escalate tension without realising it.

The best leaders regulate themselves first:

- They take a breath before responding, steadying their nervous system before influencing others.

- They use warmth in their voice—tension in tone signals threat.
- They hold open, receptive body language—crossed arms or tense shoulders send defensive signals.

They are not reactive. They are stabilisers.

The Leader's Hidden Leverage

It is tempting to think of leadership as decisive action, bold vision, and strategic moves. And while these matter, they are meaningless without the micro-skills that shape team engagement.

A leader can *declare* psychological safety, but if their tone, posture, and micro-interactions contradict their words, their team will trust what they feel, not what they are told.

Micro-skills are not trivial. They are the architecture of trust. So, the question is not *what kind of leader you believe yourself to be*. A core question is:

What does your team's nervous system know to be true about you?

Storytelling for Safety & Trust

Leadership is not merely the art of giving direction—it is the art of shaping meaning. When uncertainty rises, when pressure mounts, when teams face setbacks, a leader's job extends far beyond managing tasks. It is about framing experience in a way that preserves engagement, reinforces trust, and strengthens cohesion.

And the most powerful instrument for shaping meaning? *Storytelling.*

A story does not merely transmit information; it encodes safety, solidifies trust, and anchors a team to a shared reality. In the absence of a compelling narrative, people construct their own—

and more often than not, these are narratives of doubt, fear, and fragmentation. The most effective leaders understand that the story people tell themselves is the story that dictates their actions. Whoever frames the narrative controls how reality is perceived.

Consider a ship lost in a storm. If the captain describes the situation as hopeless, the crew panics, focus fractures, and paralysis sets in. If the captain, instead, recounts tales of sailors who triumphed over tempests, if they frame the storm as a test rather than a threat, a shift occurs. Fear gives way to resolve. The same storm, reframed, demands courage rather than despair.

This is not mere rhetoric—it is neurobiology in action.

Stories Shape Nervous Systems

The human brain does not process raw data in the same way it absorbs stories. Facts and figures engage logic, but stories ignite the limbic system—the emotional core that governs trust, motivation, and belonging.

A spreadsheet of metrics does not inspire engagement. A directive to 'work harder' does not ignite commitment. But a well-crafted narrative *does*. It activates the brain's emotional circuitry, transforming passive listeners into engaged participants. This is why leaders who master storytelling build teams that are not just compliant, but committed.

Yet not all stories unify. Some divide. Some deepen distrust. The difference lies in *how* the story is framed.

Framing for Engagement & Unity

Great storytelling for leaders follows an unspoken rhythm, a psychological sequence that moves teams from hesitation to clarity, from doubt to determination. The most effective narratives do not simply relay events—they shape the emotional landscape of a team, guiding their collective response.

A well-structured story:

- *Begins with alignment*—grounding the audience in a shared experience.
- *Creates agency*—framing the challenge as something that can be acted upon rather than suffered passively.
- *Connects individual struggles to collective purpose*—reinforcing team identity.
- *Provides a new lens for interpreting setbacks*—embedding resilience and adaptability.

Without this structure, a story risks misfiring—triggering resistance rather than engagement, scepticism rather than trust.

Cohesion Under Pressure

The story of Easy Company in *Band of Brothers* is one of leadership under extreme adversity. Facing the brutal conditions of war, these men did not survive on strategy alone—they survived on meaning.

- Their leader framed hardship as part of a larger mission, ensuring that suffering did not feel meaningless.
- Micro-moments of storytelling reinforced their shared identity, preventing doubt from fracturing their cohesion.
- Humour served as a resilience tool, shifting the emotional state of the group when pressure became overwhelming.

Elite military units, high-performance teams, and deeply bonded organisations all share this trait: a unifying narrative that transforms hardship into purpose. Without it, pressure drives fragmentation.

The lesson? *A team's ability to persist through adversity is directly tied to the strength of their shared story.*

Reframing Hardship

In *Les Misérables*, Jean Valjean undergoes a transformation—not because his circumstances change, but because the *story he tells himself* does. At first, he sees himself as a victim of injustice, condemned to resentment. But through an act of trust and forgiveness, he rewrites his identity. He ceases to be the man to whom things *happen* and becomes the man who *chooses*.

This is the essence of effective leadership storytelling:

- It does not erase hardship—it reframes it in a way that restores agency.
- It does not ignore struggle—it contextualises struggle as a path to growth and impact.

A leader who does not provide this level of narrative clarity leaves their team adrift. And when uncertainty dominates, trust and motivation erode.

Everyday Leadership Storytelling

Storytelling in leadership is not an event—it is a habit. The best leaders use narrative not as a performance, but as a rhythm woven into daily interactions. A single well-told story can reframe a crisis, restore morale, and deepen alignment.

Consider how the same situation can be framed differently:

- 'We failed to meet our target.'
- 'We discovered that our assumptions about X were incorrect —this insight now gives us a competitive advantage.'

- 'We don't know what will happen next.'
- 'Great teams are defined not by certainty, but by their ability to adapt. This is our moment to prove exactly that.'

- 'This is your role.'
- 'Let me tell you a story about how this role connects to something larger than the individual.'

A leader who does not actively shape the team's story leaves a vacuum—and a vacuum will always be filled, either by fear and doubt, or by purpose and resolve.

And so the fundamental question remains:

Are you crafting a story that strengthens your team's trust, resilience, and commitment? Or are you allowing uncertainty to write the story for you?

Because every team has a story. The only question is:

Who is telling it?

Neuro-Resilient Leader

Mastering leadership resilience is not about knowing—it is about doing. The most insightful frameworks, the most compelling theories, and the most well-reasoned strategies mean nothing if they are not woven into daily leadership practice.

A neuro-resilient leader does not merely memorise principles; they embody them. They create the conditions where trust, adaptability, and high performance emerge naturally, not as policies, but as lived realities.

Now comes the real challenge:

How do you ensure that neuro-resilience is not just a concept you appreciate, but a capability you develop and apply consistently?

The Art of Resilience

Leadership is not a fixed trait—it is a practice, much like the discipline of an athlete or the refinement of an artist. Every decision, every interaction, every reaction under pressure either strengthens or weakens the resilience of the leader and, by extension, their team.

Three pillars uphold neuro-resilient leadership:

- *Self-Regulation* – Mastering one's own nervous system before attempting to influence others.
- *Psychological Safety* – Ensuring trust is reinforced in every interaction.
- *Collective Intelligence* – Leading the Hive Mind rather than merely managing individuals.

These are not abstract ideals—they are disciplines, requiring continual refinement and a willingness to evolve.

The Leadership Anchor

A leader's emotional state is not private—it is public information, continuously broadcasted and absorbed by their team. If a leader is reactive, tense, or defensive, the team unconsciously mirrors those states. If a leader is calm, clear, and grounded, the team regulates to that stability.

Think of a jazz musician improvising in a live performance. The ability to stay in flow—to absorb unpredictability without panic—determines the quality of the music. Leadership is the same. The ability to remain composed under pressure is not innate; it is cultivated.

To lead well under stress, a neuro-resilient leader must develop:

- *Situational Awareness of Their Own Nervous System*

Can you recognise the subtle shifts in your body before stress takes over? When pressure mounts, does your voice tighten, your breath shorten, or your movements become rigid? A leader who ignores these signals is already being led—by their own biology.

- *Deliberate Recovery Strategies*

A well-regulated leader builds rituals that prevent stress from accumulating. Deep breathing before a high-stakes meeting, structured reflection at the end of the day, or even the simple act of pausing before reacting—these micro-adjustments define the difference between a leader who steers the ship and one who is tossed by the waves.

If a leader cannot regulate themselves, they cannot regulate a team.

The Daily Test of Leadership

A team's engagement is not driven solely by motivation—it hinges on whether they feel safe enough to fully participate. Without psychological safety, ideas shrink, collaboration stalls, and decision-making narrows to defensive self-preservation.

See two meeting rooms. In one, team members hesitate before speaking, calculating whether their ideas will be dismissed or ridiculed. In the other, ideas flow freely, even the flawed ones, because people trust that failure will be treated as learning, not incompetence. The difference is not in the talent of the individuals—it is in the leadership that shapes the environment.

Psychological safety is built in two ways:

- *Through Structures that Enable Trust*

Are there clear norms for participation? Do feedback loops allow learning without fear of punishment? Are mistakes treated as useful data or as evidence of incompetence? If a team does not know the answer to these questions, their leader has already answered it for them—through neglect.

- *Through the Leader's Daily Behaviour*

How often do you interrupt rather than listen? Do your facial expressions match your words? When challenged, do you appear curious or defensive? Trust is not declared; it is demonstrated, in micro-moments, over time.

Psychological safety is not a policy—it is a lived experience, shaped by what leaders reinforce in every conversation.

From Compliance to Intelligence

Managing individuals is straightforward. Leading a collective intelligence is the real test.

Consider a school of fish moving in synchrony. There is no single leader dictating each turn, yet the group moves with fluid precision, responding dynamically to threats and opportunities. A truly high-functioning team operates in the same way—not as a set of compliant individuals awaiting orders but as an intelligent, adaptive unit.

To cultivate this, a leader must ask:

- *Am I fostering an environment where people think freely, or are they filtering their ideas to fit my expectations?*
- *Do I encourage problem-solving, or am I the bottleneck for every decision?*
- *Is debate welcomed, or do people feel safer staying silent?*

High-performing teams exhibit:

- *Adaptive Intelligence* – They navigate complexity collectively, rather than defaulting to hierarchical decision-making.
- *Shared Ownership of Success and Failure* – Accountability is distributed, rather than concentrated in authority.
- *Active Challenge Without Fear* – A team that feels safe to question assumptions will always make better decisions than one that avoids conflict.

A neuro-resilient leader does not need to have all the answers. They need to create an environment where the best answers emerge.

For a leader, the true test is not knowledge—it is embodiment. Consider this:

- When faced with stress, do you react instinctively or respond deliberately?
- Do your team members feel encouraged to challenge ideas, or do they tread carefully around leadership?
- When a problem arises, does your team collaborate dynamically, or do they wait for direction?

If these questions give you pause, that is not a failure—it is an invitation to the next level of leadership mastery.

Engaging Complexity

Leadership is shifting. Command-and-control models are crumbling under the weight of complexity. Static leadership styles collapse in environments that demand adaptability.

The leaders who will thrive in the coming decades are not those who dictate; they are those who understand and harness the human nervous system at scale.

Neuro-resilient leaders will be:

- The ones who create teams that adapt to rapid change rather than resist it.
- The ones who sustain high performance even in volatility.
- The ones who transform pressure into a strategic advantage rather than a source of dysfunction.

And so, the final challenge is not theoretical—it is deeply personal:

Are you ready to embody neuro-resilient leadership?

Because leadership is not about what you know—it is about what you reinforce in every interaction, every decision, and every moment you lead.

The Leadership Promise

So now, the question is not whether you *understand* these principles—it is whether you will *embody them*.

Neuro-resilient leadership is not about *occasional moments of inspiration*. It is about *consistent, deliberate practice*. Every conversation, every micro-interaction, every leadership decision is an opportunity to either:

- Reinforce *psychological safety* or *erode it*.
- Foster *adaptive intelligence* or *trigger self-protection*.
- Lead with *clarity and stability* or react from *uncertainty and stress*.

The world is not slowing down. Complexity is not easing. But leaders who master neuro-resilience will stand unshaken in the storm—guiding their teams through change, uncertainty, and challenge with clarity, confidence, and precision.

Neuro-Resilient Imperative

Command-and-control leadership is not fading—it has already failed. The future will not belong to the most authoritative, but to the most adaptive. Not to those who impose certainty, but to those who cultivate resilience.

In a world of constant disruption, neuro-resilient leadership will be the defining edge between organisations that flourish and those that falter.

Tomorrow's strongest leaders won't just be those with technical skill or authority. They will be those who:

- Regulate their own nervous system before attempting to influence others.
- Shape team conditions to drive performance through trust, not coercion.
- Frame challenges as narratives of resilience, ensuring uncertainty fuels engagement, not fear.

Organisations that fail to develop *neuro-resilient leadership* will struggle. They will experience:

- Increased *burnout and disengagement*, as employees operate in *states of chronic stress and uncertainty*.
- Higher *turnover and loss of talent*, as people seek environments where they feel *psychologically safe and valued*.
- Slower *adaptation to change*, as teams resist uncertainty rather than leaning into it with confidence.

Meanwhile, organisations that embed *neuro-resilience* into their leadership culture will *outperform, outlast, and outthink* their competition.

The difference will not be in *IQ, strategy, or resources*—it will be in *how well leaders cultivate trust, engagement, and adaptability in the people they lead.*

Final Challenge

A leader does not sculpt results—they sculpt the conditions in which results emerge. The best leaders act as architects, designing an environment where intelligence, trust, and resilience become the natural state of the team.

And so, one final challenge remains:

You are shaping the conditions of your team's future—right now, in real time. With every word, every pause, every glance. The question is not whether you are leading.

Are you leading them forward—or watching them retreat?

Because leadership is not about what you intend. It is about what your team feels, trusts, and dares to do under your influence. And every moment—whether you notice it or not—is tipping the balance.

What will you choose?

AFTERWORD
THE LEADER YOU HAVE BECOME

There comes a moment in every leader's journey when the external noise fades, the frantic search for answers slows, and a quiet clarity emerges from within. Perhaps you have already felt it—an unshakable confidence that, regardless of what tomorrow brings, you have cultivated the resilience to meet it. If so, you have not merely read this book; you have absorbed it, wrestled with its challenges, and, most importantly, embodied its lessons.

Resilience is often spoken of as a trait—something one either possesses or lacks. Yet, as you have discovered, true resilience is not a fixed attribute. It is an evolving capacity, a skill set honed through deliberate practice, reflection, and, above all, experience. It is not about avoiding stress, nor is it about brute force endurance. Rather, it is about learning to dance with uncertainty, to become pliable and not break, to act with wisdom rather than mere reaction.

At the heart of neuro-resilience is a profound paradox: The most unshakable leaders are those who allow themselves to feel. They do not numb themselves to stress, nor do they deny the reality of pressure. Instead, they engage with their neurology fully, process it skilfully, and turn it around into clarity, focus, and decisive action. They listen to their instincts without being enslaved by them. They wield reason without becoming detached. They foster emotional connection without losing composure. They are, in the truest sense, whole.

The Road You Have Travelled

Consider for a moment where you started. Perhaps stress was something you fought against, an adversary to be subdued or ignored. Perhaps your instincts felt unreliable—prone to overreaction or misfire. Perhaps leadership felt like a constant balancing act, teetering between control and exhaustion. And now, what do you notice?

You have learned to engage your instincts rather than suppress them, to see them not as vestiges of a primitive past but as a sophisticated early-warning system. You have learned to refine your perception, to trust your ability to assess situations accurately, to sense shifts in the emotional undercurrents of a room before words are even spoken. You have trained yourself to hold steady in chaos, to remain composed in the face of uncertainty, and to lead in a way that inspires —not through fear or authority, but through presence and certainty.

Through the exercises and techniques you have practised, you have strengthened not just your mind but your entire nervous system. Your ability to regulate your state has increased. Your capacity to absorb tension without transmitting it to others has deepened. You are no longer simply reacting; you are choosing. And that, above all, is what defines a resilient leader: choice over reflex, mastery over impulse, wisdom over mere knowledge.

Beyond the Page

The journey, of course, does not end here. This book has provided the framework, but your leadership will be measured by what you do next. The challenges ahead will not announce themselves politely. They will arrive unbidden, in moments of ambiguity, conflict, and high stakes. Yet, where others may falter, you will stand firm—not because you are immune to pressure, but because you have trained yourself to meet it differently.

Picture yourself standing on the deck of a ship in a rising storm. The winds howl, the waves crash, the sky darkens. Some around you panic, their instincts screaming at them to retreat, to react blindly. But not you. You have trained for this. You plant your feet, adjust your stance, and take control—not of the storm, but of yourself. This is leadership. Not waiting for the chaos to subside, but learning to navigate within it.

You will listen more deeply—not just to words, but to the unstated, the hesitations, the hidden currents of group dynamics. You will speak with greater impact—not through volume, but through congruence, precision, and presence. You will create environments where psychological safety is not just a buzzword, but a lived experience—where your team operates not from fear, but from trust and engagement.

Most importantly, you will be the leader others turn to when the way forward is unclear. Not because you have all the answers, but because you know how to find them. Because you embody the kind of presence that reassures, the kind of clarity that cuts through chaos, and the kind of resilience that allows others to draw strength from your steadiness.

There is an old saying: *Calm seas do not make skilled sailors.* You have been tested, you have adapted, and you have emerged stronger. Yet, even as you refine your neuro-resilience, remember that leadership is not a solo act. It is, at its core, an act of service—of guiding others, of creating space for them to thrive, of forging a path where none seemed to exist.

Take a moment now. Close your eyes. Think back to a moment in your journey—perhaps a time of doubt, a time when stress felt insurmountable. Now, contrast that with the leader you are today. Feel that shift. See it. Recognise it. That transformation is real.

The work of leadership is never truly finished. But now, you possess something invaluable: the ability to lead yourself first. And that is the foundation upon which all leadership legacy is built.

Step forward with intention, not just into leadership, but into a future where your resilience is the steady pulse beneath every decision, every challenge, and every triumph. Storms will brew. Crises will come. This is your moment. This is your time to lead.

You are a crisis-ready leader.

Paul O'Neill

November 2024

APPENDIX
SUBMODALITY COMPARISON SHEETS

	Experience 1	Experience 2
VISUAL		
Number of images		
Motion/still		
Colour/black and white		
Bright/dim		
Focused/unfocused		
Bordered/panoramic		
Associated/dissociated		
Centre-weighted/wide angle		
Size (relative to life)		
Shape		
Three-dimensional/flat		
Close/distant		
Location in space		
AUDITORY		
Number of sounds/sources		
Volume		
Tone		
Tempo		
Pitch		
Pace		
Timber		
Duration		
Intensity		
Direction		
Intensity		
Direction		
Rhythm		
Harmony		
More in one ear than another		
KINESTHETIC		
Location in body		
Breathing rate		
Pulse rate		
Skin temperature		
Weight		
Pressure		
Intensity		
Tactile sensations		
OLFACTORY & GUSTATORY		
Sweet		
Sour		
Salt		
Bitter		
Aroma		
Fragrance		
Essences		
Pungency		

	Experience 1	Experience 2
VISUAL		
Number of images		
Motion/still		
Colour/black and white		
Bright/dim		
Focused/unfocused		
Bordered/panoramic		
Associated/dissociated		
Centre-weighted/wide angle		
Size (relative to life)		
Shape		
Three-dimensional/flat		
Close/distant		
Location in space		
AUDITORY		
Number of sounds/sources		
Volume		
Tone		
Tempo		
Pitch		
Pace		
Timber		
Duration		
Intensity		
Direction		
Intensity		
Direction		
Rhythm		
Harmony		
More in one ear than another		
KINESTHETIC		
Location in body		
Breathing rate		
Pulse rate		
Skin temperature		
Weight		
Pressure		
Intensity		
Tactile sensations		
OLFACTORY & GUSTATORY		
Sweet		
Sour		
Salt		
Bitter		
Aroma		
Fragrance		
Essences		
Pungency		

	Experience 1	Experience 2
VISUAL		
Number of images		
Motion/still		
Colour/black and white		
Bright/dim		
Focused/unfocused		
Bordered/panoramic		
Associated/dissociated		
Centre-weighted/wide angle		
Size (relative to life)		
Shape		
Three-dimensional/flat		
Close/distant		
Location in space		
AUDITORY		
Number of sounds/sources		
Volume		
Tone		
Tempo		
Pitch		
Pace		
Timber		
Duration		
Intensity		
Direction		
Intensity		
Direction		
Rhythm		
Harmony		
More in one ear than another		
KINESTHETIC		
Location in body		
Breathing rate		
Pulse rate		
Skin temperature		
Weight		
Pressure		
Intensity		
Tactile sensations		
OLFACTORY & GUSTATORY		
Sweet		
Sour		
Salt		
Bitter		
Aroma		
Fragrance		
Essences		
Pungency		

	Experience 1	Experience 2
VISUAL		
Number of images		
Motion/still		
Colour/black and white		
Bright/dim		
Focused/unfocused		
Bordered/panoramic		
Associated/dissociated		
Centre-weighted/wide angle		
Size (relative to life)		
Shape		
Three-dimensional/flat		
Close/distant		
Location in space		
AUDITORY		
Number of sounds/sources		
Volume		
Tone		
Tempo		
Pitch		
Pace		
Timber		
Duration		
Intensity		
Direction		
Intensity		
Direction		
Rhythm		
Harmony		
More in one ear than another		
KINESTHETIC		
Location in body		
Breathing rate		
Pulse rate		
Skin temperature		
Weight		
Pressure		
Intensity		
Tactile sensations		
OLFACTORY & GUSTATORY		
Sweet		
Sour		
Salt		
Bitter		
Aroma		
Fragrance		
Essences		
Pungency		

	Experience 1	Experience 2
VISUAL		
Number of images		
Motion/still		
Colour/black and white		
Bright/dim		
Focused/unfocused		
Bordered/panoramic		
Associated/dissociated		
Centre-weighted/wide angle		
Size (relative to life)		
Shape		
Three-dimensional/flat		
Close/distant		
Location in space		
AUDITORY		
Number of sounds/sources		
Volume		
Tone		
Tempo		
Pitch		
Pace		
Timber		
Duration		
Intensity		
Direction		
Intensity		
Direction		
Rhythm		
Harmony		
More in one ear than another		
KINESTHETIC		
Location in body		
Breathing rate		
Pulse rate		
Skin temperature		
Weight		
Pressure		
Intensity		
Tactile sensations		
OLFACTORY & GUSTATORY		
Sweet		
Sour		
Salt		
Bitter		
Aroma		
Fragrance		
Essences		
Pungency		

NOTES

1. INSTINCTUAL CONTACT

1. MacLean, P. D. (1990). *The triune brain in evolution: Role in paleocerebral functions*. Springer.
2. The enteric nervous system (ENS) is often referred to as the 'second brain' due to its extensive network of neurons in the gut. See: Gershon, M.D. (1998). *The Second Brain: A Groundbreaking New Understanding of Nervous Disorders of the Stomach and Intestine*; and
    Damasio, A. R. (1994). *Descartes' error: Emotion, reason and the human brain*. Putnam.
3. Freud, S. (1915/2001). The unconscious. In *The standard edition of the complete psychological works of Sigmund Freud*(Vol. 14). Vintage.
4. The gut-brain axis involves a bidirectional communication network between the central and enteric nervous systems. This interaction significantly affects emotional regulation and cognitive functioning under stress.
5. This emphasis on integrating instinct and cognition reflects themes from Gigerenzer's research on heuristics and intuitive intelligence. See: Gigerenzer, G. (2007). *Gut Feelings: The Intelligence of the Unconscious*.

2. INSTINCTUAL AWARENESS

1. MacLean, P. D. (1990). *The Triune Brain in Evolution: Role in Paleocerebral Functions*. This theory posits that the human brain evolved in three major parts: reptilian (survival), limbic (emotion), and neocortex (reason).
2. MacLean, P. D. (1990). *The triune brain in evolution: Role in paleocerebral functions*. Springer.
3. The 'fight, flight, or freeze' response is part of the autonomic nervous system's defence mechanism, originally mapped by Walter Cannon and later refined in trauma studies by Peter Levine and Bessel van der Kolk.
4. While the Triune Brain model is debated in modern neuroscience, it remains a useful metaphor for explaining instinctive reactions, especially in leadership and coaching contexts
5. Kahneman, D. (2011). *Thinking, fast and slow*. Farrar, Straus and Giroux.

3. INSTINCTUAL ACUITY

1. Porges, S. W. (2011). *The Polyvagal Theory: Neurophysiological Foundations of*

Emotions, Attachment, Communication, and Self-Regulation. Neuroception refers to the body's unconscious system for detecting safety, danger, or life threat.
2. This technique draws on NLP reframing strategies and pattern detection, pioneered by Richard Bandler, which treat worry as a signal from the unconscious that can be reframed and redeployed. See Bandler, R. (1985). *Using Your Brain—for a Change.*
3. van der Kolk, B. (2014). *The body keeps the score: Brain, mind and body in the healing of trauma.* Viking.
4. This story is cited by Porges as an example of neuroception in action: an embodied form of unconscious safety detection critical to survival, even without logical reasoning
5. Richard Bandler, co-creator of Neuro-Linguistic Programming (NLP), has written extensively on pattern recognition, submodalities, and altering state through reframing.
   See: Bandler, R. (2008). *Get the Life You Want.*
6. The Unconscious Navigator concept resonates with Daniel Kahneman's System 1 (fast, intuitive) thinking. See: Kahneman, D. (2011). *Thinking, Fast and Slow.*
7. Bandler, R. (1985). *Using your brain for a change: Neuro-linguistic programming.* Real People Press.
8. This process uses kinaesthetic anchoring and memory amplification techniques developed in Neuro-Linguistic Programming (NLP), particularly Bandler's emphasis on shifting emotional states through vivid mental rehearsal and body-based focus. See Bandler, R. & Andreas, S. (1987). *Using Your Brain—for a Change.*

SECTION TWO

1. This metaphor parallels the concept of self-regulation as dynamic steering—central to emotional intelligence frameworks. See Goleman, D. (1995). *Emotional Intelligence.*
2. The notion that modern stress responses are rooted in ancient neurological circuits is central to Polyvagal Theory. See Porges, S. (2011). *The Polyvagal Theory: Neurophysiological Foundations of Emotions, Attachment, Communication, and Self-regulation.*

4. CORE SKILLS

1. Jacques Lecoq (1921–1999) was a French actor and movement coach who developed a widely respected approach to physical theatre, based on body awareness and instinctive action.
2. This notion draws on the evolutionary continuity between species, notably articulated in Charles Darwin's *The Descent of Man* (1871), where he argued that humans retain the physical and behavioural residues of their ancestral past.
3. Instinct Mapping is influenced by NLP submodality techniques, which explore

how sensory details structure internal experience. See Bandler, R. & MacDonald, W. (1988). *An Insider's Guide to Submodalities.*

5. INTERMEDIATE SKILLS

1. This technique builds on cognitive distancing and visual dissociation strategies found in NLP and trauma therapy. See Bandler, R. & Grinder, J. (1979). *Frogs Into Princes.*
2. This technique draws directly on Richard Bandler's work with submodality shifts and timeline reframing in Neuro-Linguistic Programming (NLP), used to change the emotional charge of painful memories. See Bandler, R. (1985). *Using Your Brain—for a Change.*

   *It also echoes findings from trauma studies on memory reconsolidation and embodied trauma.

   Reframing emotional memory content draws from memory reconsolidation research and trauma reframing approaches. See van der Kolk, B. (2014). *The Body Keeps the Score.*
3. This inner dialogue restructuring method is derived from Bandler's pattern interruption techniques and the NLP "Meta Model," which deconstructs limiting language patterns. See Bandler, R. & Grinder, J. (1975). *The Structure of Magic, Vol. 1.*

   It also has parallels in narrative therapy that encourage the re-authoring of internal stories. See White, M. & Epston, D. (1990). *Narrative Means to Therapeutic Ends.*

6. ADVANCED SKILLS

1. *This method of noticing the "spin" of anxiety and reversing it draws from Richard Bandler's "Neuro-Hypnotic Repatterning" (NHR), a technique that builds on submodality directionality to collapse or overwrite emotional patterns. See Bandler, R. (2008). *Get the Life You Want: The Secrets to Quick and Lasting Life Change.*
2. Bandler, R. (2008). *Get the life you want: The secrets to quick and lasting life change with neuro-linguistic programming.* Health Communications.

SECTION TWO SUMMARY

1. This concept aligns with somatic psychology, which posits that the body often initiates responses before conscious cognition. See Levine, P. (1997). *Waking the Tiger: Healing Trauma.*
2. These techniques aim to restore and optimise the 'window of tolerance'—the zone of optimal arousal for functioning. See Siegel, D. (2012). *The Developing Mind.*

7. WHEN SAFETY IS RUPTURED

1. The 'freeze' response is a survival mechanism governed by the dorsal vagal system, part of the Polyvagal Theory introduced by Stephen Porges
2. MacLean, P. D. (1990). *The Triune Brain in Evolution*. This framework describes the layered structure of human emotion, with survival instincts driven by the 'reptilian brain'
3. Richard Bandler. Often used in stress-management workshops to emphasise neuroplasticity and mindset choice

8. RUPTURE REPAIR COACHING

1. **Bandler, R.** (2008). *Get the life you want: The secrets to quick and lasting life change with neuro-linguistic programming*. Health Communications Inc.
2. This culinary metaphor illustrates neuroplastic coaching: just as chefs manipulate ingredients to affect biology, skilled coaches shape subjective experience to shift emotional and physiological states
3. The PACE Protocol (Prime, Agency, Connect, Embed) draws inspiration from Richard Bandler's live demonstrations—particularly his work on emotional pacing and layered anchoring, as seen in his *Konstanz* DVD. The structure integrates NLP's pacing techniques with trauma-informed coaching, offering a fluid framework for regulating emotional states and re-patterning behavioural responses.

11. SAFETY-EMBEDDED STRUCTURES

1. Whilst engagement's purpose was inspired by *Anecdote Circles,* the framing of the Appreciative Inquiry, is very much part of PACE Strengths DNA. In execution, the PACE structure and Meta Model are preeminent.

12. SAFETY PRIMING SKILLS

1. Bandler, R. (1985). *Using your brain—for a change: Neuro-linguistic programming*. Real People Press.
2. Extending co-regulation techniques to external stakeholders helps build trust, credibility, and rapport beyond the team setting.

SECTION FOUR SUMMARY

1. Stephen Porges, Polyvagal Theory: Neurophysiological Foundations of Emotions, Attachment, Communication, and Self-Regulation.
2. The concept of 'Hive Mind' is used metaphorically to describe emergent intelli-

gence in complex adaptive systems, similar to that observed in eusocial insects and flocking birds.
3. Neuroception is a term coined by Stephen Porges to describe the nervous system's unconscious detection of safety, danger, or life threat without cognitive awareness.
4. The 'Inner Game' refers to self-regulation; the 'Outer Game' involves group-level regulation and creating safety through behaviour, language, and presence.
5. AARs were developed by the U.S. Army to extract learning from events. The model fosters shared understanding without assigning blame.
6. 'Crumple & Toss' provides anonymity to reduce power distance and elicit more honest feedback, especially useful in hierarchical teams.
7. The PACE storytelling structure highlights Permission, Agency, Connection, and Embedding—used to shift emotional states and surface group wisdom.
8. Weak signals are early indicators of emerging issues or cultural dynamics. PACE Surfacing helps detect these through story-driven exploration.
9. Conscious breath regulation is a key co-regulation skill that allows leaders to influence collective nervous system states.
10. According to Polyvagal Theory, prosodic voice patterns signal safety to the vagus nerve, facilitating social engagement.
11. Mirroring metaphors and emotional intensity enhances empathy and psychological safety by demonstrating attunement.

SECTION FIVE

1. Paul Ekman's research on micro-expressions and universal emotional displays has shown how non-verbal cues trigger emotional judgments before verbal content is processed.
2. Joseph LeDoux and Antonio Damasio have demonstrated that emotional appraisal of threat and safety begins in subcortical structures before conscious awareness, reinforcing the evolutionary basis of non-verbal perception.
3. Daniel Goleman's model of emotional intelligence identifies self-awareness and self-regulation as foundational competencies for effective leadership and influence.
4. Chris Argyris and Donald Schön describe the gap between 'espoused theory' and 'theory-in-use,' suggesting leaders may unconsciously send signals that contradict their stated intentions.

SECTION FIVE SUMMARY

1. Antonio Damasio's somatic marker hypothesis shows that physiological cues are processed before language, anchoring decisions in bodily experiences.
2. Albert Mehrabian's communication model suggests that trustworthiness is largely judged by non-verbal alignment between tone, expression, and content.
3. Bandler, R., & Grinder, J. (1975). *The Structure of Magic, Vol. 1*. Science and Behavior Books.

4. Bandler, R., & Grinder, J. (1979). *Frogs into Princes: Neuro Linguistic Programming*. Real People Press.
5. Grinder, M. (1993). *ENVoY: Your Personal Guide to Classroom Management*. Michael Grinder & Associates.
6. Bandler, R. (2008). *Get the Life You Want*. Health Communications; Grinder, M. (2003). *A Cat in the Doghouse*. Michael Grinder & Associates.
7. Grinder, M. (1993). *ENVoY: Your Personal Guide to Classroom Management*.
8. Grinder, M. (2004). *The Elusive Obvious: The Science of Nonverbal Communication*. Michael Grinder & Associates.
9. Grinder, M. (2004). *The Elusive Obvious: The Science of Nonverbal Communication*. Michael Grinder & Associates.

    Stephen Porges' Polyvagal Theory highlights how breathing patterns modulate vagal tone, which in turn influences how others perceive safety or threat in social interactions.
10. Bandler, R. (1993). *Time for a Change*. Neuro-Linguistic Programming Training Institute.

    NLP practices, as introduced by Richard Bandler, train perceptual flexibility through peripheral vision and subtle non-verbal pattern recognition, enhancing interpersonal calibration.
11. Grinder, M. (2005). *Charisma: The Art of Relationships*. Michael Grinder & Associates.
12. Synthesised concept based on Michael Grinder, Paul Ekman & NLP observation of "clusters" – cf. Ekman, P. (2003). *Emotions Revealed*. Times Books.

    Virginia Satir's work on communication stances suggested that congruent body-language patterns influence relational impact and perception of authority.
13. Robert Dilts' behavioural modelling in NLP includes coordinated gesture-use to enhance linguistic anchoring and direct group attention during communication.

    See Grinder, M. (2004). *The Elusive Obvious*.
14. Grinder, M. (2004). *The Elusive Obvious*, esp. in police training & de-escalation chapters.
15. The 'Milton Model,' developed by Bandler and Grinder, includes embedded command structures and tonal shifts such as pauses and whispers to guide attention below the level of conscious resistance.

    Grinder, M. (2004). *The Elusive Obvious*.

SECTION SIX

1. Ralph Stacey, *Complexity and Organizational Reality*, Routledge, 2001.
2. Dave Snowden, "The Cynefin Framework: Decision Making in Context," *Harvard Business Review*, 2007.
3. Stephen W. Porges, *The Polyvagal Theory: Neurophysiological Foundations of Emotions, Attachment, Communication, and Self-Regulation*, Norton, 2011.
4. https://www.richardbandler.com/
5. Paul D. MacLean, *The Triune Brain in Evolution*, Springer, 1990.

17. "BAND OF BROTHERS"

1. Dave Snowden, cited in "The Use of Narrative in Knowledge Management," *KM World*, 2000.
2. Based on a real merger case story (anonymised), where leadership narrative helped stabilise emotional uncertainty and define the new shared identity.

18. "LES MISÉRABLES"

1. Dave Snowden, "Narrative and Complex Systems," *Cognitive Edge Blog*, 2009.
2. Nelson Mandela, Rivonia Trial Speech, April 20, 1964.
3. Mahatma Gandhi, Speech during the Quit India Movement, August 8, 1942.
4. Abraham Lincoln, Gettysburg Address, November 19, 1863.
5. The 4Cs—Compassion, Credibility, Cognition, and Campaign—are adaptive leadership traits for narrative engagement developed by the author to accompany the FOCUS UP framework.
6. Composite leadership narrative drawn from multiple team transformation projects led by the author between 2018–2022.
7. The story of Jerry illustrates how psychological safety ruptures propagate through teams if left unresolved—an example of emotional contagion in social neuroscience
8. The Triune Brain model (Reptilian, Mammalian, Primate) was first developed by neuroscientist Paul MacLean and has since been applied in organisational and leadership studies
9.

SECTION SIX SUMMARY

1. See: Porges, S. (2011). *The Polyvagal Theory*; also Snowden, D. (2005). "Narrative as Sense-Making in Complex Systems." These works underpin the role of narrative in triggering safety responses

BIBLIOGRAPHY

Books

Aristotle. (2009). *The Nicomachean ethics* (W. D. Ross, Trans.). Oxford University Press. (Original work c. 4th century BCE)

Bandler, R. (1985). *Using your brain for a change: Neuro-linguistic programming*. Real People Press.

Bandler, R. (2008). *Get the life you want: The secrets to quick and lasting life change with neuro-linguistic programming*. Health Communications.

Bandler, R., & Grinder, J. (1975). *The structure of magic I: A book about language and therapy*. Science and Behavior Books.

Bandler, R., & Grinder, J. (1979). *Frogs into princes: Neuro linguistic programming*. Real People Press.

Bandler, R., & LaValle, J. (1996). *Persuasion engineering*. Meta Publications.

Bion, W. R. (1961). *Experiences in groups: And other papers*. Tavistock Publications.

Breen, M. (2003). *Coaching mastery in NLP*. MBNLP Publishing.

Brown, B. (2012). *Daring greatly: How the courage to be vulnerable transforms the way we live, love, parent, and lead*. Gotham Books.

Cuddy, A. J. C. (2015). *Presence: Bringing your boldest self to your biggest challenges*. Little, Brown and Company.

Damasio, A. R. (1994). *Descartes' error: Emotion, reason and the human brain*. Putnam.

Damasio, A. R. (1999). *The feeling of what happens: Body, emotion and the making of consciousness*. Heinemann.

Dana, D. (2018). *The polyvagal theory in therapy: Engaging the rhythm of regulation*. W. W. Norton.

Darwin, C. (1871). *The descent of man, and selection in relation to sex*. John Murray.

Dawkins, R. (1976). *The selfish gene*. Oxford University Press.

Dawkins, R. (1982). *The extended phenotype: The long reach of the gene*. Oxford University Press.

Dawkins, R. (2006). *The God delusion*. Bantam Press.

Dennett, D. C. (1991). *Consciousness explained*. Little, Brown and Company.

Dennett, D. C. (1995). *Darwin's dangerous idea: Evolution and the meanings of life*. Simon & Schuster.

Dennett, D. C. (2003). *Freedom evolves*. Penguin Books.

Edmondson, A. C. (2018). *The fearless organisation: Creating psychological safety in the workplace for learning, innovation, and growth*. Wiley.

Franklin, B. (n.d.). *Poor Richard's almanack*. (Quoted aphorism: "An ounce of prevention is worth a pound of cure.")

Freud, S. (1915/2001). The unconscious. In J. Strachey (Ed. & Trans.), *The standard edition of the complete psychological works of Sigmund Freud* (Vol. 14, pp. 159–215). Vintage. (Original work published 1915)

Goffman, E. (1959). *The presentation of self in everyday life*. Anchor Books.

Goleman, D. (1995). *Emotional intelligence: Why it can matter more than IQ*. Bantam Books.

Goleman, D. (2006). *Social intelligence: The new science of human relationships*. Hutchinson.

Grinder, M. (1996). *ENVoY: Your personal guide to classroom management*. Michael Grinder & Associates.

Grinder, M. (2006). *A healthy classroom: Educational group dynamics*. Michael Grinder & Associates.

Grinder, M. (2009). *Charisma: The art of relationships*. Michael Grinder & Associates.

Huxley, A. (1965). *Island*. Chatto & Windus.

Jacobs, B. (2014). *The embodied leader: A somatic approach to developing your leadership*. Jossey-Bass.

Kahneman, D. (2011). *Thinking, fast and slow*. Farrar, Straus and Giroux.

Lakoff, G., & Johnson, M. (1980). *Metaphors we live by*. University of Chicago Press.

LeDoux, J. (1996). *The emotional brain: The mysterious underpinnings of emotional life*. Simon & Schuster.

Levine, P. A. (1997). *Waking the tiger: Healing trauma*. North Atlantic Books.

MacLean, P. D. (1990). *The triune brain in evolution: Role in paleocerebral functions*. Springer.

Mandela, N. (1994). *Long walk to freedom: The autobiography of Nelson Mandela*. Little, Brown and Company.

Mandelbrot, B. B. (2004). *The (mis)behaviour of markets: A fractal view of financial turbulence*. Profile Books.

McKenna, P. (2009). *Control stress: Stop worrying and feel good now!*. Bantam Press.

McKenna, P. (2017). *Freedom from anxiety*. Hay House.

McKenna, P. (2010). *I can make you confident*. Sterling Publishing.

Orwell, G. (1949). *Nineteen eighty-four*. Secker & Warburg.

Porges, S. W. (2011). *The polyvagal theory: Neurophysiological foundations of emotions, attachment, communication, and self-regulation*. W. W. Norton.

Rowling, J. K. (2008). *The tales of Beedle the Bard*. Bloomsbury.

Siegel, D. J. (2010). *The mindful therapist: A clinician's guide to mindsight and neural integration*. W. W. Norton.

Sinek, S. (2009). *Start with why: How great leaders inspire everyone to take action*. Penguin Books.

Snowden, D. J., & Boone, M. E. (2007). A leader's framework for decision making. *Harvard Business Review*, 85(11), 68–76.

Stacey, R. D. (2007). *Strategic management and organisational dynamics* (5th ed.). Pearson Education.

Sun Tzu. (2009). *The art of war* (L. Giles, Trans.). Arcturus Publishing. (Original work c. 5th century BCE)

Sutton, R. I. (2007). *The no asshole rule: Building a civilised workplace and surviving one that isn't*. Business Plus.
van der Kolk, B. A. (2014). *The body keeps the score: Brain, mind and body in the healing of trauma*. Viking.
Wheatley, M. J. (2006). *Leadership and the new science: Discovering order in a chaotic world* (3rd ed.). Berrett-Koehler Publishers.
White, M. P. (1990). *White heat*. Ebury Press.
Zhuangzi. (2009). *Zhuangzi: Basic writings* (B. Watson, Trans.). Columbia University Press. (Original work c. 4th century BCE)
Zinsser, W. (2006). *On writing well: The classic guide to writing nonfiction* (30th anniversary ed.). Harper Perennial.

Audio/CD Recordings
Bandler, R. (2000). *Soften Too!* [Audio CD]. Excellence Quest Training International.
Bandler, R. (2003). *Medicine Show* [CD set]. Business NLP Ltd.
Bandler, R. (2011). *Persuasion Engineering* [CD set]. NLP Life Training.
McKenna, P. (2022). *Positivity* [Audio program]. Audible Originals.
McKenna, P., & Breen, M. (1998). *The power to influence* [Audio recording]. Nightingale-Conant.

Video/DVD Recordings
Bandler, R. (1992). *The adventures of anybody* [Video]. NLP Comprehensive.
Bandler, R. (1993). *Anxiety relief and phobia cure* [Video]. NLP Seminars Group International.
Bandler, R. (1994). *Personal enhancement series* [DVD series]. NLP Comprehensive.
Bandler, R. (2002). *Trance-formations live* [DVD]. NLP Life Training.
Bandler, R. (2004). *Richard Bandler in Konstanz: Advanced NLP Seminar* [DVD]. NLP Life Training / NLP Seminars Group International.

INDEX
(TOOLS, TECHNIQUES & SKILLS IN BOLD AND ITALICS)

Above (Pause) Whisper: 343, 354, 362
After-Action Reviews: 221, 252, 274, 301, 466
Allan: 395–405
Anchoring States: 189
Angus: 121, 320-322
Aristotle: 161
Band of Brothers: 367, 393, 413, 475
Ben: 39-40
Beth: 425
Body Scanning: 186
Breath & Perception: 361
Breathing: 25, 272–273, 279–280, 303–304, 330–334, 327, 340, 350

- ***4-7-8 Breathing***: 32, 41, 58, 162–164, 170–171, 195, 210
- ***Box Breathing***: 162–164, 170–171, 200, 280

Bruce: 313–314, 323–324
Calm: High-Frequency Topics by Chapter
Co-Regulating Humour: 189, 224, 290, 467
Co-Regulation: 126-131, 186-198, 223, 281–301, 310, 472
Complex Adaptive Systems: 375, 388, 417, 441, 443
Congruence, metabolic: 12–13, 29, 52–53, 316, 323, 360–361, 489
Connect with Yourself: 13, 48, 52–53, 178
Crumple & Toss: 222, 252-257, 274, 301
Cynefin: 366
Daniel Kahneman: 31, 364, 448
Dave Snowden: 257, 274, 364-367, 373-374, 381-383, 386, 390, 406, 438–441, 446, 449
Decision Journaling: 35–39, 53
Eye Contact: 288, 291, 316-331, 352, 360, 361
Eye-Hand Coordination: 333, 362
Fear: see *High-Frequency Index by Chapter*
Finding Home: 66, 104-109, 123, 195, 247
FOCUS UP: 368- 455
Future Pacing: 138, 159, 189, 356
Gazelle (metaphor): 65, 69–70, 103
Get Rid of It: 176, 209, 211
Get to Sleep: 176, 189, 210

Gold Seam Mining: 252, 262-267, 275, 301
Gut feeling: 12, 16, 25, 32–33, 43–44, 46, 52–53, 58–59, 61
How Not to Get Shot: 297, 353, 362
Immobilisation: 62, 96, 115, 121–122, 187
Instinct: see *High-Frequency Index by Chapter*
Instinct Mapping: 103–105, 124, 127, 195
Jerry: 114–119, 133–148,
Joy light: 41–42, 55–56
Living Systems: 388, 417, 435
Meg Wheatley: 220, 356–357, 364, 441, 448
Michael Grinder: 341-343, 349, 351, 378, 386
Mick: 35, 36, 40
Mobilisation: 58, 60–62, 96, 121–122, 187–188, 194–195,
Neuroception: see *High-Frequency Topics by Chapter*
Neuro-Hypnotic Repatterning (NHR): 85
Neuro-Linguistic Programing (NLP) – 59-60, 63, 84-85, 126–133, 155–156, 186, 198, 250–252, 368–370, 378–380
Non-Verbal Congruence: 361
Non-Verbal Pattern Clusters: 332, 362
PACE Protocol: 156, 162, 163, 185-189, 206, 277, 345-360, 380, 385
PACE Storytelling: 363-368, 383, 387, 421-423, 445-451
PACE Strengths: 258-275, 301, 381
PACE Surfacing: 258-274, 301, 374, 381
PACE Yourself: 165, 189
Peripheral Awareness: 331, 362
Points of Focus: 330
Polyvagal Theory: 38–39, 186 , 345 , 352, 387, 439, 447, 451, 459
Posture Awareness: 361
Primate Brain: 12, 24, 30–31, 38, 41, 52, 60, 81, 186, 188, 193, 196, 199–203, 224, 352, 366, 371–372, 446
Psychological safety: High-Frequency Topics by Chapter
Ralph Stacey: 356-357, 364-365, 441, 447-448
Reptilian Brain: 12, 20, 24–25, 29, 31, 37–38, 43, 52, 80, 122, 186–188, 194–197, 202–203, 352, 366, 371–372, 451
Resilience: see *High-Frequency Index by Chapter*
Richard Bandler: 36 , 64 , 85–87, 92, 107, 117-121, 126–130, 136, 175, 186, 194, 239–240, 283, 365–376, 382, 390, 449
Rise & Shine: 168, 189
Robert Dilts: 369
Safety Priming: 131-143, 157, 184-198, 216-223, 240, 260, 277-301, 466
Safety Rupture: 113–125, 133–175, 236–266, 289, 414,
Safety: see *High-Frequency Index by Chapter*
Sarah: 159
Sharon: 16, 25, 30, 38–39, 78

Silencing the Storm: 104, 105, 197

Social engagement: 25, 92, 104, 122, 140, 164, 186, 217, 224, 288–289, 320, 347, 350, 352, 447

Socialisation: 156, 415

Somatic Honing: 53, 195

Stephen Porges: 30-31, 38, 40, 289, 447, 459

Stepping Out of Fear: 104, 125, 127, 201, 211

Steve Jobs: 362, 382

Steve (Coach): 133–135, 141-152,

Stress: see *High-Frequency Topics by Chapter*

Taming Vicious Memories: 67, 104–105, 126–127

Tension Releasor: 6, 12, 26, 41, 52–53, 186

The Bliss List: 165, 189

The Power of the Pause: 335, 361

Tone Modulation: 361

Triune Brain: 12, 185, 193, 376, 378–379, 408, 413, 437, 441, 449

Turning Anxiety Around: 67, 104, 105, 118, 175

Unconscious Navigator: 38, 42, 48, 52, 64

Unity BRIDGE: 367-390, 395-398, 402-408, 450-453

Verbal Empathy: 284, 285, 302, 312

Vocal Prosody: 135, 149, 223, 283, 290, 300-302, 312, 466

Worry Solver: 39, 42, 52–53, 201, 211, 294

Wrapped in Serenity: 97, 101-105, 118, 158

Zhuangzi: 121

High-Frequency Index by Chapter

Calm
- — Chapter 1: Instinct and Attention: 6, 7, 19, 25, 26, 27, 29
- — Chapter 2: Emotional Regulation: 32, 33, 41, 42, 49, 50, 53, 56, 57, 58
- — Chapter 3: Elementary Control: 64, 73, 75, 76, 77, 78, 79, 81, 83, 86, 87
- — Chapter 4: Adaptive Thinking: 96, 97, 98, 99, 100, 104-105, 109-118
- — Chapter 5: Controlling Stress Under Pressure: 124, 126, 135, 143-146
- — Chapter 6: Long-Term Vision, Short-Term Calm: 152-175
- — Chapter 7: Social Cohesion: 180-197, 207-208
- — Chapter 8: Adaptive Leadership: 210, 224
- — Chapter 10: Applied Neuro-Resilience: 279-299
- — Chapter 11: Adaptive Resilience: 301-302, 312-316, 323-324
- — Chapter 12: The Neuro-Resilient Culture: 337-351, 355-357
- — Part Five: Implementing Resilience: 362, 432, 437, 459, 463, 472, 480, 490

Fear
- — Chapter 1: Instinct and Attention: 6, 15, 16, 29
- — Chapter 2: Emotional Regulation: 45
- — Chapter 3: Elementary Control: 61-81
- — Chapter 4: Adaptive Thinking: 94-111

- — Chapter 5: Controlling Stress Under Pressure: 125-128
- — Chapter 6: Long-Term Vision, Short-Term Calm: 173
- — Chapter 7: Social Cohesion: 191-199, 201-205
- — Chapter 8: Adaptive Leadership: 211, 221-237
- — Chapter 9: Resilient Horizons: 243-245, 253-256
- — Chapter 10: Applied Neuro-Resilience: 271, 274
- — Chapter 11: Adaptive Resilience: 307
- — Chapter 12: The Neuro-Resilient Culture: 344, 345
- — Part Five: Implementing Resilience: 363-364, 374-383, 399-408, 411-422, 437, 438-455, 463-89

Instinct
- — Chapter 1: Instinct and Attention: 5-7, 11-25
- — Chapter 2: Emotional Regulation: 30-55
- — Chapter 3: Elementary Control: 61-80
- — Chapter 4: Adaptive Thinking: 91-107
- — Chapter 5: Controlling Stress Under Pressure: 122-127, 138, 143
- — Chapter 6: Long-Term Vision, Short-Term Calm: 164-165, 173
- — Chapter 7: Social Cohesion: 186-195, 201-209
- — Chapter 8: Adaptive Leadership: 210-239
- — Chapter 9: Resilient Horizons: 243, 262-265
- — Chapter 10: Applied Neuro-Resilience: 294, 299
- — Chapter 11: Adaptive Resilience: 316-329
- — Chapter 12: The Neuro-Resilient Culture: 338-357
- — Part Five: Implementing Resilience: 360-372, 383, 390-391, 408-423, 437-457, 471, 483-489

Neuroception
- — Chapter 1: Instinct and Attention: 13
- — Chapter 2: Emotional Regulation: 38-52
- — Chapter 5: Controlling Stress Under Pressure: 139, 142
- — Chapter 7: Social Cohesion: 194
- — Chapter 8: Adaptive Leadership: 218-236
- — Chapter 10: Applied Neuro-Resilience: 281
- — Chapter 11: Adaptive Resilience: 300-301, 320
- — Part Five: Implementing Resilience: 463

Psychological safety
- — Chapter 1: Instinct and Attention: 7
- — Chapter 5: Controlling Stress Under Pressure: 126-130
- — Chapter 6: Long-Term Vision, Short-Term Calm: 163
- — Chapter 7: Social Cohesion: 180-185
- — Chapter 8: Adaptive Leadership: 215-239
- — Chapter 9: Resilient Horizons: 240-262
- — Chapter 10: Applied Neuro-Resilience: 271-277, 282-297
- — Chapter 11: Adaptive Resilience: 300-301
- — Chapter 12: The Neuro-Resilient Culture: 359

INDEX

- — Part Five: Implementing Resilience: 367, 422, 430, 448, 458-489

Resilience
- — Chapter 1: Instinct and Attention: 1-13, 20
- — Chapter 2: Emotional Regulation: 51, 53
- — Chapter 3: Elementary Control: 65-68, 78-89
- — Chapter 4: Adaptive Thinking: 103-105, 110, 117-119
- — Chapter 5: Controlling Stress Under Pressure: 123, 128-141
- — Chapter 6: Long-Term Vision, Short-Term Calm: 157-179
- — Chapter 7: Social Cohesion: 181-208
- — Chapter 8: Adaptive Leadership: 211-219, 226
- — Chapter 9: Resilient Horizons: 240, 247-254, 260
- — Chapter 10: Applied Neuro-Resilience: 286, 290-299
- — Chapter 11: Adaptive Resilience: 301
- — Chapter 12: The Neuro-Resilient Culture: 345, 347, 358
- — Part Five: Implementing Resilience: 361, 367-390, 400-490

Safety
- — Chapter 1: Instinct and Attention: 7, 13, 20
- — Chapter 2: Emotional Regulation: 38, 50, 52
- — Chapter 3: Elementary Control: 60-67, 85, 89
- — Chapter 4: Adaptive Thinking: 92-96, 117-119
- — Chapter 5: Controlling Stress Under Pressure: 121-143
- — Chapter 6: Long-Term Vision, Short-Term Calm: 157-163, 174
- — Chapter 7: Social Cohesion: 180-201, 205-206
- — Chapter 8: Adaptive Leadership: 210-239
- — Chapter 9: Resilient Horizons: 240-262
- — Chapter 10: Applied Neuro-Resilience: 271-299
- — Chapter 11: Adaptive Resilience: 300-06, 312-320
- — Chapter 12: The Neuro-Resilient Culture: 332, 347-359
- — Part Five: Implementing Resilience: 361-367, 380-390, 409-422, 430-489

Stress
- — Chapter 1: Instinct and Attention: 1, 6, 12-19, 26
- — Chapter 2: Emotional Regulation: 33, 41, 48-59
- — Chapter 3: Elementary Control: 60-67, 75-88
- — Chapter 4: Adaptive Thinking: 99-119
- — Chapter 5: Controlling Stress Under Pressure: 122-130, 141, 148
- — Chapter 6: Long-Term Vision, Short-Term Calm: 156-176
- — Chapter 7: Social Cohesion: 180-205, 209
- — Chapter 8: Adaptive Leadership: 210, 223, 225
- — Chapter 9: Resilient Horizons: 247
- — Chapter 10: Applied Neuro-Resilience: 279-294
- — Chapter 11: Adaptive Resilience: 310-312
- — Chapter 12: The Neuro-Resilient Culture: 334-353
- — Part Five: Implementing Resilience: 384, 428, 435-490

ACKNOWLEDGMENTS

My sincere thanks to **Francinne Kaye Gacilo**, whose sharp eye and creative mind brought this book to life in more ways than one.

As a digital media specialist with a flair for graphic design, Francinne not only proofread the manuscript with care but also contributed a series of interior graphics that added clarity, elegance, and visual depth to the pages.

Her work helped turn concepts into compelling visuals, and for that, I'm deeply grateful.

ABOUT THE AUTHOR

Paul O'Neill is trusted by professionals in business, heavy industry, medical and mental health, and elite sports as consultant, coach and guide. For more than twenty-five years, he's been doing exactly that: guiding individuals, teams and entire organisations through the thickets of change, chaos and contradiction with a calm intensity that refuses to settle for surface solutions.

His leadership record spans continents and industries, yet his work never follows a formula. That's the point. Real transformation, he insists, can't be imposed or standardised. It must be built, brick by deliberate brick, in the language, rhythm, and logic of those who live it.

Clients across Australia, New Zealand, the UK, North America, and South Africa describe him as 'visionary', 'invaluable', 'a lifelong friend' - though the word most often repeated is 'transformational'. Not because Paul performs miracles, but because he hands the tools over. He trains people to recognise patterns, to respond to pressure with composure, to build resilience that sticks - not just in the individual nervous system, but in the culture of entire teams.

Paul's training and coaching in neuro-resilience skills, verbal and non-verbal skills, group dynamics, complex problem-solving, stakeholder engagement and adaptive strategic leadership has helped professionals across sectors rewrite their stories - by both negating the harsh effect change can have on the leaders, as well as by navigating their group through it differently. He's known for making the complex understandable, for challenging the status quo with warmth and rigour, and for turning the work of change into something deeply human and fiercely practical.

He remains, above all else, a practitioner. Someone who steps in, shoulder to shoulder, as a guide; and he stays until the work is done.

If you've reached the edge of what you know and understand, Paul is someone you want in the room.

THEY MIGHT FOLLOW YOUR STRAT[EGY]

[Le]adership doesn't begin when you speak—it begins when you [enter] the room.

[Lo]ng before a decision is made, your team is reading you. [N]ot your clever plans or polished slides. You. They read your walk, [your fa]ce, your silence.

[Th]is book begins with that signal, the one you send without mean[ing].

[Yo]u'll learn how to shift it. To steady it. To make grounded your base [ev]en when the pressure builds and the stakes tilt.

[Th]ese aren't abstract ideas. They're practical, embodied skills way[s to cl]ear your head, reset your body, and think when others can't. [Th]at's only the beginning.

[Be]cause resilience, in leadership, is never just personal. [Yo]ur state spills. It spreads.

[An]d if you're not ready for that, you won't be ready for them.

BUT THEY ALWAYS FOLLOW YOUR STA[TE]

[Pa]ul O'Neill helps leaders stay clear, calm, and connected—and [build te]ams that move as one. Paul is the Author of the Six Pillars [of Su]ccessful Executives and the Human Flourishing series.

www.ingramcontent.com/pod-product-compliance
Lightning Source LLC
Chambersburg PA
CBHW061147170426
43209CB00011B/1583